Bluegrass B

Bluegrass Banjo

by Peter Wernick

Oak Publications
New York • London • Sydney

This book is dedicated to:
Bill Monroe and Earl Scruggs, without whom there would have been nothing to write about; my parents, William and Ruth Wernick, who tolerated my practicing for hours as I learned to play; my wife, Nondi Leonard, who tolerated my typing and working on the tablature for hours as I prepared this book; and finally, this book is dedicated to dedication itself, which is responsible for these fine people doing what they did.

Acknowledgements:
Thanks: to John Ellis of the Guitar Workshop in Ithaca, for help with the sections on choosing and caring for instruments; to Will and Marie Provine for help with photographs. The publisher wishes to thank Jack Baker of the Fretted Instrument Music School in New York for his kind help and the loan of his banjo for the photograph that appears on the cover.

Photographs

Ira Haskell	Cover, 56
Eric Levenson	15, 50, 91
Marie Provine	20, 31, 55, 94, 123, 125
Don Kissil	33, 35, 37, 69 bottom, 105, 109, 111, 117, 129, 142
Hank Holland	47, 77
David Gahr	53, 101
Ed Badeaux	69 top
Unknown	75
David I. Stewart	113
Gil Golen	119
Carol Siegal	121

Book design by Iris Weinstein

US International Standard Book Number: 0.8256.0148.7
UK International Standard Book Number: 0.7119.0297.6
Library of Congress Catalog Card Number: 73-92396

Exclusive Distributors:
Music Sales Corporation
24 East 22nd Street, New York, NY 10010 USA
Music Sales Limited
8/9 Frith Street, London W1V 5TZ England
Music Sales Pty. Limited
120 Rothschild Street, Rosebery, Sydney, NSW 2018, Australia

Printed in the United States of America by
Victor Graphics

Contents

Introduction, 7

Getting ready to play, 9

Elementary songs, 13
- *Red River Valley*, 14
- *Skip to My Lou*, 16
- *Worried Man*, 16
- *Oh Susannah*, 16
- *Mountain Dew*, 16
- *Tom Dooley*, 17
- *Go Tell Aunt Rhody*, 17
- *She'll Be Coming Round the Mountain*, 17
- *When the Saints Go Marching In*, 17

Basic right hand techniques, 18
- Picking out a melody, 18
- *She'll Be Coming Round the Mountain*, 19
- Getting your hand to play a flow of notes, 19

Basic bluegrass style, 22
- *She'll Be Coming Round the Mountain*, 25
- *Worried Man*, 26
- *Ballad of Jed Clampett*, 27
- *Will the Circle Be Unbroken*, 28

Left hand techniques, 29
- Hammer-ons, 29
- Slides, 29
- Pull-offs, 31
- Lead-ins, 32

Licks and improvising, 34
- Licks, 34
- Improvising, 37

Intermediate tablature section, 38
- *Cripple Creek*, 38
- *Worried Man*, 39
- *She'll Be Coming Round the Mountain*, 40
- *Will the Circle Be Unbroken*, 41
- *The Ballad of Jed Clampett*, 42
- *Mountain Dew*, 43
- *Jesse James*, 44
- *Little Maggie*, 45

Using records to learn, 46

Playing with other people, 48
- The role of the banjo in a bluegrass band, 48

Some other techniques you should know, 51
- Unorthodox rolls, 51
- *In My Mind to Ramble*, 52
- *Old Joe Clark*, 54
- Choking, 55
- Endings, 55
- Harmonics, 56
- Scruggs-Keith pegs, 57

Music theory, 58

Up the neck, 62
- Fretting the fifth string, 65
- *Cedar Hill*, 66

Playing in different keys, 70
- *Little Birdie*, 70
- *Rabbit in the Log*, 71
- C tuning, 72
- D tuning and other tunings, 73

Slow stuff, 74
- *Dark Hollow*, 74
- *Banks of the Ohio*, 76
- Medium Tempo, 78

Three-quarter time, 79
- *All the Good Times Are Past and Gone*, 80

Melodic style ("Keith style," "chromatic style"), 81
- *Devil's Dream*, 84
- *Sailor's Hornpipe*, 85
- *Orange Mountain Special*, 86
- *Chromania*, 89

Single string style, 90

Double banjo, 92
- *Jesse James* banjo harmony, 92

Muted banjo, 94
- *Dark Hollow*, 95

Advanced tablature section, 96
- *Lonesome Road Blues*, 96
- *Will the Circle Be Unbroken*, 97
- *John Hardy*, 98
- *John Henry*, 99
- *Buffalo Gals*, 100
- *Cripple Creek*, 102
- *Pow Wow the Indian Boy*, 103
- *Salt Creek (Salt River)*, 104
- *Huckling the Berries*, 106
- *November Cotillion*, 107
- *Armadillo Breakdown (first break)*, 108
- *Armadillo Breakdown (second break)*, 110
- *Tequila Mockingbird*, 112
- *Kentucky Bullfight*, 114
- *Six Mile Creek*, 116
- *Barrel of Fun*, 118
- *Parson's Duck*, 120
- Paul's Banjo (poem), 122

(cont'd)

Appendices, 124
Appendix 1: Buying your first banjo, 124

Appendix 2: Banjo Accessories:
What else you should get, 125

Appendix 3: How the banjo works and how to maintain it, 127

Appendix 4: Getting a better banjo, 128
What should you look for in a quality banjo? 128

Appendix 5: *Gibson Banjo Information,* by Tom Morgan, 130
Stretcher band (tension hoop), 131
Wood rim construction, 131
Tone rings, 131
Getting the best sound from a banjo, 134
Adjustment of string height, Gibson banjo, 134
Correcting neck warp, 134
Tuning gear, 134

Appendix 6: *Bluegrass Instruments: Original vs. Reproduction*
by George Gruhn (with Douglas Green), 135
Styles of tone ring, 135
Styles of headstock shape, 135
Style numbers, 135

Appendix 7: Records, 138
The major groups, 138
New banjo records, 141

Index of songs and tunes in tablature, 143

Introduction

This is a book designed specifically to help you become a good bluegrass banjo player. Hopefully, it will have something in it for everyone, be they beginners with no musical experience, or seasoned banjo players looking for new ideas.

The book will start off with the assumption that you are a beginner. If you're not, pick it up where you see fit (though you might find it worthwhile to check out the beginning anyway).

Reading this book will be something like taking lessons. That is, it will show you what to practice, and, more importantly, show you *how* to practice; it will not somehow automatically turn you into a good bluegrass banjo player. There's just no way of learning how to play this music well without lots of practice.

Some people learn faster than others. People who start off with agile hands or a good ear for music definitely have a head start. Anyone who has played another instrument before, especially a guitar, has a good background. This is not to discourage people who don't have those advantages. These assets can be acquired . . . through practice. I can't stress this fact enough. Anyone can learn how to play good bluegrass banjo, *if* he or she is willing to practice. That includes people who can't hold a tune or a rhythm (that was me when I started), youngsters (there are some eight and nine year olds who can really play!), oldsters (Paul Cadwell and Snuffy Jenkins are among the most respected banjo players today), people with small hands, even people with some fingers missing (Django Rhinehart, the legendary jazz guitarist of the 30's and 40's, had only two fully functional fingers on his left hand. Rock guitarist Jerry Garcia, who also plays fine bluegrass banjo, is missing the end of his right middle finger and picks with his ring finger instead). Plenty of blind people have mastered instruments—Doc Watson is the best example in the bluegrass-old time field, and he is one of the greats on both guitar and banjo.

If you don't feel you'll have too much time to practice don't even start. Bluegrass banjo is not something you can learn halfway. It really needs some commitment, no matter how fast a learner you are. There are plenty of banjo and guitar styles that are fun and musically satisfying without requiring sustained effort to learn. So if you don't think you'll have time to practice much, try another style (check out the Pete Seeger banjo book or one of the Oak Publications guitar books) and save yourself the effort of starting and then quitting bluegrass banjo.

If, on the other hand, you think you have the time but you aren't sure, go ahead and try. If you really like what you're doing, you will start *finding* the time to play, even if none seems there. You'd be surprised how much television you don't have to watch, and how much ten minutes here and fifteen minutes there can add up to, even when you lead a busy life.

Getting ready to play

If you don't have a banjo or you don't know how one works, start off by consulting the first three appendices. If you don't have at least a few good bluegrass records, you should get some as soon as possible. Consult **Appendix 7** before buying records.

Before you can play any instrument it has to be in tune, so you have to learn whether a banjo is in tune or not, and if it's not, how to tune it. An instrument can be "in tune with itself" or "in standard (or concert) pitch". Here's the difference: Standard or concert pitch means that if the banjo is supposed to be tuned GDGBD, the notes produced are actually equivalent to the standard notes GDGBD (standard A = 440 c.p.s.). But when you don't have a tuning standard like a pitch pipe, tuning fork, in-tune piano or other instrument where the notes are in accurate standard pitch, you can still tune the strings so that they sound correct in relation to each other, even though they are not tuned exactly to Standard GDGBD. The banjo is then "in tune with itself."

Most of the time you don't have to be tuned to standard, and it's good enough for the banjo to be in tune with itself. In fact, whole groups of people can play together without being in standard pitch, as long as they are tuned to each other. Bluegrass bands have been known to record above standard pitch because they feel the instruments sound better when tuned higher.

The first band of the record included with this book gives the proper notes for standard G tuning. The fifth string (the one with the peg part way up the neck) is tuned to G above middle C. The D just above middle C is the pitch of the *first* string, the one furthest from the fifth string and closest to the floor with the banjo in playing position. The second string is tuned to the next lowest B. The third string is tuned to the next lowest G, an octave below the fifth string G note. The fourth string, the lowest note on the banjo, is the D below the third string G, and one octave lower than the first string D.

If you happen to have an in-tune piano around you can tune the banjo to standard pitch by tuning each of the banjo strings to the corresponding piano notes:

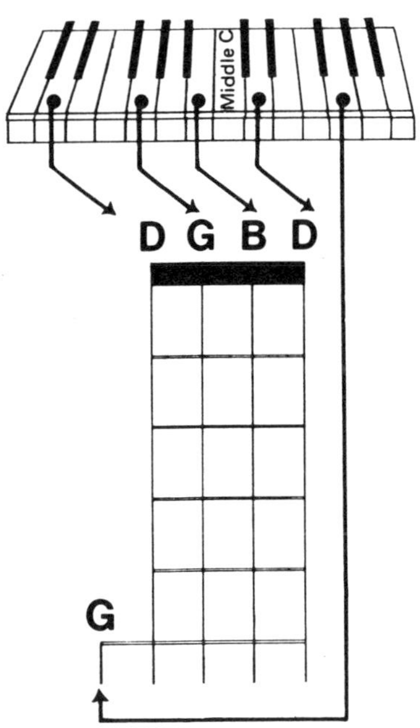

If all you have is one standard note (it would have to be G, B, or D), get the appropriate string in tune with the note. Then the rest of the strings can be tuned to each other. Standard notes can come from a tuning fork, an in-tune guitar (the 2nd, 3rd, and 4th strings of a guitar are tuned to B, G, and D, just like a banjo), or even from a record – I sometimes use Scruggs' *Fire Ball Mail* to get a standard G note. If the only standard note available is one other than G, B, or D you'll have to compare the note to one of the banjo strings *fretted.* For instance, the second fret of the third string should be A, the first fret of the second string should be C, and the first or fourth string, second fret should be E.

In tuning the strings to each other, the thing to remember is that when a banjo is in tune,

The 5th fret of the 4th string should match the 3rd string open (G)

The 4th fret of the 3rd string should match the 2nd string open (B)

The 3rd fret of the 2nd string should match the 1st string open (D)

The 5th fret of the 1st string should match the 5th string open (G)

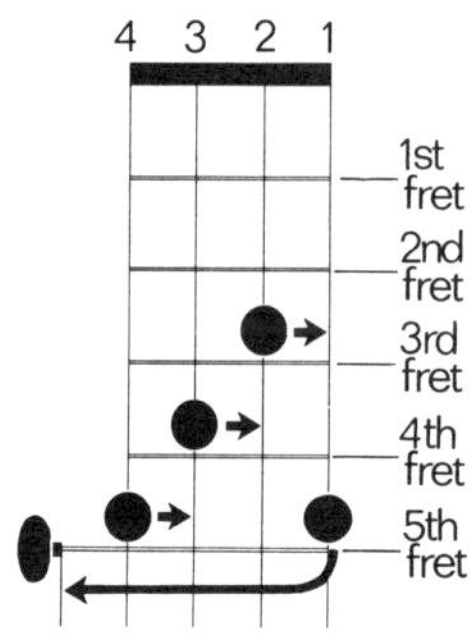

When I get my banjo in tune I check to make sure that certain chords sound good. I always try a D chord:

D

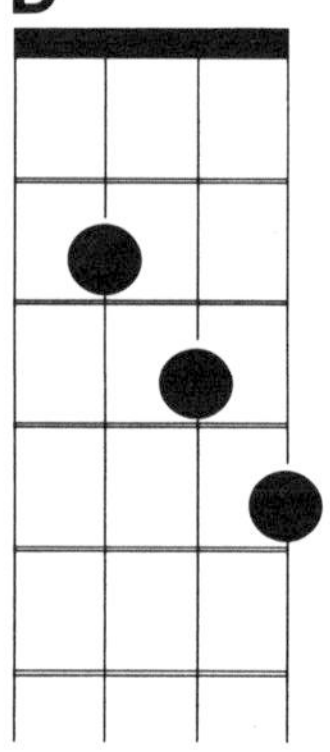

and sometimes a couple of G chords:

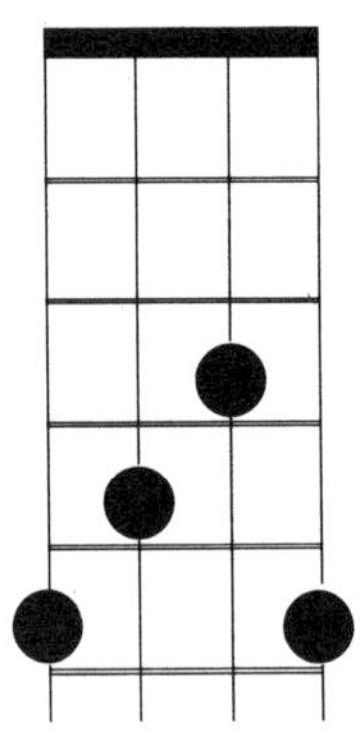

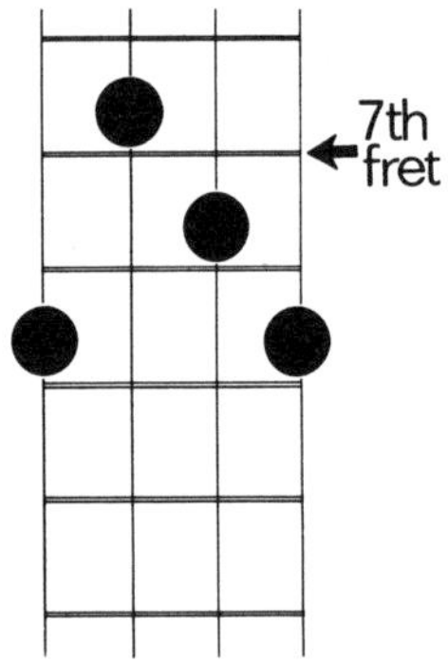

playing one string at a time to see if anything sounds a little off. Sometimes even though the strings sound all right using the matching method I just described, you must modify the tuning a bit to get the chords sounding right. If the chords sound more than a little off, it may mean that the strings are too old and are in need of changing, or that the bridge may be in the wrong place.

When you tune a string, first play the note you're tuning *to* and listen carefully. Then play the string being tuned and see whether it is too high or low. Start twisting the peg in the appropriate direction, constantly playing the string to see how you're doing. If you need to, go back and listen to the note you're tuning to and then resume tuning. Don't play the two notes together – it's hard to tell that way if the notes are exactly the same, and even if you can tell that they aren't, you won't be able to determine which is higher and which is lower.

If you have trouble tuning, get some assistance from a friend or teacher. Don't worry if your sense of pitch is not what you would like it to be, it will improve with practice.

Now that your banjo is in tune it's time to learn chords. The first chord couldn't be easier – the banjo in G tuning (which is the tuning you have it in) gives you a G chord when you strum it with open strings.

To play most simple songs in the key of G you need just two other chords: C and D7 or D.

C

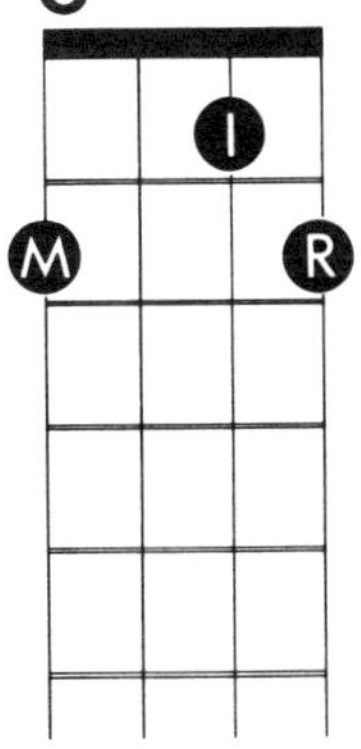

D7

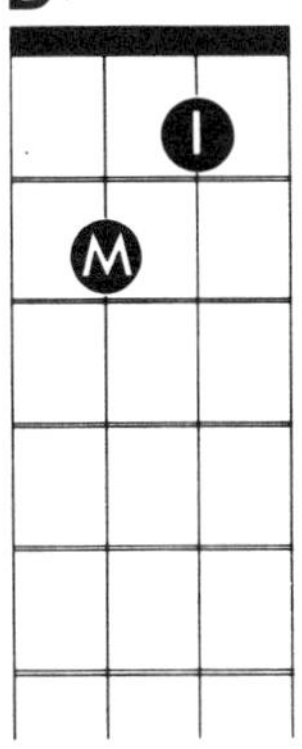

D

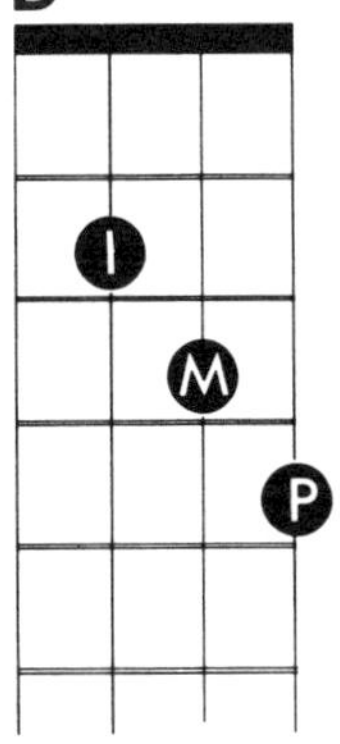

When playing in the key of G, D7 and D are interchangeable. I know D is more difficult to play, but you'll be needing it later so practice it now.

To play in the key of C you need just C, F, and G or G7. Here are F and G7. The F chord can be difficult to learn at first, but it's an important one.

F

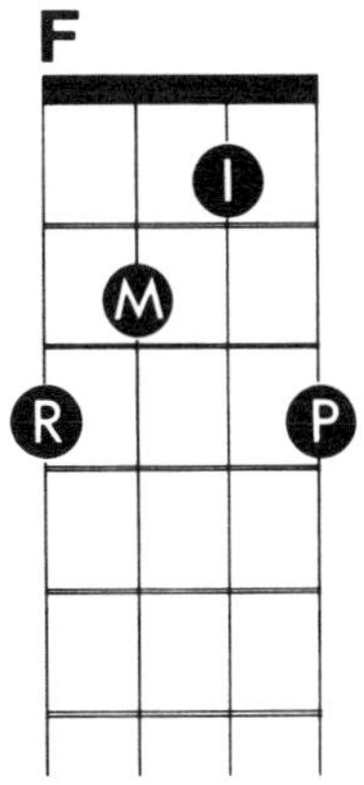

G7

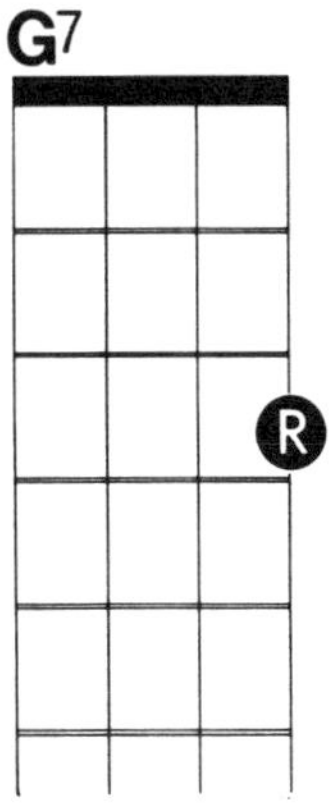

You'll have to practice these chords so that they become second nature to you. In the long run (well, it shouldn't take you *that* long), you should be able to play them without looking. quickly (in a split second) and accurately. Accuracy means your fingers should be right behind the frets, and that each note of the chord sounds clearly. When you first practice them, play the chords *one string at a time* (rather than strummed as a whole) because that way you'll be able to hear whether each string of the chord is right. When you have a few chords memorized, try changing them quickly back and forth (always checking for accuracy). When that becomes easy, try doing it without looking. Once you can do that, you're ready to start playing songs.

The reason I gave you two different sets of chords (one for G and one for C) is that in some of the songs you'll be playing you might find one key more comfortable than the other for singing. A song can be played in any key. The choice is generally based on what is comfortable for singing, and sometimes on what key's easiest to play in. The process of switching a song from one key to another is called *transposing.*

Most Western music is built around three chords, the I, IV and V chords. In the key of G, the I, IV and V chords are G, C, and D. In the key of C, they're C, F, and G. (Sound familiar?) The chord numbers refer to notes in the scale of the key being played in. This means the I, IV, and V chords are the chords built around the first, fourth, and fifth notes of the scale.

The chords used in any song can be expressed in numbers (such as I, IV, V, II, VI, etc.). What the actual chord names are (G, C, D, A, E, etc.) depends on what key you've chosen to play in.

Many song books give chords by name but not by number. In other words, they pick the keys of the songs and don't tell you what to do if you can't play or sing the song easily in the key they provide. This can be especially rough for beginning banjo players who would rather not have to cope with keys like B (using B, E and F♯ chords) or E♭ or E.

Here is a small version of a transposing chart, which is all you'll need for the time being. There is a more complex chart in the next chapter, and more complete information about transposing in the chapter about music theory.

Key of	**I**	**IV**	**V or V7**
G	G	C	D or D7
C	C	F	G or G7

Now here are some songs to practice. Pick the key that seems the best for singing, plug in the chords for that key, and do what you can. Don't worry about a right hand strum now. Just flail away, doing whatever comes naturally with the right hand. Have a good time! You might try tapping your foot where the markings are. Aim to be able to play a song from start to finish without stopping and preferrably without having to look at the banjo or at the chord changes in the book. If you memorize some of the songs (including chords) in the following section it will help you develop an ability to hear when chord changes are supposed to happen, and that's important.

Elementary songs

Of the nine songs in this section you probably know the melody to at least four or five. For those songs, learn the chord changes well enough to get through the song with ease from start to finish. If you find yourself stopping or hesitating to change chords, keep practicing.

You might want to try some more songs and for this purpose I can recommend two books: Pete Seeger's *American Folk Ballads* (Oak Publications), which contains 85 of the best-known folk songs, many of which should be familiar to you, and my own *Bluegrass Songbook* (Oak Publications), which is a collection of 140 of the best-known bluegrass songs, with melodies in simple tablature. Unless you can read music I don't recommend these or any books containing but a few familiar songs. It's pretty useless to have the words and chords to songs if you don't know the melodies.

If the two books I just mentioned aren't available or don't suit your needs, you may still find a book that will be useful – just take a good look in your local music shop. Beware of over-arrangements or books with chord changes on every word or two.

If you use a songbook you'll encounter many songs with chords other than I, IV and V. You'll also find that the chords they give you are often for keys other than G and C. So here is a more elaborate transposing chart than the one on page 12. It will help you through most chord problems you may encounter. (If you still have problems check out the music theory chapter.)

		I	IV	V	II	VI	VII♭
	A	A	D	E	B	F♯	G
	B	B	E	F♯	C♯	G♯	A
	C	C	F	G	D	A	B♭
keys	D	D	G	A	E	B	C
	E	E	A	B	F♯	C♯	D
	F	F	B♭	C	G	D	E♭
	G	G	C	D	A	E	F

If you see a song in a book you might like to play, take a look at what key it's in (that will be the same as the last chord in the song, because songs almost always end on a I chord). If it's one of the keys listed in the above chart, fine. (If it's in B or some other key I didn't list you'll have to check the music theory chapter for a more complete transposing chart.) Find the key you're in in the left hand column of the chart and look across the row. Those are the chords most likely to be used in that key. If the song has no chords other than those in it, you can transpose using this chart. For instance if a song you want to play is in D, using the chords D, G, A, and E (the I, IV, V, and II chords), you can transpose it to the key of G with the chords G, C, D, and A. If the II chord were a II minor chord – Em in the key of D – you'd transpose it to Am for playing in the key of G. It works the same with seventh chords – an E7 in the key of D becomes an A7 chord in G (although in the case of seventh chords you can always drop the seventh if you want to).

Here are some chords you may need:

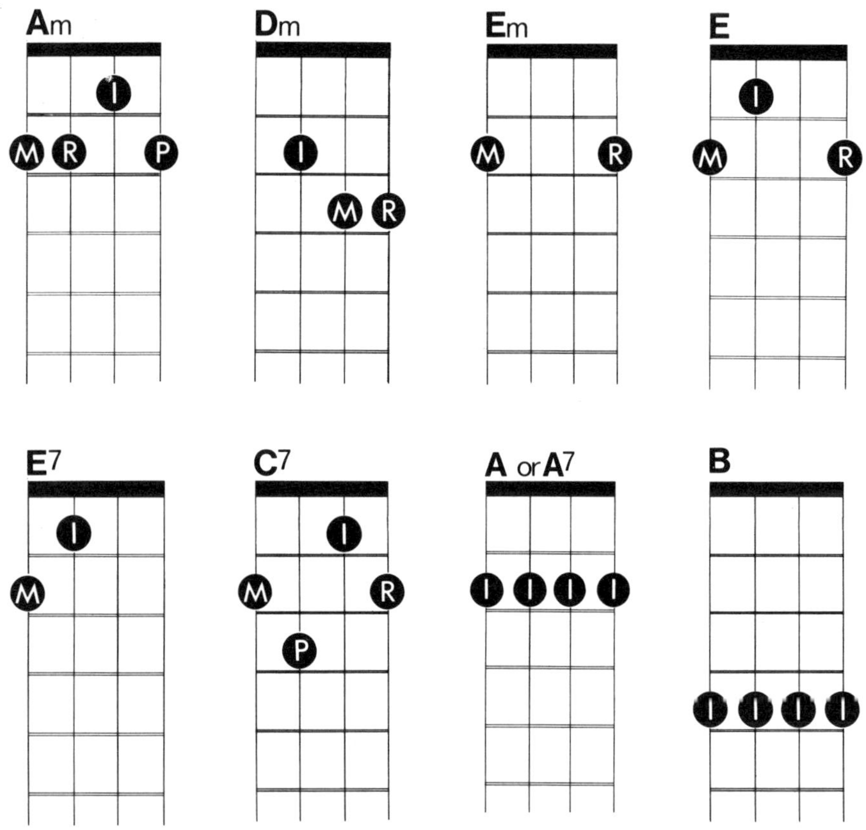

Anyone who plays the guitar may notice that guitar chords and banjo chords have something in common: The notes played on the second, third and fourth strings are the same for the banjo and guitar on every chord. That's because on both banjo and guitar the second, third, and fourth strings are tuned to B, G, and D.

If you want to learn the chords to a song which you can't find in a song book and if you have a pretty good ear, you can sometimes work them out by experimenting. If the song is a blue-grass, country, or folk song the chances are good that you can play it with the I, IV, and V chords. Most songs start on I, and nearly all end by going to V and then I. With a bit of trial and error you'll probably stumble on the right chords for most songs.

Red River Valley

I IV
From this valley they say you are going . . . . . .
/ / / / / / / /

I V
We will miss your bright eyes and sweet smile . . . . . .
/ / / / / / / /

I IV
For they say you are taking the sunshine . . . . . .
/ / / / / / / /

I V I
That has brightened our path for a while
/ / / / / /

Come and sit by my side if you love me,
Do not hasten to bid me adieu,
But remember the Red River Valley,
And the cowboy who loved you so true.

Don Reno and Red Smiley

Oh Susannah

I V
Oh I come from Alabama with a banjo on my knee . . .
/ / / / / / / /

I V I
I'm going to Lou'sianna, my true love for to see . . .
/ / / / / / / /

IV I V
(Chorus:) Oh Susannah, . . . oh don't you cry for me . . .
/ / / / / / / /

I V I
I come from Alabama with a banjo on my knee . . .
/ / / / / / / /

It rained all night the day I left, the weather it was dry,
The sun so hot I froze myself, Susannah don't you cry.

Skip to My Lou

I
Lou, Lou, skip to my Lou,
/ / / /

V
Lou, Lou, skip to my Lou,
/ / / /

I
Lou, Lou, skip to my Lou,
/ / / /

V I
Skip to my Lou my darling.
/ / / /

Lost my partner, what'll I do (etc.)
Flies in the buttermilk, shoo fly, shoo (etc.)

Mountain Dew

I
Oh they call it that good old mountain dew . . . . . .
/ / / / / / / /

IV I
And them that refuse it are few . . . . . .
/ / / / / / / /

I'll hush up my mug if you fill up my jug
/ / / / / / / /

V I
With that good old mountain dew . . . . . .
/ / / / / / / /

My uncle Mort, He's sawed off and short,
Measures 'bout four foot two,
But he thinks he's a giant if you give him a pint,
Of that good old mountain dew.

The preacher came by with a tear in his eye,
Said his wife had been down with the flu,
We said that he ought to give her a quart,
Of that good old mountain dew.

My Aunty June has a brand new perfume,
It has a sweet-smelling pu [author's note:
I don't know just what a "pu" is either],
Imagine her surprise when she had it analyzed,
It turned out to be that good old mountain dew.

Worried Man

I
It takes a worried man . . . to sing a worried song . . .
/ / / / / / / /

IV I
It takes a worried man . . . to sing a worried song . . .
/ / / / / / / /

It takes a worried man . . . to sing a worried song
/ / / / / / /

V I
I'm worried now . . . . . . but I won't be worried long . . . .
/ / / / / / / / / /

I went across the river and I laid down to sleep, (3x)
When I woke up, I had shackles on my feet.

I asked the judge, what's going to be my fine, (3x)
Twenty-one years on the Rocky Mountain line.

If anyone should ask you should write this song, (3x)
Tell them it was me, and I sing it all day long.

Tom Dooley

(the commercial folk version,
not the Doc Watson version)

I
Hang down your head Tom Dooley,
/ / / /

V (or V7)
Hang down your head and cry,
/ / / /

Hang down your head Tom Dooley,
/ / / /

I
Poor boy you're bound to die.
/ / / /

This time tomorrow,
Reckon where I'll be,
Down in some lonesome valley,
Hanging from a big oak tree.

Go Tell Aunt Rhody

I
Go tell Aunt Rhody,
/ / / /

V I
Go tell Aunt Rhody,
/ / / /

I
Go tell Aunt Rhody,
/ / / /

V I
The old gray goose is dead . . .
/ / / /

The one she's been saving, (3x)
To make a feather bed.

She died in the mill pond, (3x)
Standing on her head.

When the Saints Go Marching In

I
Oh when the saints . . . . . go marching in . . . . . .
/ / / / / / / /

V
Oh when the saints go marching in . . . . . .
/ / / / / / / /

I IV
Oh I want to be in that number . . . . . .
/ / / / / / / /

I V I
When the saints go marching in . . . . . .
/ / / / / / / /

Oh when the sun refuse to shine (etc.)
Oh when that trumpet sounds the call (etc.)

She'll Be Coming Round the Mountain

I
She'll be coming round the mountain when she comes . . . . . .
/ / / / / / / /

I V
She'll be coming round the mountain when she comes . . . . . .
/ / / / / / / /

I
She'll be coming round the mountain,
/ / / /

IV
She'll be coming round the mountain,
/ / / /

I V I
She'll be coming round the mountain when she comes . . . . . .
/ / / / / / / /

She'll be driving six white horses (etc.)
Oh we'll kill the old red rooser (etc.)
Oh we'll kiss an armadillo (etc.)

Basic right hand techniques

Now that you've learned a little left hand technique and made your way through a few songs, you're ready to focus on bluegrass style.

First, you should have an idea of what is actually happening when a person plays bluegrass banjo.

From listening to it, it's easy to hear that there are a lot of notes being played. Some of these notes are accented and carry the melody. The others are really just background notes – when added between the melody notes at a fast pace, they give the effect of a flow of sound, the sound of a bluegrass banjo.

The idea, then, is to play melody notes and fill the spaces between them with a lot of background notes. That means learning two skills – the skill of picking out a melody and the skill of getting your hand to play a flow of notes. Both of these skills have to be fairly well-developed before you can play a tune in coherent bluegrass style.

Picking out a melody

Learning how to do this right is a trial and error process. Some people will get it right almost instinctively (especially if they've played another instrument). Others (especially those with pitch problems) may have some trouble at first.

It helps to be able to sing on key. If you can, you may find yourself guessing your way through a melody line with a fair amount of accuracy, just by thinking the melody in your head and picking out notes on the banjo. Try picking out the melody to a few of the songs in the last chapter. If you don't have too much trouble, fine. You can skip the rest of this section.

If not, try this: Play the chords for the song and sing along. Repeat that a couple of times to get thoroughly used to the melody. Then start to sing the song very slowly, still playing the chords. For each melody note, hunt down the note you're singing on the banjo neck. A very good hint is that it is more than likely to be one of the notes in the chord you are playing. If you have trouble finding it, *sing the note loud and clear* (making sure to hold the pitch), and try out a variety of notes – slowly, one at a time. It's helpful to be aware that for almost any simple song in G you'll find all the melody notes among these nine notes:

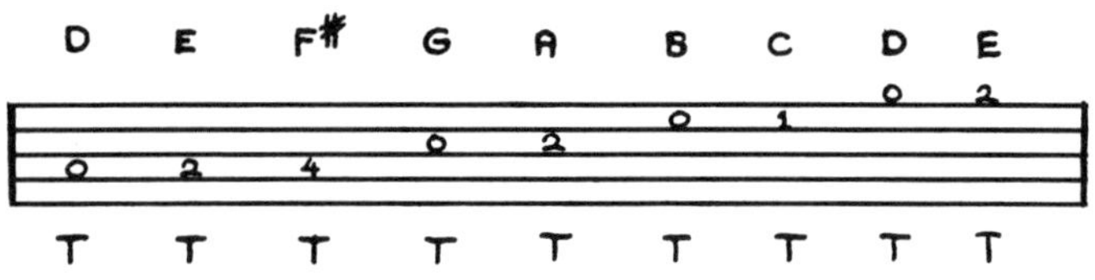

The notes are written not in musical notation, but in *tablature* form. This is standard banjo notation, and here's how it works: Each of the five lines represents a string (the top line is the first string, the bottom line is the fifth). The number above the line indicates which fret of the string is being played ("O" means the string is open). The letter below each note indicates how the note is played with the right hand. Here, all the notes are played by the thumb ("T"). More on tablature later, when the need arises. (Incidentally, tablature doesn't tell you how to get the notes with your *left* hand. That's for you to decide.)

So in trying to pick out a melody, you can limit your experimenting to those nine notes above.

Try playing different sequences of those notes and you may very well start running into fragments of songs. Another helpful idea is to try to get a sense of whether a note in a song is higher or lower than the one that came before it. That limits the notes you have to pick from.

If the going is slow, keep at it. Work on it every day for a while, and you'll get it. Here's a sample version of *She'll Be Coming Round the Mountain* with the melody notes already picked out for you:

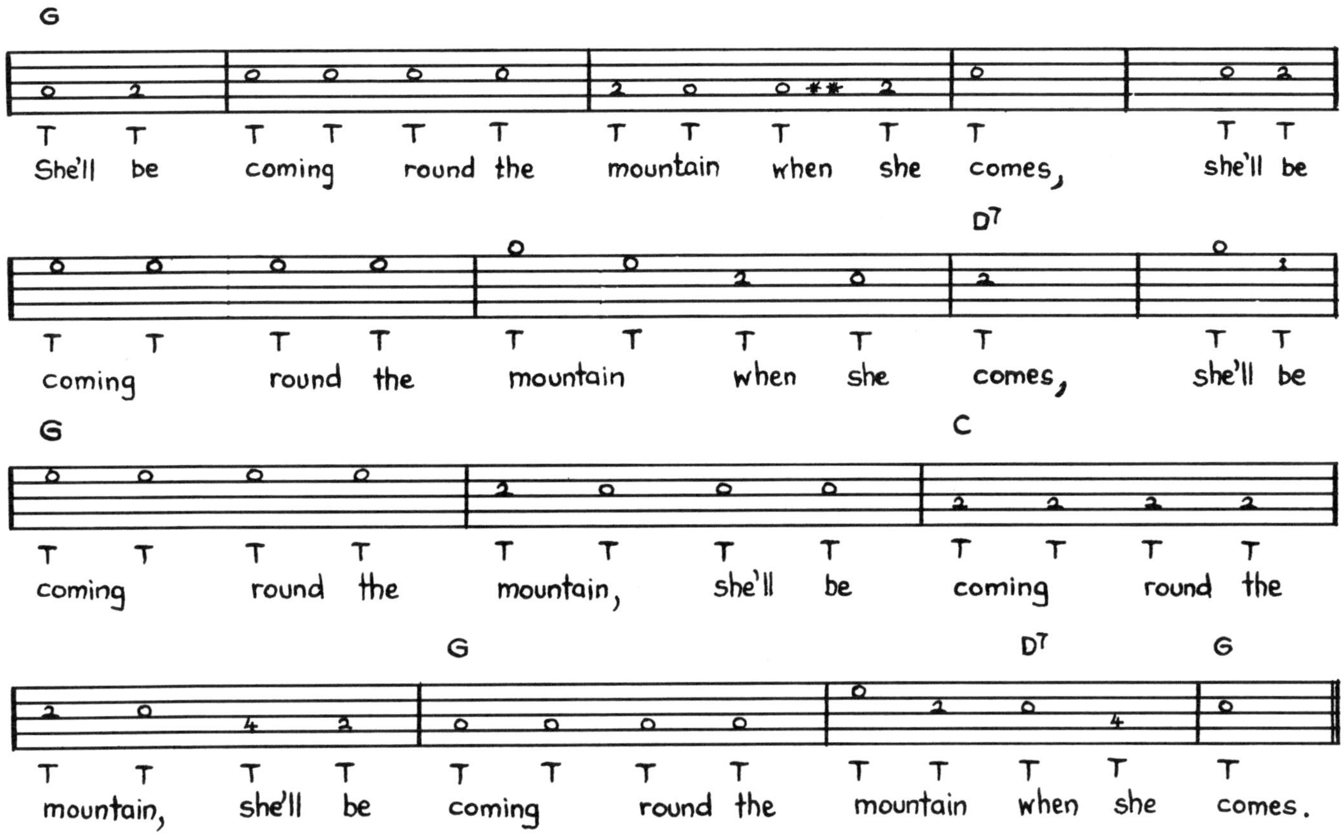

**This note is actually supposed to be a B and not a D, as is written here. The B, however, is below the normal banjo range, so I chose the nearest note available – D. This sort of compromise happens all the time in bluegrass banjo playing, so get used to it. My technical term for it is *fudging*.

Getting your hand to play a flow of notes

What I'll give you here is a set of practice rolls to play. They each have eight notes, which is just the number of notes that conveniently fits into one measure of 2/4 time (the time used for up-tempo bluegrass). This variety of rolls is by no means all that your right hand will be called upon to do. There are endless variations, and we'll get to some of those later. But this is a group of some of the patterns which are used most frequently, and which you'll find most convenient to use at this stage. I have given them names for future reference, but you don't have to worry about remembering each roll's label.

Thumb in and out

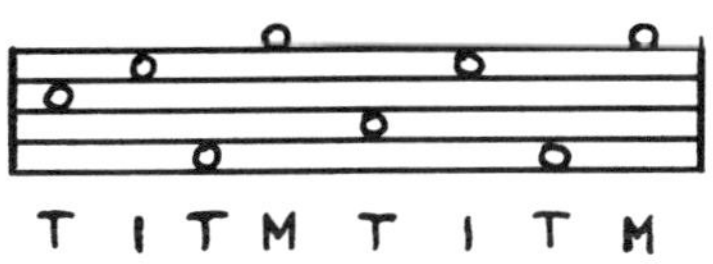

Forward Backward I

Forward Backward II

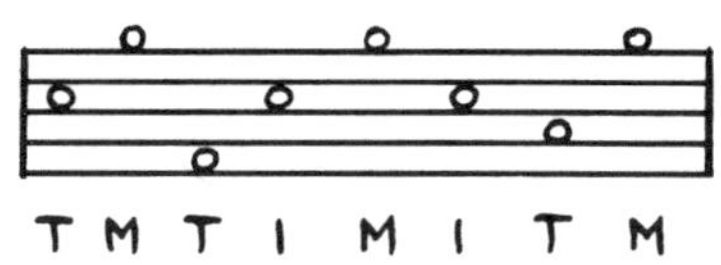

Forward I

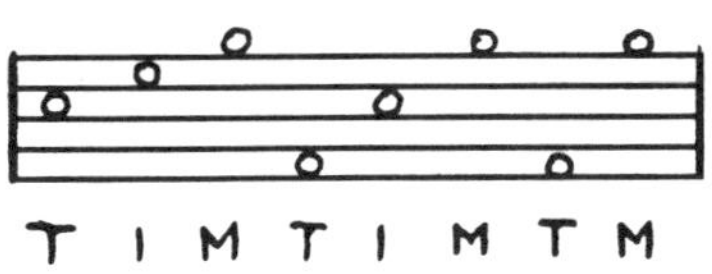

Forward II

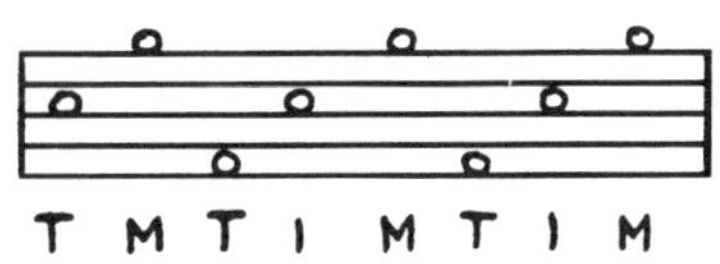

***Foggy Mt. Breakdown* Roll**

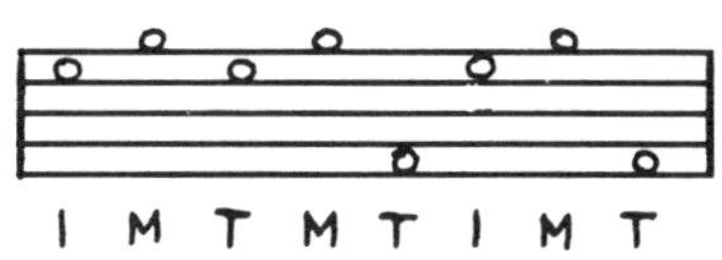

These rolls all use three fingers: thumb, index, and middle. The tablature symbols are T, I, and M.

Before practicing the rolls, make sure your right hand is in the correct position.

First, keep either your ring or little finger (or both) planted firmly on the head next to, but not touching, the bridge. Have the palm of your hand well above the head by a good couple of inches. This means keeping your wrist bent and well off the head. Your index and middle fingers should end up touching the strings about two inches from the bridge, and at about a sixty degree angle from the strings. This positioning may be a little awkward but it makes for a steady hand and a clear sound once you're used to it. It's *very* important for accuracy to have your hand positioned firmly. See the photograph.

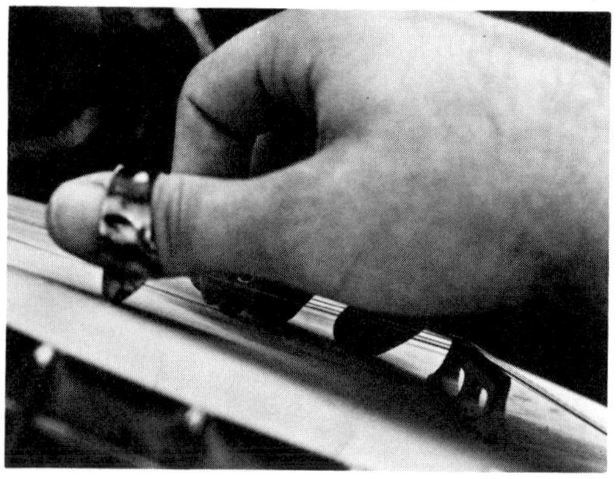

Another thing that's very important is to wear your finger picks when you practice. Again, it may be uncomfortable at first, but you'll have to get used to it sometime, so the sooner you do it the better. Practicing bluegrass banjo without picks is like practicing a golf swing without a club.

Practice the rolls and practice them a lot. Go for clarity, evenness and accuracy at first. Once you're comfortable, try for a little speed. When you can play the roll clearly, evenly, and accurately about five times in ten seconds (that's about four notes a second), you're doing fine. On the first side of the record included with this book I've recorded each of the six rolls. Check yourself against them.

A few words about speed

When a banjo is being played really fast, it may be playing close to fifteen notes a second. Normally, though, it's more like six or eight or ten. That might sound terribly fast, and of course when you hear the banjo playing, it does sound very fast. But it's not really as extreme as you might think. To prove it to yourself, try drumming your thumb, middle and index fingers on a table in rapid succession. If you can do it three times in a second (do it while looking at the second hand of a watch or clock), you're already moving your fingers nine times a second – quickly enough for respectable bluegrass banjo playing. And you can be sure that as you play more and more, your fingers will get looser and respond more quickly.

One of the reasons bluegrass banjo picking sounds so fast is that on a banjo, every note that's played is distinct. A banjo is set up to sound sharply and quickly. In the long run, the ability of a banjo player to play fast is of undeniable value – some material is supposed to be played quite fast, like *Rawhide* or *Foggy Mt. Breakdown.* But most bluegrass is not played as fast as that, and shouldn't be. There comes a point where the faster you play, the more subtlety you sacrifice; so speed is not automatically a virtue. The idea is to play to suit the material. Do whatever is necessary to put the right feeling behind what you're playing. That goes not just for speed, but for loudness and every other musical characteristic.

For now, while you're still a long way from worrying about playing too fast, also bear in mind that it won't hurt you to start off *slowly.* Make sure that what you're doing is right. If you sacrifice accuracy for speed, you're making a big mistake. As you feel more comfortable, pick up the speed a bit. But don't push yourself. Speed comes automatically, with a lot of practice. Be patient and keep your mind on sounding good and being accurate.

The thumb generally gets the melody in bluegrass style, except when it is playing the fifth string. When you practice rolls, try giving the accent to the thumb notes on the inside strings (and especially to the first note of the roll, which is almost always the most important melody note in the roll).

Sometimes the index finger gets melody notes, but its main job is to provide fill-in notes. The middle finger rarely gets melody (except in some kinds of advanced playing) – it usually just keeps on hitting the first string, to keep the flow of notes going.

The basic pattern of each roll can be varied. For instance, the first forward backward roll can be played as written:

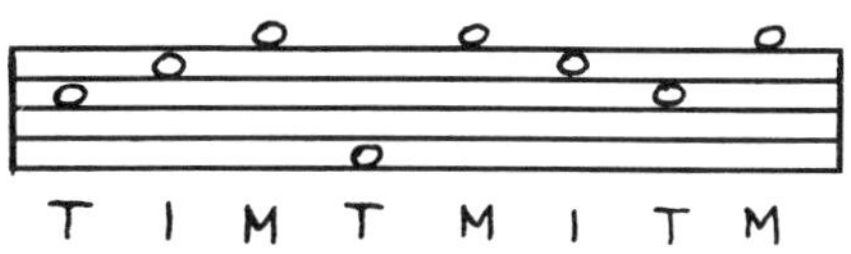

or it can use the fourth string instead of the third when appropriate (that is, when a melody note you want is on the fourth string):

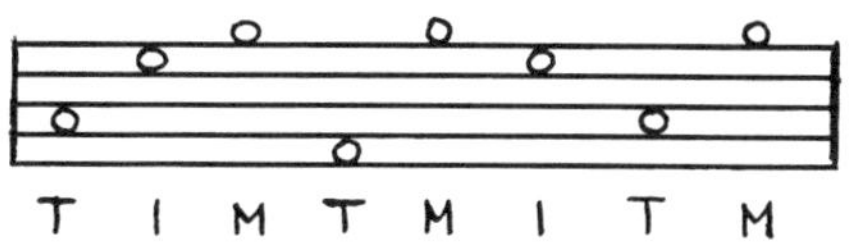

Any roll can be (and often is) varied to work in a melody note. If a melody note is on the second string, you can vary the second forward roll or the second forward backward roll as follows:

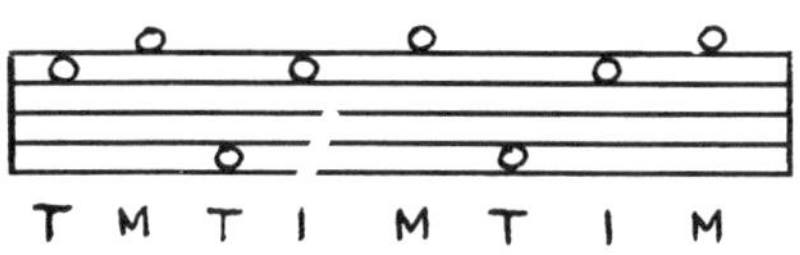

Try these variations and make up other ones yourself. You'll soon be needing them. One of the most important things a banjo player should strive to develop is a *free right hand* – that is, one which is not stuck in a few limited patterns, but which can go from pattern to pattern very freely at will, almost to the point of not moving in patterns at all. By exercising your hand on many variations of rolls (you don't need to memorize them), you are teaching your right hand to be versatile.

As each roll becomes comfortable and smooth, try changing chords with the left hand while playing. *Without stopping,* play the roll twice through on a G, twice on a C, twice on a D or D7 and so forth. If you can do that consistently you're ready to plug a roll into a song. Go back to the song section and select a song. For openers, start doing the thumb in and out roll and sing the song while you play the roll and change chords. The rhythm markings below the words should be your guideposts. Since the heavier lines mark out the measures and each eight-note roll fits into one measure, make sure the first note of the roll comes right at the heavy marking. If you do that, you're in rhythm. With the thumb in and out roll, the second inside thumb note (the fifth note of the roll) should line right up with the lighter markings.

The thumb in and out roll with its regular alternating thumb is the easiest roll to accompany songs with (in fact, it makes a very nice accompaniment for singing, just as it is). Now try the first forward backward roll, which is harder but more commonly used in actual playing. Try it on a few songs, aiming to make it smoothly through the song *without breaking the roll.* Once you can do this, you're ready for your first bluegrass tune using melody and rolls together.

Reminders: Is your hand in the right position? Are you chording neatly? Is each note sounding clearly? Are you enjoying yourself??

Basic bluegrass style

When playing bluegrass banjo the idea is to make the melody (or most of it) prominent, as your right hand keeps rolling along, pouring out notes. This means to play the melody with your thumb, and fill in the spaces so that there is a total of eight notes per measure in the song. There is no set method that makes this happen. It's up to you to experiment, trying to eliminate what sounds wrong and rigorously practicing what sounds right.

Some general hints to remember:

The first note of every measure in a tune is usually an important melody note. When working out your arrangement of a tune, start each eight-note roll with the melody note. What roll you play is not always important. It *is* important when you want to include one or more other melody notes in the measure. Then the roll has to allow the thumb (or possibly the index finger) to hit the proper note or notes at the right time. The example later in this chapter will show you how to select your rolls.

After a while you will not need to carefully work out every measure you play. Eventually you will learn to keep your right hand going almost effortlessly while you think mostly about the melody notes you want to play.

An important rule: Within each eight-note roll you have to keep switching fingers. If you try to play two consecutive notes in an eight-note roll with the same finger you'll have trouble, especially at high speed. Also, for now don't play the same string twice in a row (with different fingers); it can sound good, but at the beginning you should avoid it.

It is rare for a bluegrass banjo player to render a melody with perfect accuracy. Because the rolls include mostly fill-in notes (that is, first string notes, fifth string notes, and most index finger notes), there aren't many opportunities to play melody notes. So you'll have to forego playing part of the melody of most tunes. Sometimes you'll have to play a note with your thumb which is not actually a melody note. This is not a calamity – just an example of *fudging,* a fact of life for a bluegrass banjo player. Hopefully you'll be able to keep as many melody notes as are necessary to leave the melody recognizable.

Because *Coming Round the Mountain* is a song everyone knows, I have selected it for close-up treatment. The following is an example of how to work out a tune in bluegrass style.

The first words are "She'll be coming". Since the first important beat (foot-tap) doesn't happen until the word "coming", the phrase "She'll be" doesn't take up a whole measure, and it won't need a full eight notes. Just play the melody:

Or, put in some fill-in notes, such as:

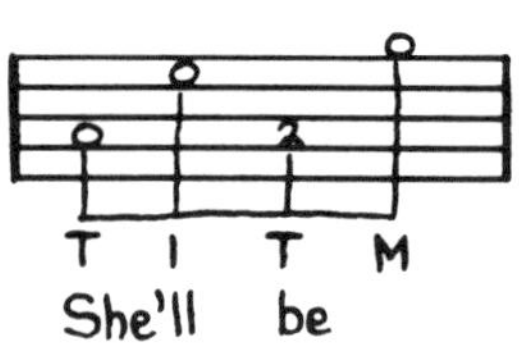

The vertical lines in the tablature are grouped in fours to help you see the rhythm.

For the first full measure, "coming 'round the," just pick any roll (I suggest the first forward backward roll), starting it off with the thumb on the third string (G). In the next measure ("mountain when she"), the melody (or a fudged version of it) is on the fourth string, second fret. Try one of the forward backward rolls, playing both inside (non-fifth string) thumb notes on the fourth string.

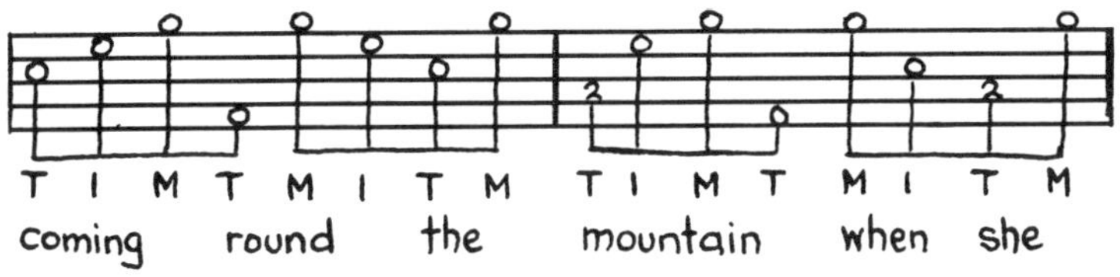

The next two measures are for the word "comes", though you'll have to sneak in something for the "she'll be" at the end of the second measure. Try any roll, starting with the thumb on the third string open (that's the melody). For the second roll try to get something in for "she'll be" or at least "be." Those notes are:

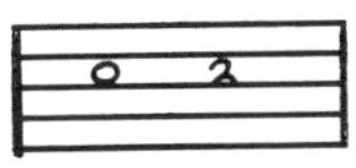

and they should be the fifth and seventh notes of the roll. If you use a thumb in and out roll for the second measure, you can easily move the thumb to get both notes. If you use a forward backward roll you can get in the "be" easily enough.

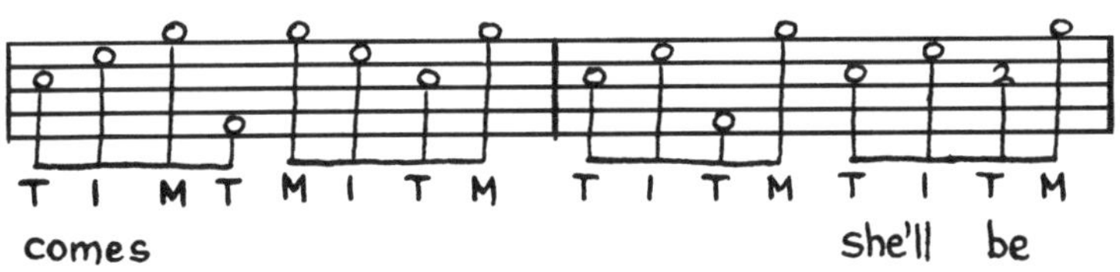

The next measure is "coming round the", and the notes are all B, which is the second string open. Pick a roll which allows you to start with the second string. If you choose the second forward roll you can get the second string three times in the roll, coinciding perfectly with the words.

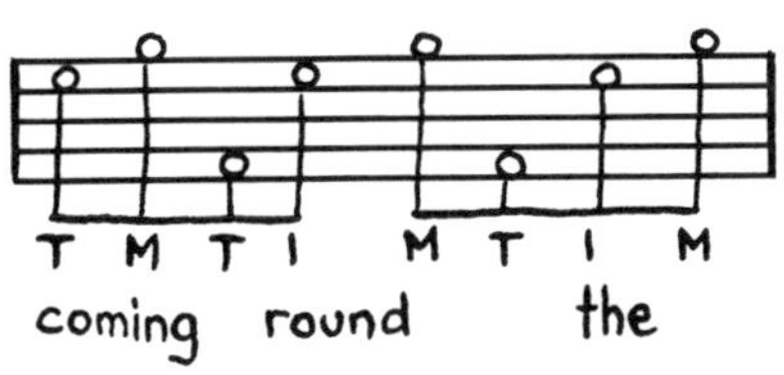

The next measure, "mountain when she", can present problems because it contains four important melody notes. One easy way to deal with this is to lapse into a two finger strum, where you simply alternate melody notes played by the thumb with fill-in notes played by the middle finger on the first string. Or you can use a variant of the *Foggy Mt. Breakdown* roll to get a pretty close approximation to the melody:

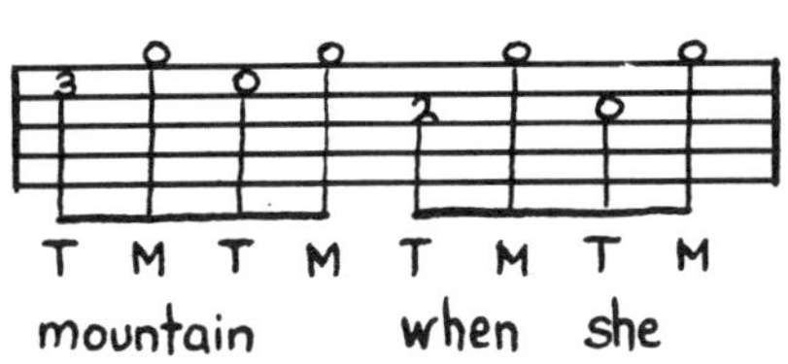

or

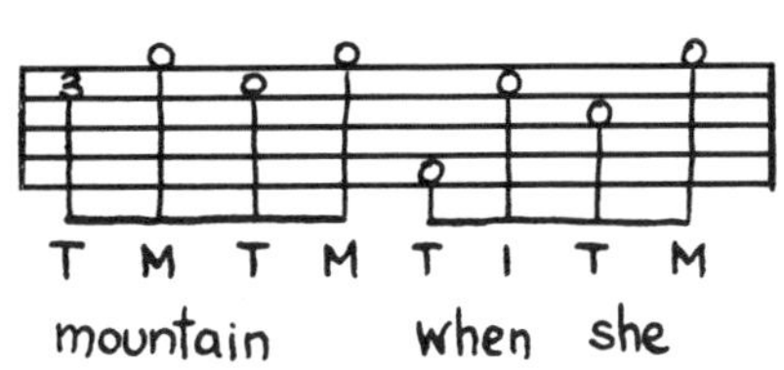

You'll notice that the first syllable of the word "mountain" is played on the second string, third fret. Another, possibly more obvious place to get it is the first string open, but I chose to get the note on the second string because it's easier to deal with melody notes when they are on the second, third, or fourth strings. Until you are comfortable with more advanced rolls it's better to take any melody notes that fall on the first string and put them on the second string: First string open = second string, third fret. First string, second fret = second string, fifth fret, etc.

For the next two measures, we again have the word "comes" with the desirable option of sneaking in "she'll be" at the end of the second measure. The song switches to a D chord here, and the melody is right on the third string when you're holding either a D or a D7 chord. Again, choose any roll which allows you to start your thumb on the third string (the first forward backward roll is a good choice) and roll away. As before, the "she'll be" happens at the fifth and seventh notes of the second roll. You can play the first four notes of any roll, and use the thumb or index finger (whichever is available) to get the fifth note for "she'll" on the second string, third fret. Follow that with a fill-in note on the first string and then play the note for "be" on the second string, first fret with your thumb. Follow that with another fill-in note on the first string and you've made it through the measure. (We're halfway through the song now.)

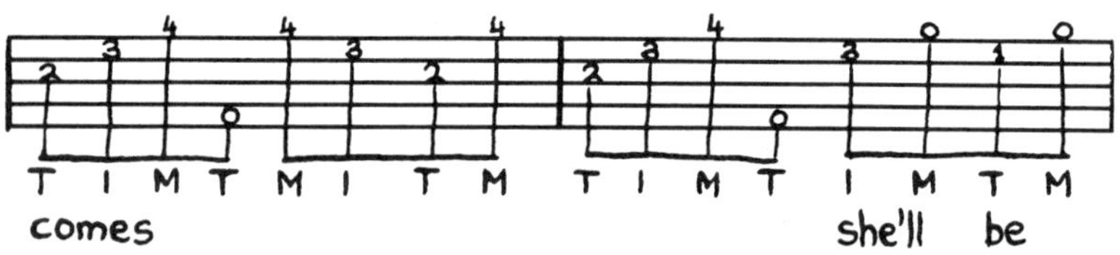

The next measure is "coming round the", all on a B. You can do just what you did last time when you had the same phrase.

For "mountain she'll be", it's time for yet another fudge. Do a forward backward roll and on the first note play the third string, second fret. It's not perfect but it certainly works.

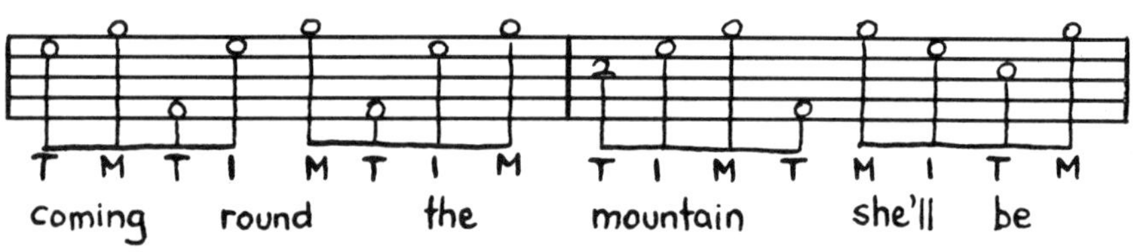

It's time now for a C chord, and you can get through two measures ("coming round the mountain she'll be") using forward-backward rolls with the thumb, playing melody notes on the fourth string.

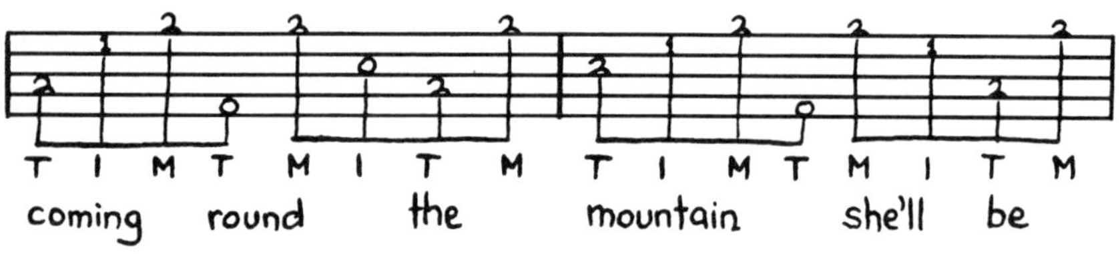

For "coming round the mountain when she comes", I leave you on your own, since you should have started to get the idea by now. One hint, though – you can get almost all of the melody with a thumb in and out roll (sometimes varying it so that the thumb stays in – doesn't hit the fifth string). Keep in mind that you don't have to play all of the melody. For the final note of the song, pick any roll; start with the third string open (G), and roll through to the end.

Here is the whole sample version in tablature:

She'll Be Coming Round the Mountain

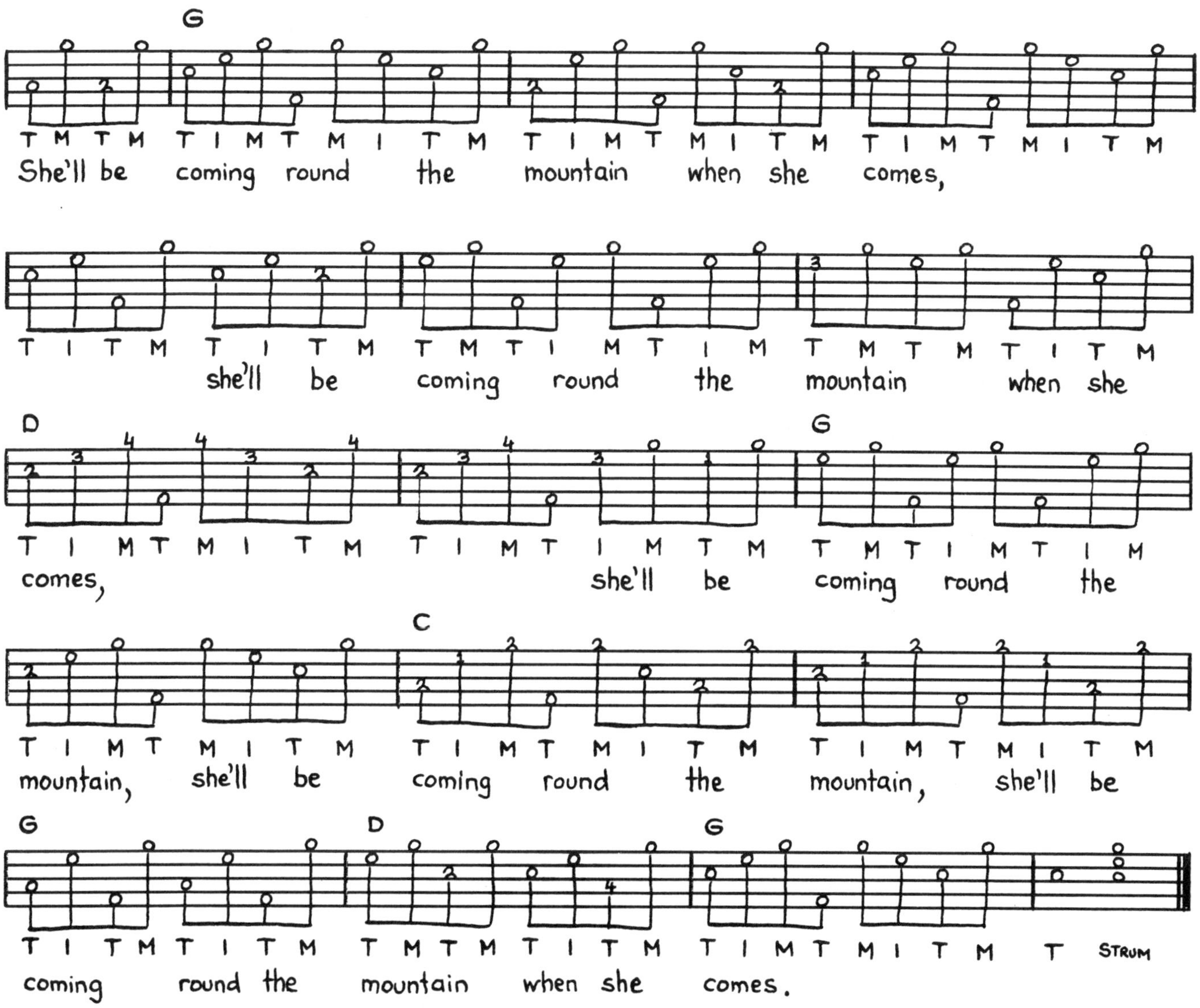

This arrangement, played slowly, is recorded on Side I, Band 3 of the record included with this book.

Here are easy arrangements for some songs you probably know: *Worried Man Blues, The Ballad of Jed Clampett* (Beverly Hillbillies theme), and *Will the Circle Be Unbroken.* However, rather than working them out from the tablature, first try to figure them out *on your own.* It's better to develop your arranging skills than to copy the music from a piece of paper. Remember, you're working toward the time when you won't have to rely on tablature at all.

When you feel you can play through your arrangement steadily, put on Side II of the record included with this book and play along with it. The side contains *Coming Round the Mountain, Worried Man* and *Will the Circle Be Unbroken.* The banjo is recorded by itself in one channel, so by adjusting the balance knob on your stereo you can eliminate the banjo or leave it in and compare what you play with what's on the record. For each of the three songs on Side II the first banjo break corresponds to the tablature from this chapter, while the second one follows the arrangement in the *Intermediate Tablature Section.*

When you work out this or any tablature, you'll probably learn faster and better by following these tips:

1. Do it a measure or two at a time. Learn each part well before moving on to the next.

2. As you learn each new part, try putting it together neatly with everything up to that point. Don't move ahead until you've got it smooth.

3. If you have a rough spot, don't ignore it – *concentrate on it.* Work repeatedly on just the rough spot, until it's smooth.

4. Continually go back and review what you've learned, to keep it fresh in your mind.

5. Try to rely as little as you can on the tablature. The idea is to teach your fingers how to move smoothly and accurately *on their own.*

Worried Man

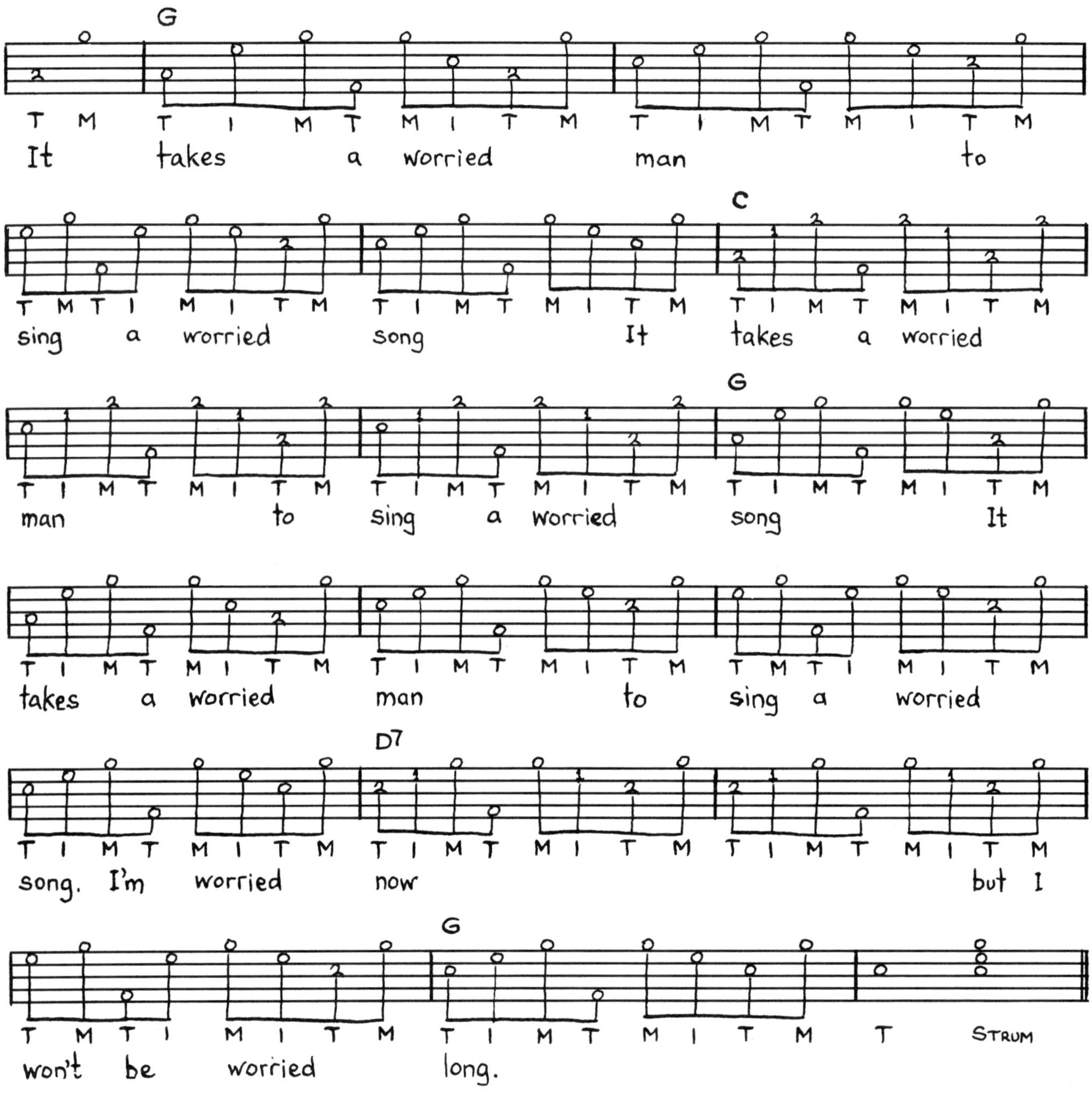

This is the first banjo break in the version of this song which appears on the record included with this book.

Ballad of Jed Clampett

Paul Henning

Based on Earl Scruggs' version.

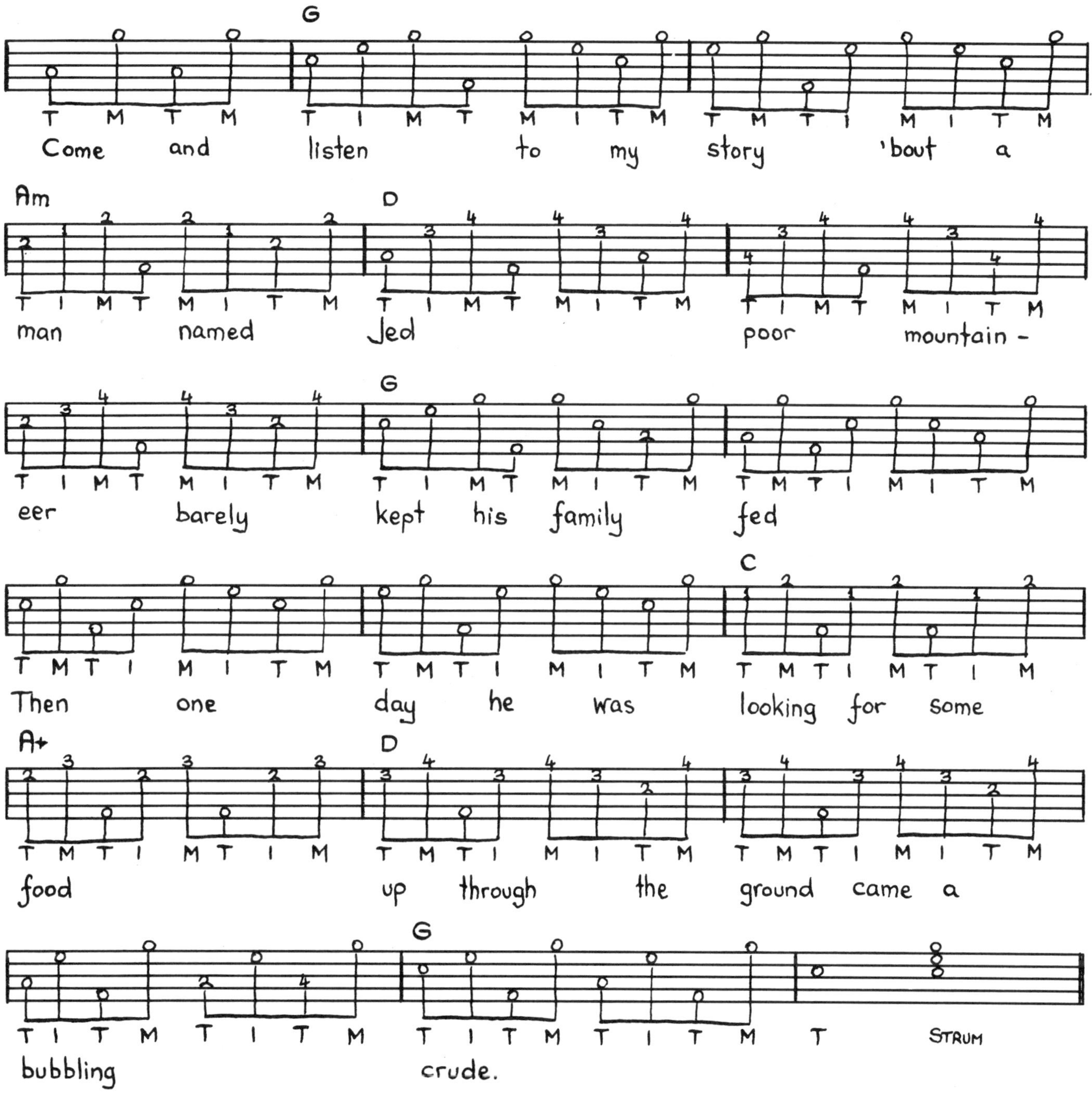

Will the Circle Be Unbroken

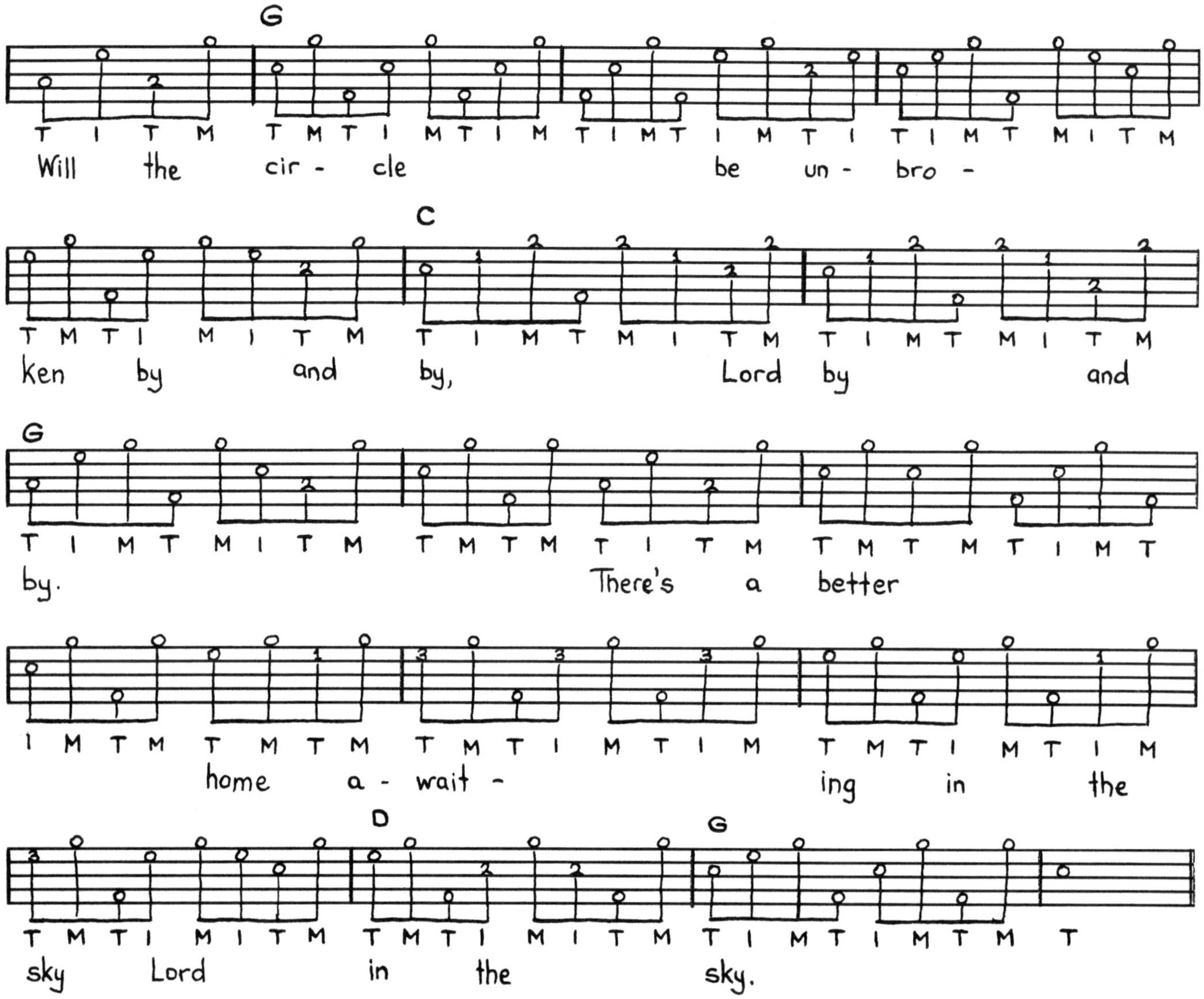

This is the first banjo break in the version of this song which appears on the record included with this book.

Left hand techniques

Slides, hammer-ons and pull-offs are very important embellishments without which bluegrass banjo just couldn't sound like bluegrass banjo. It's important to learn them well if you want your playing to have the right sound. All of the examples and exercises in this chapter are recorded on the first side of the record included with this book.

In each of these exercises, your right hand plays a note as usual and then your left hand quickly modifies it.

Hammer-ons

Play the first string with your right hand. After the string has sounded for a split second, quickly fret the string at the second fret. You should get a distinct note when you do the hammer-on. If you do it too slowly you will just dampen the string instead of getting a clear second note. If you say the word "bottom" along with the hammer-on, it may help you to start getting the sound right. Here is the tablature for the hammer-on you just did:

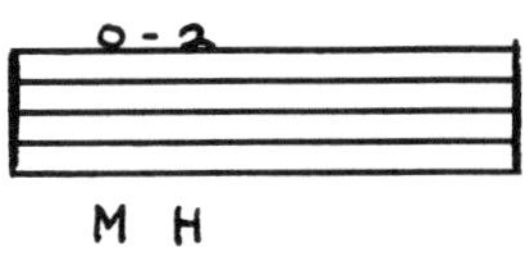

A hammer-on may also start from a fretted string. Here is a common hammer-on: Fret the second string at the second fret with your index finger. With your right index finger pick the second string and hammer on your left middle finger onto the third fret. This is how that hammer-on looks in tablature:

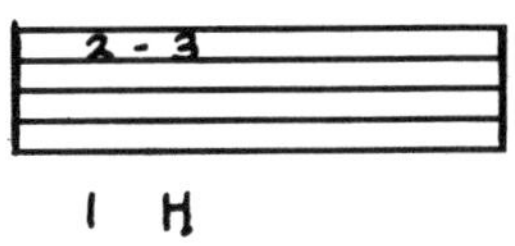

Here are two often-used licks which use the hammer-on. Notice in the tablature that the H and the M are written in the same space. This is because they are supposed to happen at just about the same time. That is, the middle finger note does not *follow* the hammer-on – they happen simultaneously. If you don't play them at the same time, it will sound as though you are trying to put nine notes into one eight-note measure.

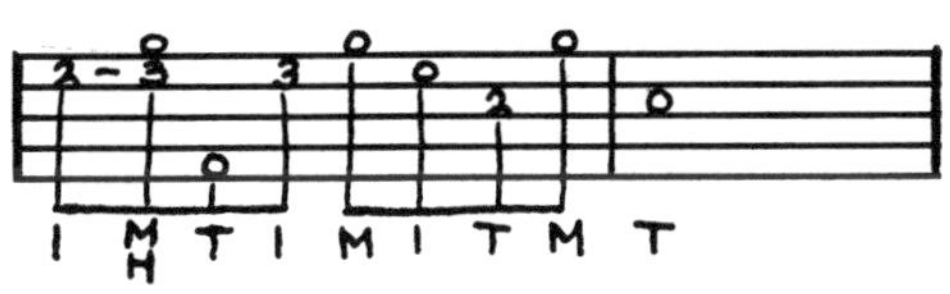

You may recognize the second of the two licks printed above as sounding like the beginning part of *Foggy Mt. Breakdown.* Notice that the third right hand note in that lick is played with the *thumb* although the first note was played with the index finger. That's the way it's usually done, but if it feels more comfortable to use your index finger instead, do it that way.

Slides

Slides are similar to hammer-ons, except that instead of using another finger to get the second note, you simply slide the finger you're fretting with up to the note you want. Slides are rarely used to lower a note. When a slide raises a note one fret it sounds just like a hammer-on. Sliding up more than one fret gives a quick sequence of the notes you pass as you slide up.

The slide from the second to the third fret of the third string is one of the most common movements in bluegrass banjo playing. An open note on the second string usually follows this slide. The effect is a slide from an A (second fret of third string) to an A♯ (third fret of third string) up to a B (second string open). This move is almost always used as a replacement for an ordinary B note (second string open).

Instead of playing:

most banjo players would play:

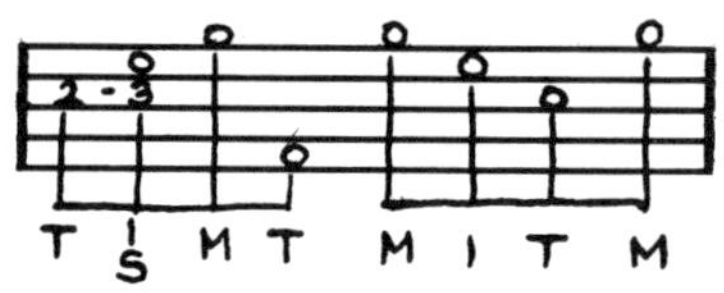

And instead of playing:

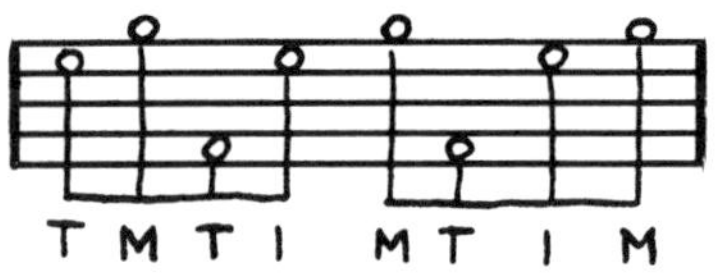

they would play:

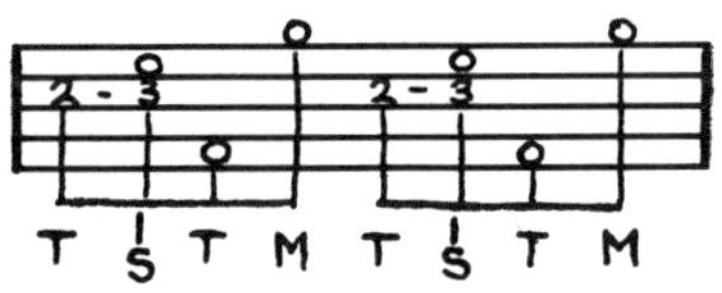

or:

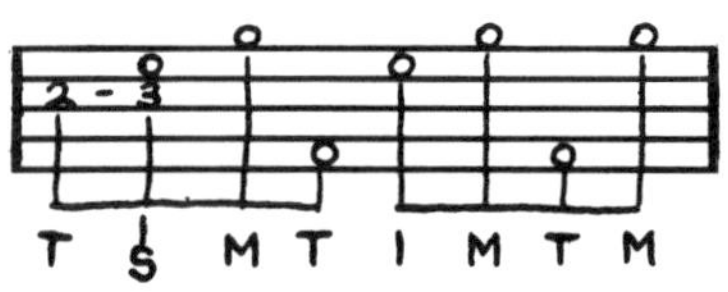

Notice that the slide goes up only to the third fret, not the fourth. Many beginners feel inclined to slide up to the fourth fret because that's where they get a B note (which sounds better with the B note of the open second string than an A♯ does). They end up sounding the two B notes in unison. The trouble is that most banjos don't fret accurately at that fret and the unison doesn't sound quite right. Some banjo instruction books say to slide up to the fourth fret, but the slide usually goes up only to the third fret (A♯) at which point the finger doing the sliding relaxes for a split second, lifting up slightly and damping the string. Just at that point, the second string is played, and the effect is the sound of a slide up to the B note. The damping effect is important because if the string isn't damped, the A♯ note on the third string clashes with the B note on the second.

Here are some other commonly used slides:

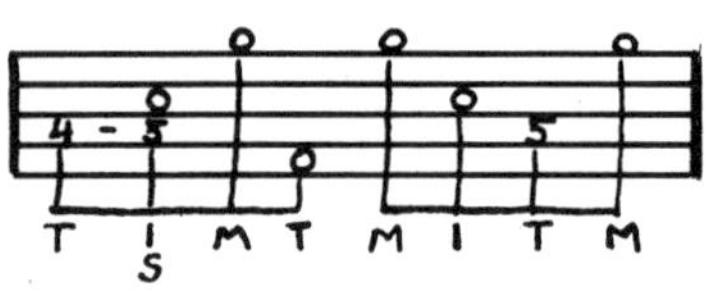

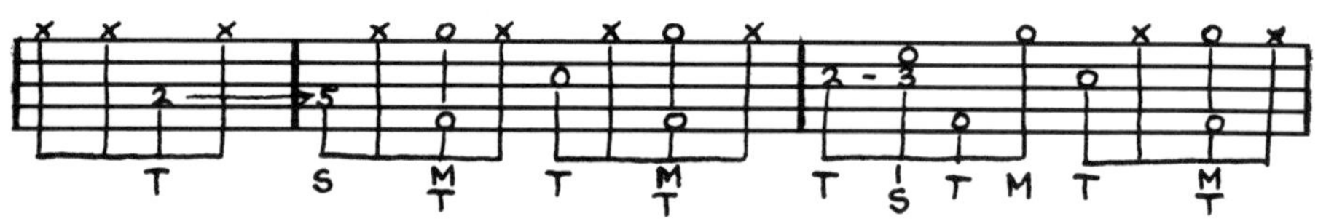

Tablature note:

The second lick contains several X's. This tablature symbol stands for *rest.* When you see an X, simply leave a space the equivalent of one note, so that even though you aren't *playing* eight notes to a measure, you will be leaving space for eight, and taking the same amount of time to play a measure. Rests are used fairly often in bluegrass banjo playing. Without them the banjo would have a machine-like sound. Rests create breathing space and allow for more variation in pacing. It's also true, however, that beginning banjo players are prone to leaving too many rests. Their playing sounds choppy as a result. In order to help you develop the ability to keep a steady flow of notes going when you want to, I won't be using many rests in the tablature for now.

Pull-offs

Pull-offs are fairly difficult to get just right. Although just about everyone does slides the same way, there are some banjo players (like J.D. Crowe and Porter Church) whose pull-offs are unmistakably crisper and snappier than others.

As you might have guessed, a pull-off is when you play a fretted string and then take your fretting finger off the string to get a different note.

You can pull off to an open string:

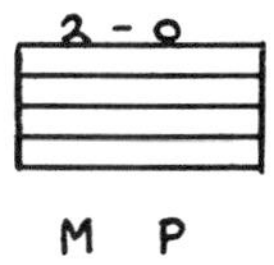

or to a closed string:

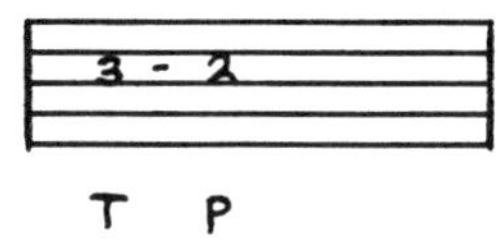

This last example is the most commonly used pull-off. Start with your left middle finger on the third fret with the index finger right behind it on the second fret. When you pull the third fret note off do not just lift the finger off; try to get under the string a bit and *snap* it slightly, as though you were picking the string with your left hand. If you get a sort of picking sound on this pull-off, you're doing well.

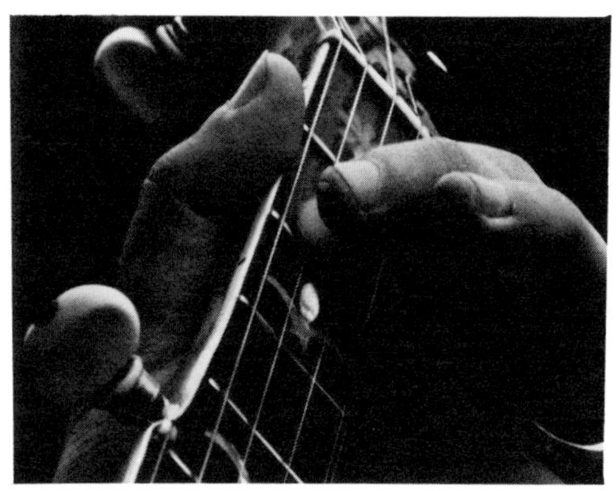

Here is a variant of a commonly used lick from before, using a pull-off this time:

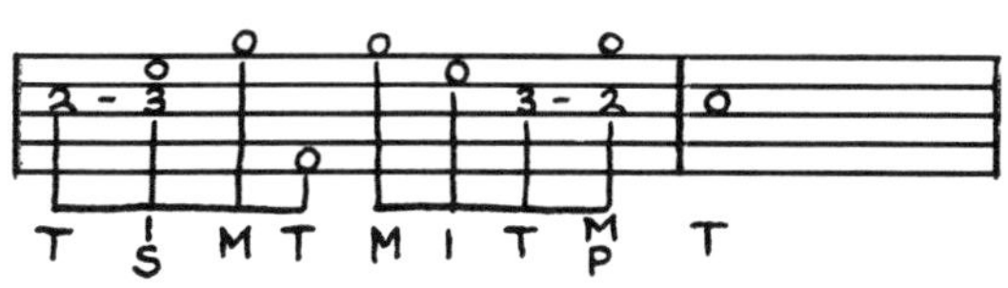

Since this is a difficult move to do just right I suggest you take plenty of time to practice the hardest part of it. Play this over and over:

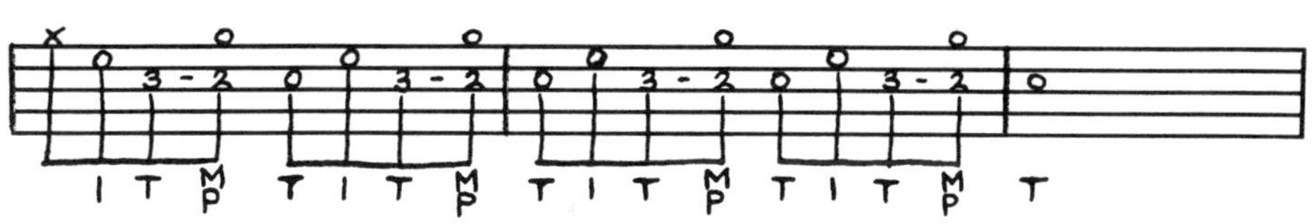

A reminder: With hammer-ons, slides and pull-offs, the left hand move should happen at about the same time as the next right hand note, otherwise you'll be adding a ninth note into the measure.

Now here is another group of commonly used licks which make use of slides, pull-offs, etc. To begin with, some *tag licks:*

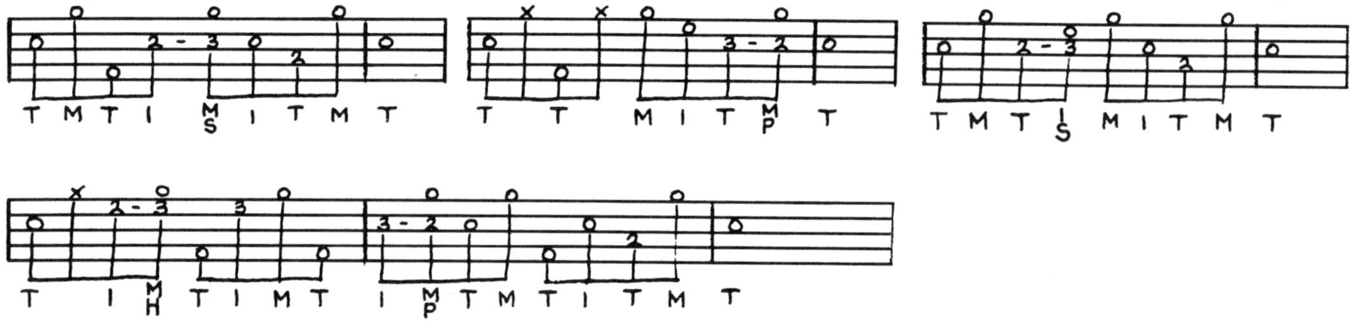

These are called tag licks because they fit well at the end of a break. At the end of a break there is always a bit of time which needs to be filled up. You can use any of these tag licks at the end of any of the songs you've worked out. Start the tag lick at the final note of the song ("comes" in *Coming Round the Mountain,* for example).

Tag licks are quite useful in spaces other than the end of a break, where you'd otherwise be playing a full measure of open G. An example of such a place is after the word "comes" in the first line of *Coming Round the Mountain.* As another example, in the opening break of *Foggy Mt. Breakdown,* Earl Scruggs uses the first in the above group of tag licks *three* times in addition to his use of it at the end of the break.

Lead-ins

When beginning a break, don't start right in on the melody, but play a few notes leading into the first full measure of the song. For example:

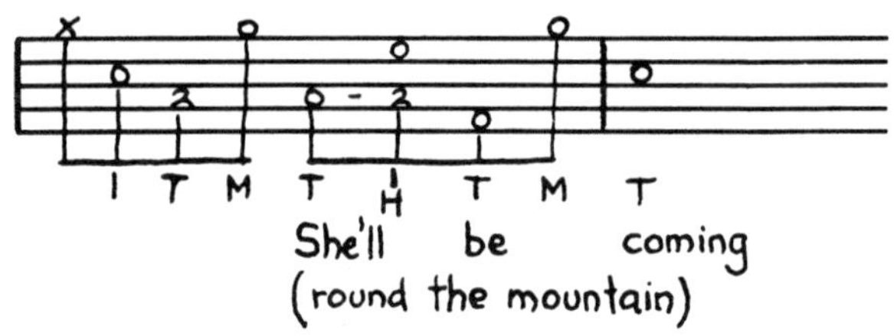

The first two lead-ins are for songs in which the note being led into is G ("coming" and "listen"). The lead-ins written above are used often for songs where the first note of the first full measure is G. The lead-in for *Red River Valley* leads into a B ("valley"), and that lick is very common for lead-ins into a B.

Here is a standard lead-in for a high D note:

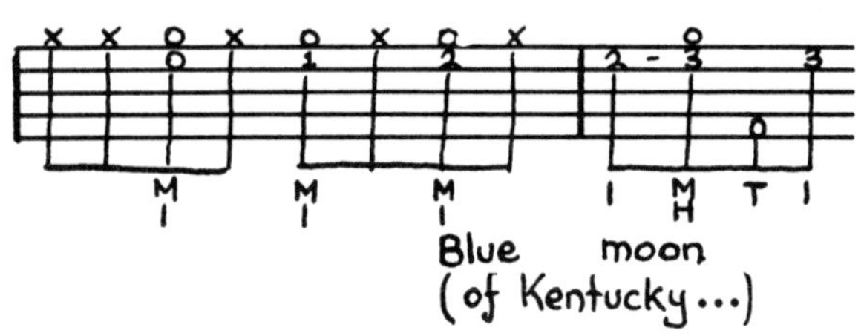

Here is one for a low D note:

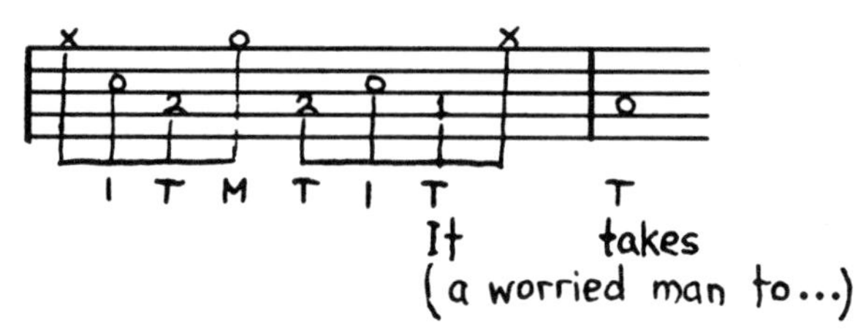

Bill Monroe and the Blue Grass Boys. Lamar Greer on banjo, Richard Greene on fiddle, Peter Rowan on guitar.

Licks and improvising

So far I've been showing you how to play a *melody* bluegrass style. By now, if you hear any simple bluegrass-type tune you should be able to produce a simple arrangement of it without too much trouble. (If you can't, I suggest you backtrack and practice working out simple arrangements before you go ahead.)

At this point, you probably want to put more variety in your playing – a little decoration on the solid foundation you've built. One way to do this is to use . . .

Licks

A lick is any musical phrase which sounds particularly good, good enough to use in places instead of the melody. Musicians use licks for variation (though some licks are used so often they are sometimes called *clichés*). Just as magicians have bags of tricks which they pull out to surprise people, musicians have bags of *licks* which they frequently dip into to brighten up their performances. Rather than play the pure melody at a certain point, they may pull out a musical phrase which is interestingly different from the melody, yet which still fits the chords and rhythm of the tune. For example, tag licks (from the last chapter) are substitutes for playing a straight roll based around the G note on the open third string.

Any part of any melody can have a lick substituted for it. The only musical requirement is that the lick fit the chords and rhythm. This is not to say that any lick will work as well as any other lick, or that it will work as well as the straight melody. These are matters of musical taste. In fact, it sometimes happens that the sound of a particular lick will delight the person who is playing it but will sound to others out of place musically with the rest of the playing. There are certainly some musicians who overuse licks – they are so intent upon showing what tricks they can do that they lose sight of the main thing, which is to play coherent, good-sounding music.

Licks are easiest to categorize by the chords they fit in with. For instance, there are some licks you can put in any time you have a measure of D to fill up. There are some licks to use for two measures of G going into a C. The following is a series of some of the most commonly used bluegrass banjo licks, stuck back to back as though they were all part of a break to a song. The chord changes are the same as for the songs *Coming Round the Mountain* or *Roll in My Sweet Baby's Arms.* This is a handy format in which to present a rather large number of licks. (It's also a way of showing how licks can be overused and sound tasteless.) By seeing where in the arrangement they fit, you can get a good idea of how to use them in your arrangements.

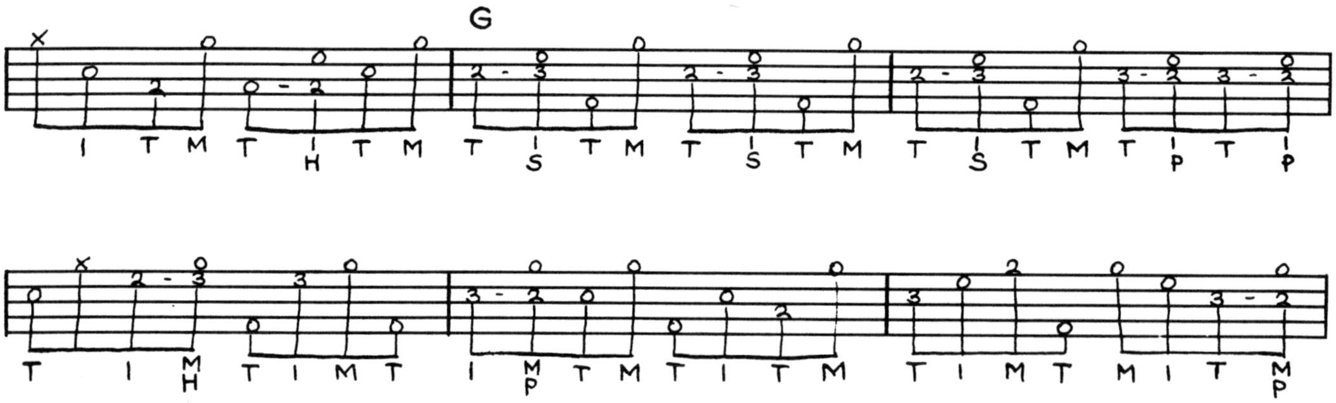

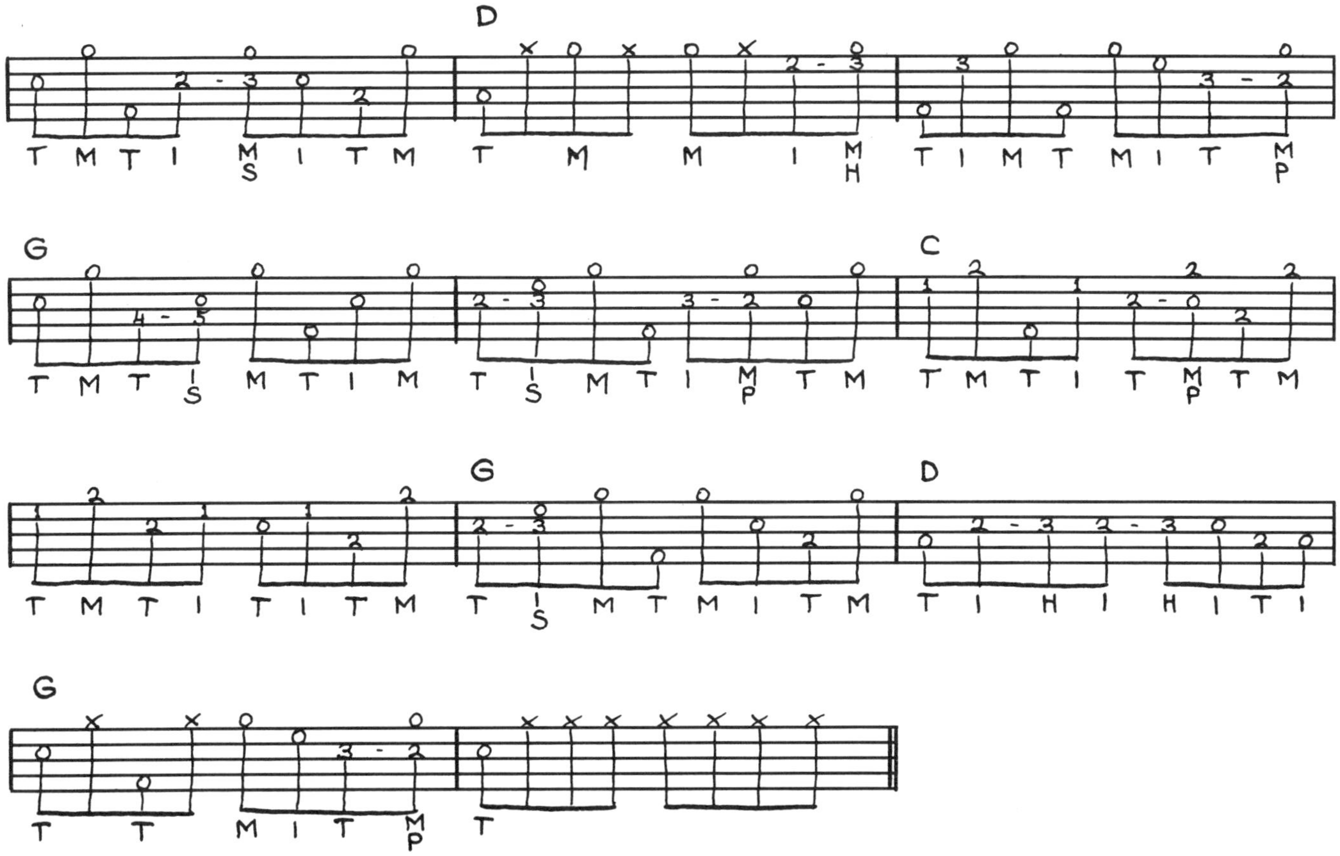

J. D. Crowe

Now here's another arrangement for the same chord progression with other licks:

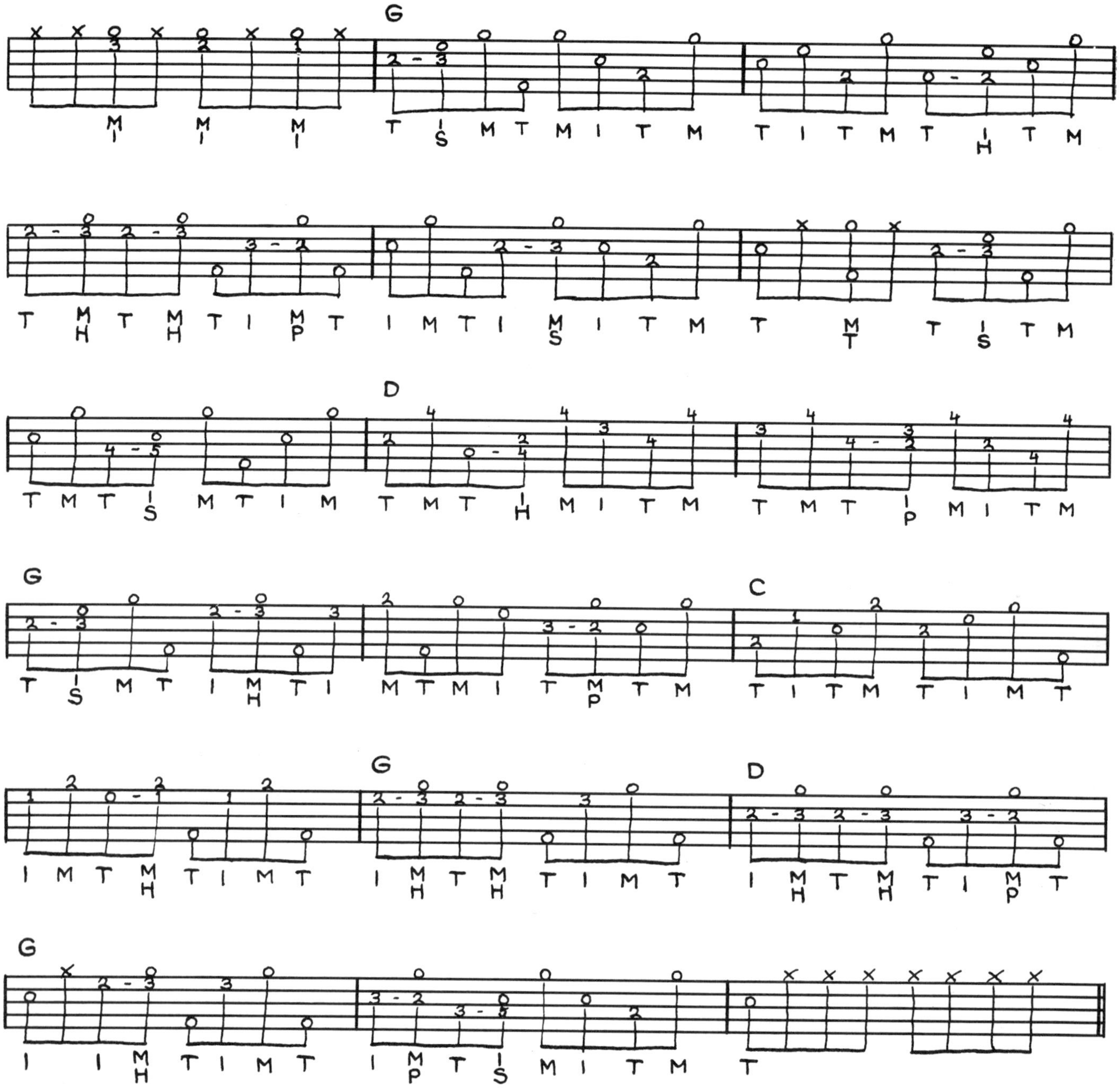

Playing music is like talking, or, more accurately, giving a speech. When you play music you try to get a certain idea across – the melody line. In music, as in speech, there are many different ways and degrees to which an idea can be embellished. There are a few who give the idea in as straight a way as possible. Most people give the idea in a fairly straight way but add a few special touches – a different word or phrase (like saying "off his rocker" or "really wigged out" instead of saying "peculiar"). Some people prefer to present ideas in highly elaborate form such as parables, analogies, or highly complicated or stylized language.

So it goes with putting together a *musical* thought. Licks are used like fancy words, analogies, or sayings – they get the idea across but they can add something extra. Beware of the pitfalls: if you use them when they don't quite fit, you can sound really pretentious; and if you overuse a lick or a phrase, it turns from something special into something boring.

Improvising

Musicians often play the same song or tune many times. Like public speakers who also have to repeat the same idea frequently, they may look for ways to vary their presentation. In the same way a speaker sometimes talks off the cuff, some musicians like to improvise instead of playing a worked-through arrangement each time.

Licks are obviously a help in improvising. In playing situations a musician can reach into the lick bag and pull out whatever seems to fit the music at the time. Some musicians make an important point of learning new licks all the time by listening to others or by simply working new ideas out themselves. They accumulate large storehouses of licks which enable them to vary their playing a great deal.

Improvising doesn't have to rely so heavily on pre-planned musical phrases. In fact, I like it best if it isn't. Like many banjo players (as well as other musicians) I don't usually know what I'm going to play until just about the moment I play it. I often try to make up a counter-melody as I go along – a melody which fits the rhythm and chords of the tune but which is different from it.

For an example of what I mean by a counter-melody, go through the second of the two tablature arrangements in this chapter. The licks I used in that arrangement have enough melody in them so that when they are put together, a fairly coherent melody line can be heard. This line would never be confused with the tune *Coming Round the Mountain,* but it can be thought of as a distant variation based on the chord scheme.

Courtney Johnson

Intermediate tablature section

Here are arrangements using some of the ideas introduced in the last two chapters. The rolls used are less repetitive and there is generally more variation than in the arrangements on pages 22-28, *(Basic bluegrass style).* It might be interesting to compare the arrangements for the songs in that chapter with the ones for the same songs in this one, to see how far you've come.

Learning the pieces as written here will help you to loosen up your playing, and you may start seeing the variations you are capable of creating yourself. You may even stumble across some nice variations while trying to work out what I have written. These discoveries are important, but don't neglect the exercises given here. At all times, try to be aware of how you're sounding. It's not enough to simply play the notes. You have to make them sound good. This is what sets Scruggs apart from so many of his imitators. Try for a sound that is smooth, clear and crisp. Don't hesitate to practice a tune again and again, until you are satisfied with it.

As with the other tablature arrangements you've worked out, try to play only a bit at a time rather than going through the whole piece at once. First, work on the first two to four measures until you are able to play them smoothly and to remember them easily. Then do the same for the next two or four measures and put them all together. Most people learn the tunes best this way.

Cripple Creek

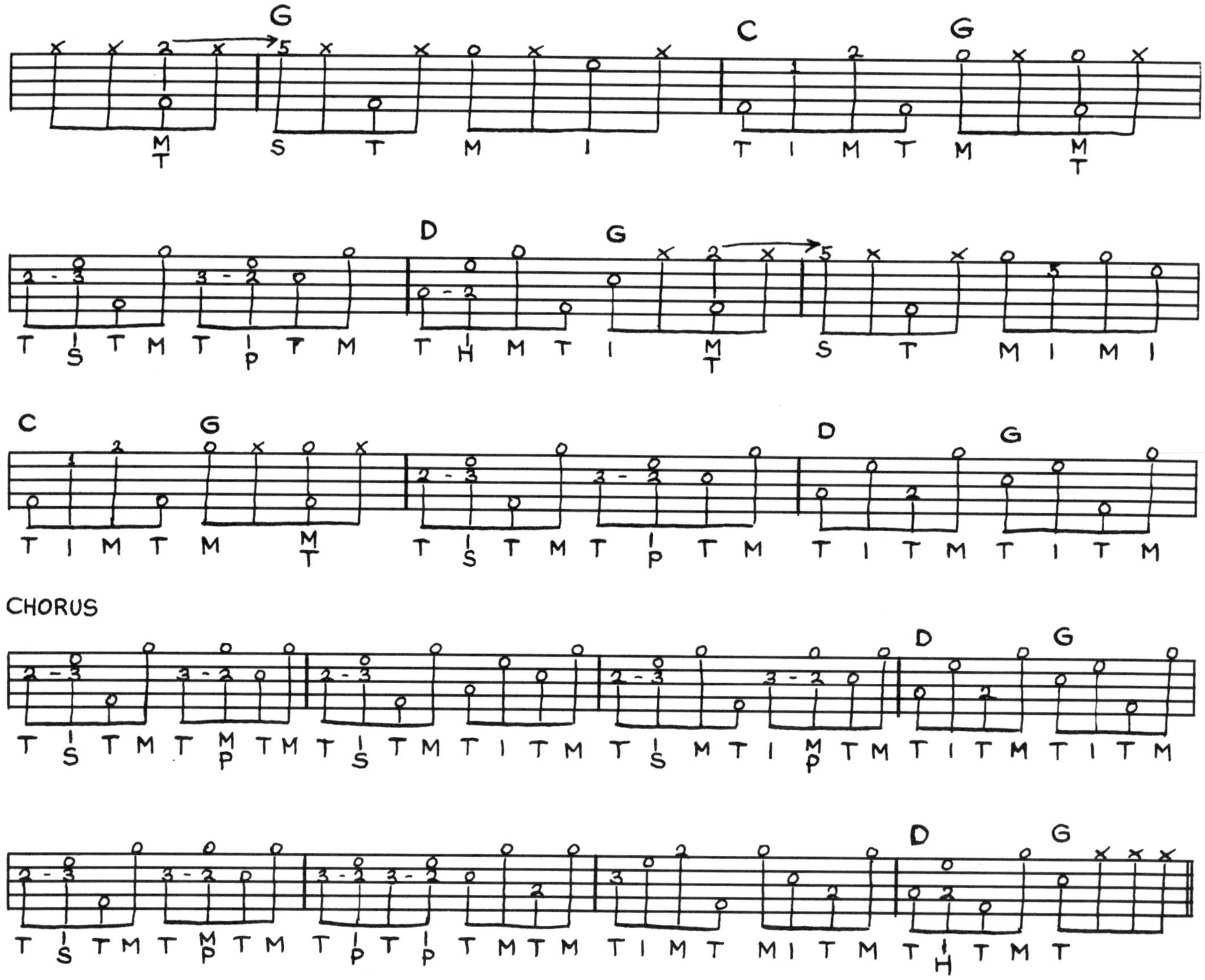

Worried Man

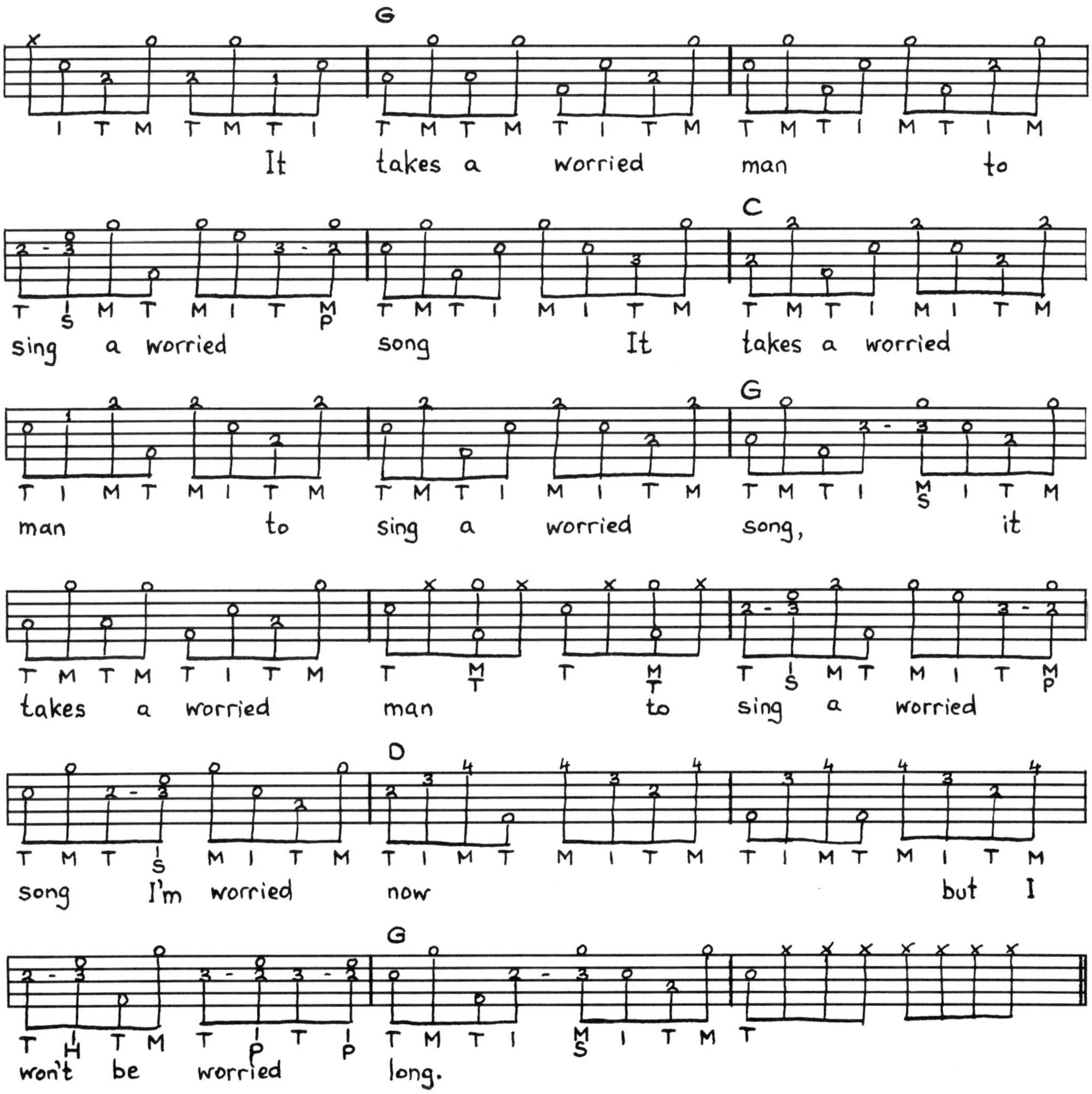

This is the second banjo break in the version of this song on the record included with this book.

She'll Be Coming Round the Mountain

This is the second banjo break in the version of this song on the record included with this book.

Will the Circle Be Unbroken

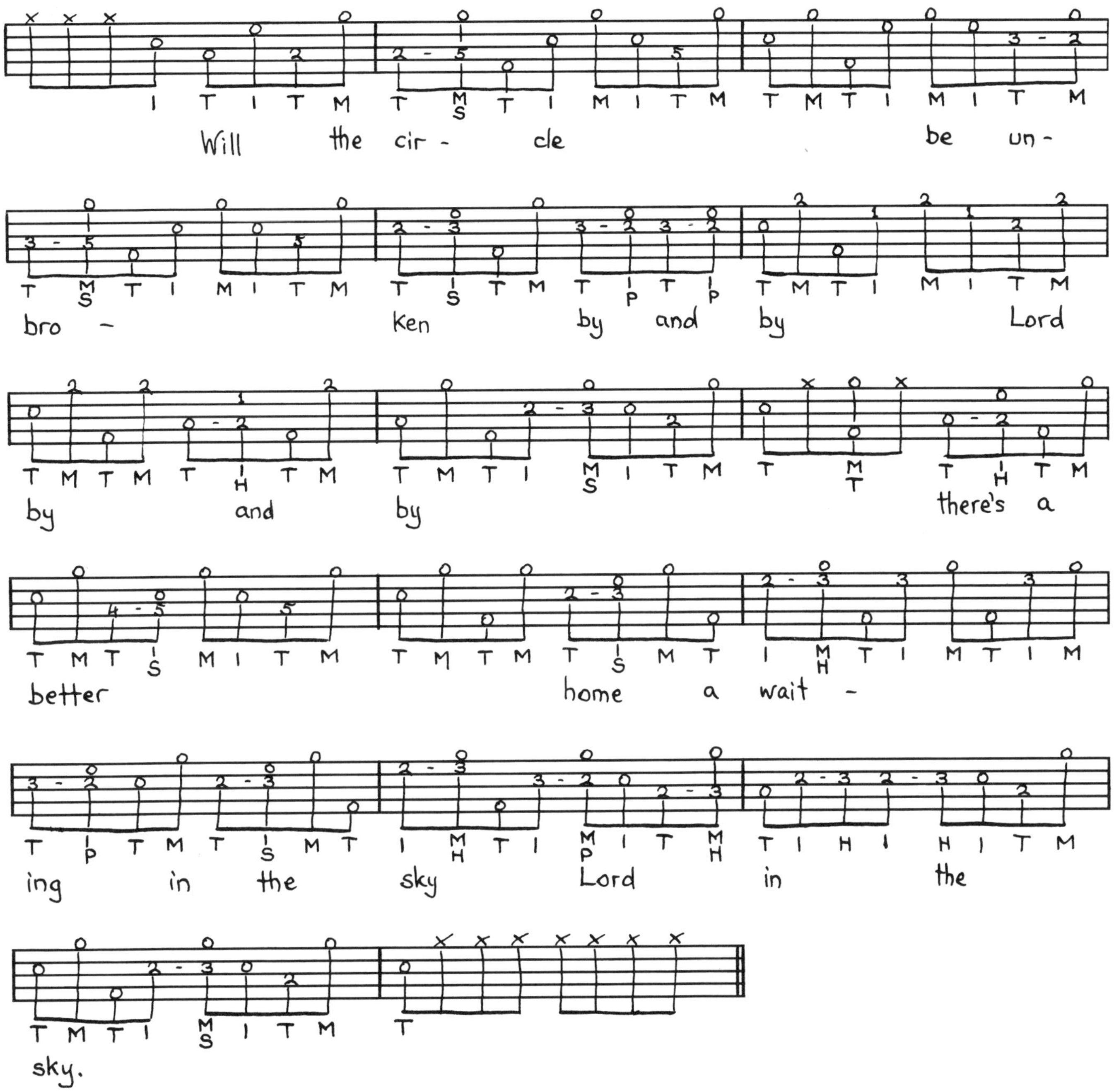

This is the second banjo break in the version of this song on the record included with this book.

Ballad of Jed Clampett

Paul Henning

Based on Earl Scruggs' version.

Mountain Dew

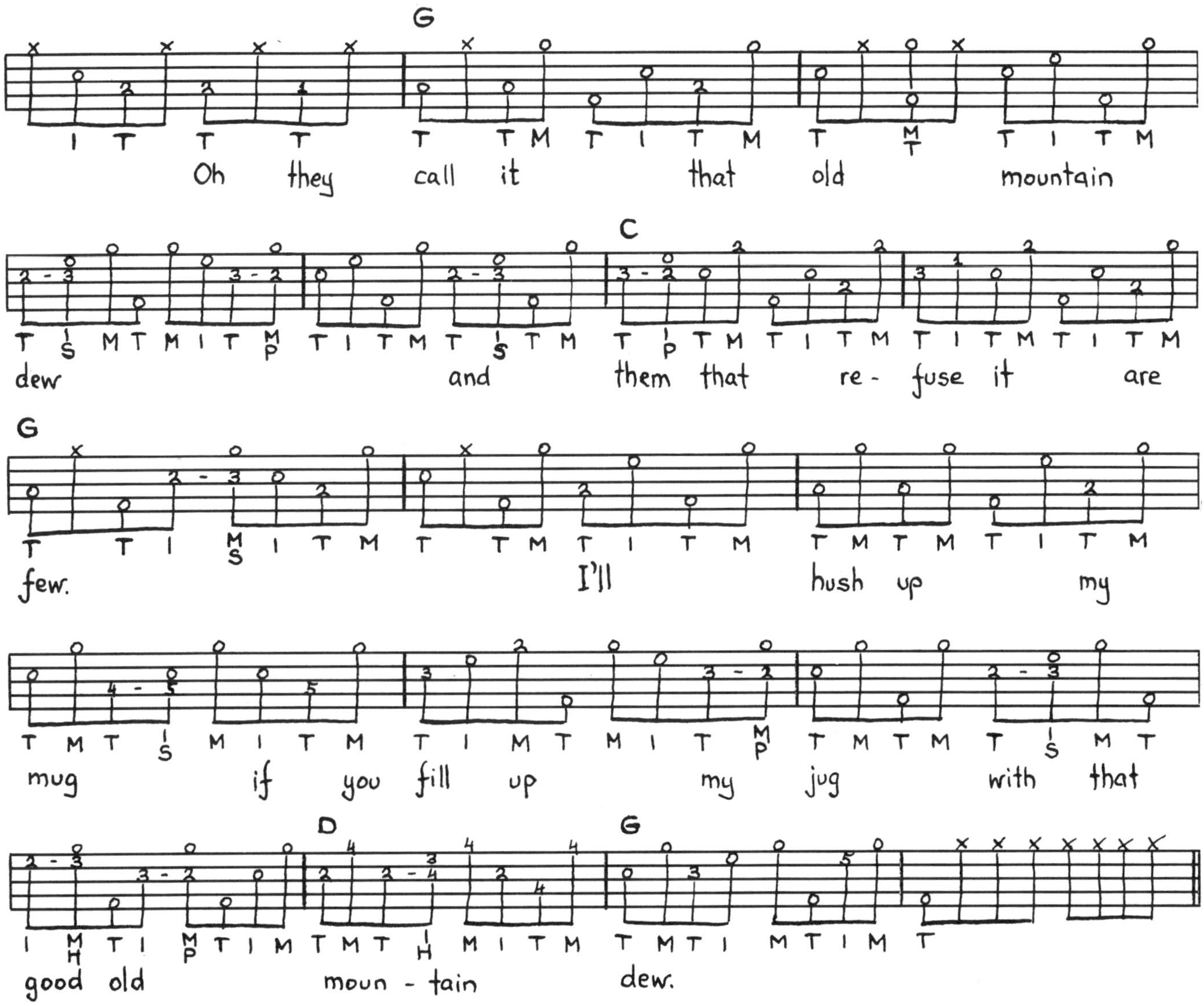

Jesse James

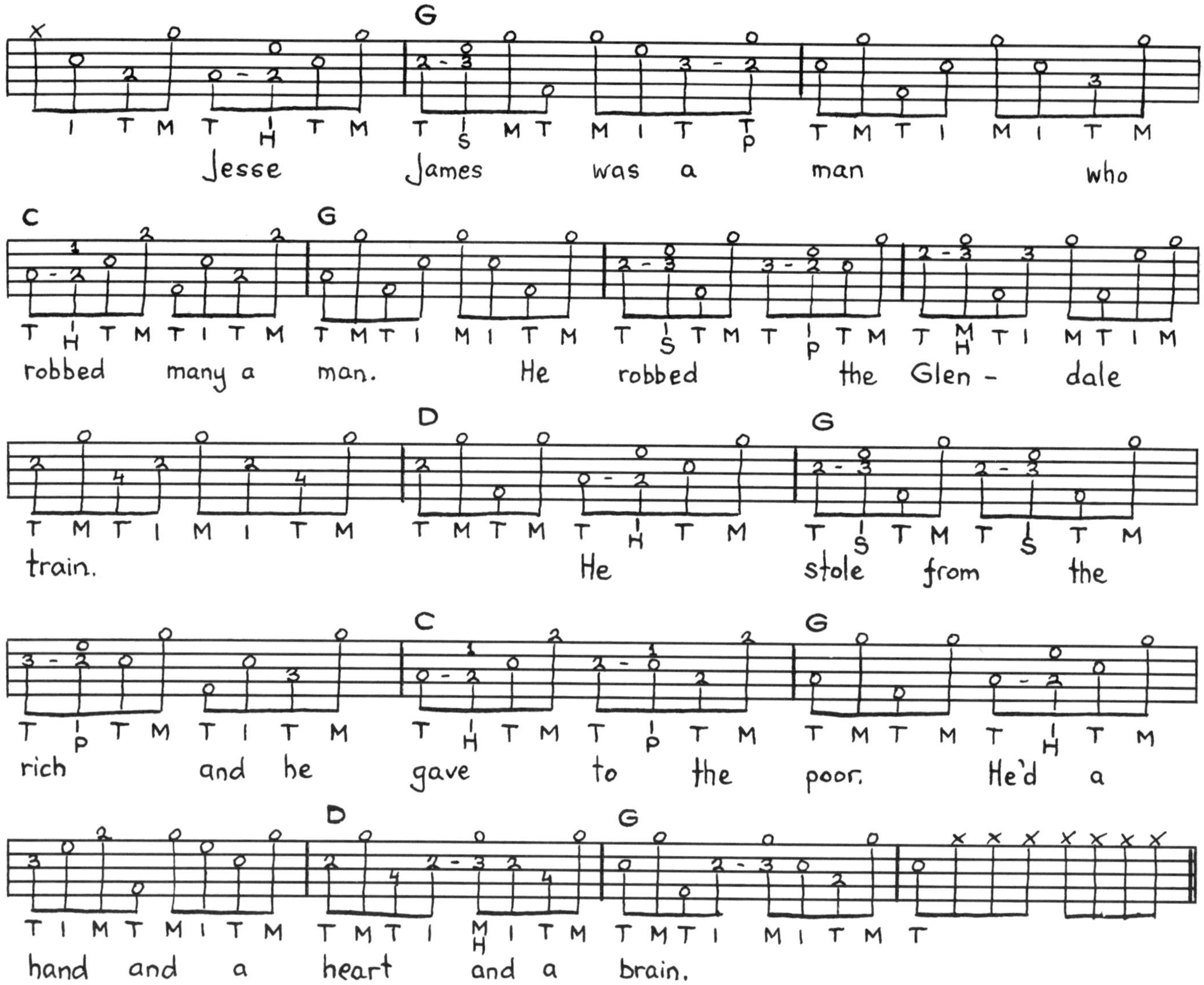

This is one half of the double banjo version of *Jesse James* on Side I of the record included with this book.

Little Maggie

Using records to learn

By this time you should have spent a good deal of time listening to your bluegrass records. Hopefully, you have learned the melodies to some of the songs. If so, you are now ready to start making up your own breaks to songs that you run across on your records. The method is the same as for the earliest songs you learned: Figure out what the chords are (they'll almost always be I, IV, and V), figure out the melody, and try to play the melody while filling up the spaces with notes. You may get some ideas from listening to what the banjo player on the record is doing. Having worked out a break, try comparing it to the break on the record, and see if you can pick up some new pointers.

Records can play a very important part in learning how to play. They can provide, in effect, the first bluegrass musicians you ever play with. With a record player or tape recorder that plays at half-speed, you can also learn banjo technique from them.

One of the problems of playing with records is getting in tune with them. The bands do not always play in G. They often use keys like A and B, which requires the use of a capo and the re-tuning of the fifth string. For instance, playing in A requires that you put your capo on the second fret and that you raise the fifth string two half steps, from G to A. You can then play as you do in G and *the strings will sound in A.* For playing in B raise everything four frets and for C raise everything five. In each case, if you play as you would in G (pretending the capo is the nut), the music will sound in whatever key you've capoed into.

To simplify raising the pitch of the fifth string (and to avoid the risk of breaking the string by too much tightening), most banjo players use either a fifth string capo or a pair of small nails placed behind the seventh and ninth frets of the fifth string. (For more information about these, see Appendix 2.)

To get in tune with a band on a record you first have to find out what key they're in. If the song is an up-tempo one, the key will almost always be somewhere between G and C. You can usually find the key easily by humming the last note of a verse or chorus and checking the first five frets of the third string to see which one it's closest to in pitch. That's the fret where the capo should go. The fifth string should then be tuned to match the pitch of the first string five frets up from the capo. Now get the banjo *exactly* in tune with the record. Listen once more to the last note of a verse or chorus, and tune the third string to that pitch. Tune the rest of the strings using that pitch as a standard and you're ready to go.

Play the record through again, experimenting with the G, C, and D chords to get an idea of the chord progression. After a little while you probably will find the right chords, and you can start playing along with some assurance. Play a basic roll along with the music at first, and then let your own ideas lead you where they may. You may want to try a break, or you may be content to just play along. It's great practice for what you're working toward – playing in a bluegrass band. This band is very patient – it will play the same song over and over as often as you like and it won't mind when you make mistakes. For those beginning banjo players who have problems keeping in rhythm (and who generally can't hear their mistakes) playing along with records is ideal for working at the problem. Just keep playing along with the record, and if you get out of time you know you made a mistake. Go back over the same part until you find a way of getting back on.

The second side of the record included with this book provides three medium-speed tunes to play along with. By adjusting the balance knob on your stereo to eliminate the banjo (recorded by itself on one channel) you can be the only banjo player in the band. The better you play, the better the whole band will sound.

Playing along with the banjo player on a record can lead to plenty of discoveries. You may often find yourself doing something similar to the record, completely by accident, and you will be just a step away from learning to duplicate it.

When you want to learn *exactly* how a banjo player on a record is playing something, slowing the record down to half-speed can be a big help. One result of playing a record at half-speed is that the sound comes out a full octave lower, with the singers sounding like incoherent elephants and the banjo sounding like twangy rubber bands, but it's a lot easier to pick out the exact pitch of each note when it is not at full speed. It's possible (if you're very patient) to go through a whole break note by note and figure out every last move. You can stop a tape recorder exactly where you want and come back to it later. Most tape recorders have numerical counters to help you find your place. Using a record player requires more guessing and more patience in finding the exact spot you want to hear.

Whichever you use, you can let the machine run right to the first note you want to learn, quickly shut off the sound (to avoid getting confused by the notes which follow), and find the note on the banjo. Then go back and do it with the note that follows, and so on. Often you can find patterns of notes without having to hunt each one down separately. It takes a while, but I can tell you that sessions with my record player and tape recorder had a lot to do with my learning how to play. It always seemed well worth the time I had to spend on it.

John Hartford

Playing with other people

Once you've achieved a level of ability which enables you to play a number of songs or tunes in rhythm and at a reasonable speed, it's time to find other people to play with. Keep practicing with your records, by all means, but there is no substitute for playing with other people. Interacting with other musicians (not just musically, but socially as well) is really what being a musician is all about. People who learn to play bluegrass alone are usually pretty strange to play with until they've adjusted themselves to the musical and social aspects of playing with others.

Now that I've convinced you . . . find yourself a guitar player.

Why a guitar player? Bluegrass banjo does not lay down a clear chordal and rhythmic basis for music the way a guitar does. The chords and the rhythm from a guitar provide a solid basis for the single notes of the banjo to stand out against or interplay with. Getting together with a guitar player will lead you into a new way of making music.

Playing with a guitar player will also probably help you to become aware of and to eliminate any musical problems you have, especially rhythm problems – the most common plague of beginners.

Aside from the direct musical benefits there are less direct ones: having someone to trade records with, to learn material from, to comment favorably about your progress, to talk bluegrass with, to drive to bluegrass shows and festivals with, etc.

How to find this guitar player? If you don't already know someone who fills the bill, why not advertise? It's a common practice and it's easily done. Some good places to start are bulletin boards, such as the one at your friendly local music shop (or any other local music shop), any paper that takes classified ads, especially a college paper or any other publication that caters to a music-oriented audience. In several parts of the country (Colorado, Indiana, New York, Virginia, Massachusetts, to name a few) there are bluegrass clubs where people get together once a month or so to exchange licks and sometimes to hear a visiting group. Then there are the bluegrass shows that come to your area. In the audience at any of these shows there are probably a few guitar players who would be ready, willing and able to play with you if you are outgoing enough to find them. A regular feature of bluegrass festivals has become the many pickup groups in the parking lot. Remember, there must be ten times as many guitar players in the country as there are banjo players, so the odds are with you.

If you are lucky you may run across more than just a guitar player. If you find a mandolin player, a fiddle player or a bass player you can form a little band. However, at this early stage it's probably better not to play with more than two others. If you are all relatively new to bluegrass you'll probably need a little experience playing in small combinations before you move up to larger ones.

The role of the banjo in a bluegrass band

When you're ready for it, playing with a full-size bluegrass band (banjo, fiddle, mandolin, guitar, and bass) is a great experience. In my opinion it is this combination of instruments which bluegrass style banjo tends to be most at home in (and I have heard and done plenty of experimenting with it in other musical settings). That isn't surprising when you consider that when the banjo style was originally developed by Scruggs in the mid-40's, its purpose was to add to and enhance the sound of a *bluegrass* band (Bill Monroe's) which until then had lacked that type of banjo sound.

Each instrument in a bluegrass band makes its own special contribution to the overall sound. There are three parts to this sound:

1. the rhythmic basis,
2. the chordal basis (the general ensemble sound – the "hum" of the band),
3. the lead, or featured part (can be vocal or instrumental).

In a conventional bluegrass band the guitar, mandolin and bass are the chordal and rhythmic foundation. The bass plays big resonant notes just on the downbeats (except for occasional runs). The guitar plays bass notes on the downbeats, strums full chords on the offbeats and also plays runs. The mandolin's usual function is as a percussion instrument – it plays brisk chords on the offbeats with occasional rhythmic variations. Together the guitar, bass and mandolin create the basic "Boom-chick" sound that sets the time in a bluegrass band. (The "boom" is the bass note on the guitar and bass; the "chick" is the chord hit by the mandolin and guitar.)

The banjo and fiddle have more leeway as backup instruments. Depending on what fits, either might be:

1. percussive, and hit chords on the offbeat (*choonk* or *pop* is what many musicians call it),

2. playing continuously and smoothly to fill out the ensemble sound, or

3. playing loudly and interestingly enough to stand out a bit from the ensemble sound. This can be done continuously (acting as a "second lead" behind a lead instrument or vocal), or sporadically (doing occasional "fills" when the lead instrument or vocal is in a short musical pause).

In other words, the banjo and fiddle can contribute to any of the three main parts of the sound – rhythmic, chordal, or lead.

To hear what I mean, listen to what the banjo does in the songs on Side II of the record included with this book.

Playing in a band involves a lot of listening to what is going on at all times. In a good band everyone pays constant attention to all parts of the sound. If an instrument isn't playing lead it should be doing everything it can to help the band sound good behind the lead. That means paying attention to the overall volume and energy level of the music, the balance of instruments, the heaviness of the rhythm, the fullness of the sound, etc. Different songs and tunes have different "feels" to them and everyone in the band has to get a sense of that feel (driving, coasting, sparse, pretty, lonesome, bouncy, warm, etc.), and make their contribution to it. Sometimes the best contribution is to play very quietly or not at all.

In this section I will give you some general tips about playing with others, but almost everything you learn will be from your own playing experience and from listening to others. The more of both you do the better a band musician you will be.

The banjo has a sound all its own, but that sound can be varied to fit different musical situations. When you play alone or with others you should experiment a little with the types of sound you can get out of your instrument. Vary the volume just by digging in harder when you pick. You can also put an edge on the tone by hitting the strings more sharply, more crisply and more closely to the tips of the finger picks than usual. The easiest way to give a hard or soft flavor to your playing is to vary the distance from your picks to the bridge. The closer to the bridge your picks hit the strings, the sharper the notes will sound, the further from the bridge, the more mellow. On most banjos if you play with your middle finger hitting the strings at about 1-1/2" from the bridge you will find the happy medium – a crisp, full sound. But when the occasion calls for harder or softer sounds you can vary the distance from the bridge accordingly. The further from the bridge you play, the longer the notes last. When you play several inches from the bridge these longer notes blend into each other and produce more of a humming sound than a crackling one.

You should be aware that the instrument you play can be made to sound sharper or more mellow by the way you set it up. See the article by Tom Morgan (Appendix 5).

Accenting notes is another way to vary the overall sound you get. Hard and regular accents right on the beats give a driving sound (a la Don Stover). Accenting notes on offbeats gives a bouncier sound (a la Allen Shelton or any Jimmy Martin banjo player). Varied accents can produce a freer but possibly more disorganized sound (watch out!). Easing off a little on accents while maintaining a smooth flow of notes at a good volume can give a relaxed coasting effect.

As you get experience playing you will find the best way to produce the different types of sounds you like, and you will develop a sense of when to use them. No two musical situations are the same and it's necessary to adapt yourself to the situation at hand. Consider the type of song you're playing, the energy level of the musicians, the acoustic properties of the room you're in, the relative volumes of the other instruments and the amount of rhythm, chordal and lead-type sounds the group is producing. All these things should go into determining how you play.

One of the most common pitfalls for the banjo player is clashing with other instruments. When the banjo isn't playing lead (and that's 90% of the time) it shouldn't get in the way of the singing or the lead being played by other instruments. By playing smoothly and without unusual notes or rhythms you can stay out of the way and contribute to the backup sound. Sometimes you should just "choonk" on the offbeats or lay out altogether if no extra rhythm is needed.

Sometimes, of course, it sounds good for the banjo to stand out in backup, almost as though it were playing a second lead. The sounds of a fiddle and a banjo complement each other very well and whenever the fiddle is playing lead the banjo sounds good against it. (Fiddle and banjo alone is a combination which goes back a long way. It has a very pleasing, lilting sound. In this situation the banjo usually plays smoothly and steadily, following the chords and weaving in a few simple melodic ideas.)

When played against singing or another instrument's lead, the banjo can sound good by playing harmony or a counter-melody or notes which closely approximate the melody. Playing second lead this way should be done sparingly and with careful attention to avoid producing a cluttered sound or getting in the way of the first lead. There are few things more frustrating than playing with a musician who contributes more than a fair share to the sound of the music.

Here are some things to remember:

1. Bluegrass is *not* built around the banjo. It's a band style and the banjo is one of the instruments in the band. Give everyone else a chance.

2. Instrumental work is not more important than vocals. Bluegrass is made up mainly of songs and if you can sing (if only well enough to help out on harmonies) you're making a good contribution.

3. Music is for everyone to participate in and get something out of. It's not (only) to show off your ego. If you get too hung up trying to amaze and astound you will revile and repel.

Ralph Stanley and Raymond McLain. (Note that Ralph, picking lead, has his hand close to the bridge. Ray, backing up, has his hand further away.)

Some other techniques you should know

Note: If you've gotten this far in the book it's fair to say that you are a serious banjo player. By now you can fully appreciate the difference between a fine-sounding, well-made banjo and a beginner's model. If you are still playing the latter type, I suggest you consider moving up to a better model. It will make a difference in the sound of your playing and in the enjoyment you get out of it. On the other hand, it can cost an arm and a leg. See Appendix 4.

To round out what you've learned so far, this chapter will deal with four techniques which are not absolutely essential but which are commonly used: Unorthodox rolls, choking, special endings, and harmonics.

Unorthodox rolls

On page 22 I gave a general rule about melody notes on the first string: Find the equivalent note on the second string and play that note instead, since it's easier to handle melody notes on the first string than ones on the second string. I added: "Until you are comfortable with more advanced rolls." It is now time for you to learn and become comfortable with those advanced rolls.

Here are four rolls that start with the middle finger:

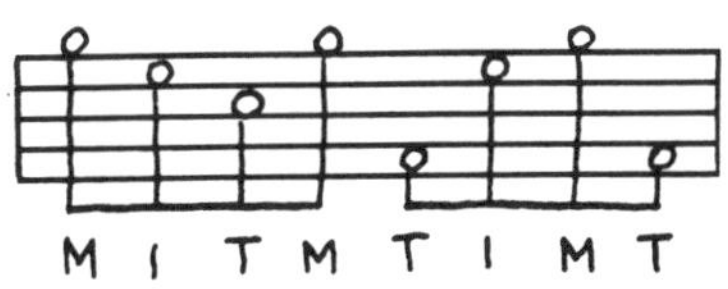

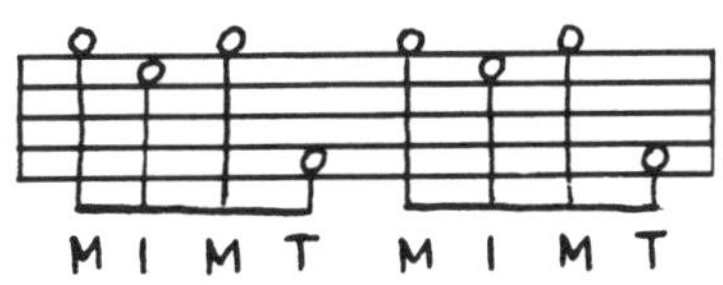

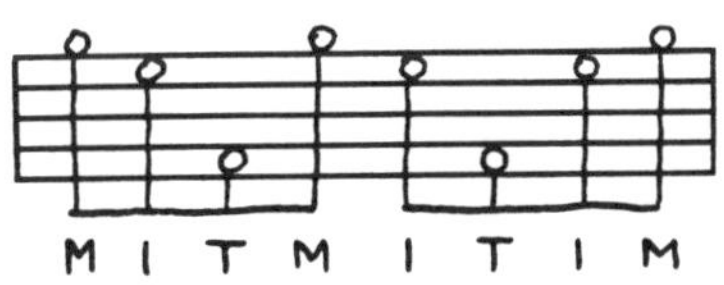

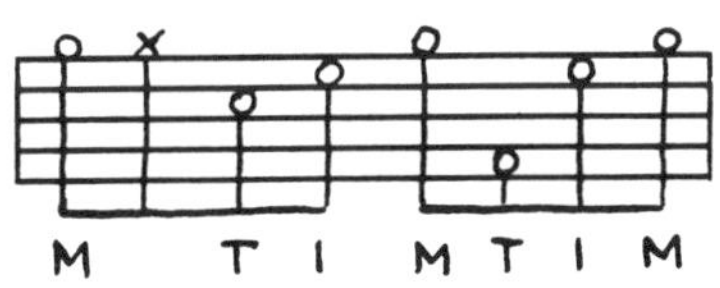

There is no need to memorize these rolls, but it would be a good exercise to go through each one until you can play it comfortably. If your hand has difficulty getting accustomed to starting a roll with the middle finger, that's all the more reason to practice them. Your right hand should eventually learn to be comfortable with *any* sequence. If you can loosen up your right hand so that it can pick up and adapt to a pattern quickly, many new possibilities are opened to you. To see what I mean, play each of the four rolls I have just given you on a simple D7 chord. Each one has a markedly different sound, and it all happens using just one simple left hand formation. Imagine what can happen when you apply a wide variety of right hand patterns to a wide variety of left hand ideas! Endless possibilities. Another thought which may inspire you to work on loosening up your right hand: Melodic style banjo ("chromatic", "Keith style") requires the right hand to be able to play any sequence of strings rapidly and flawlessly.

Here are two more rolls to practice. They both start with the index finger *followed by the thumb* (not beginning with the thumb, as you have been doing so far).

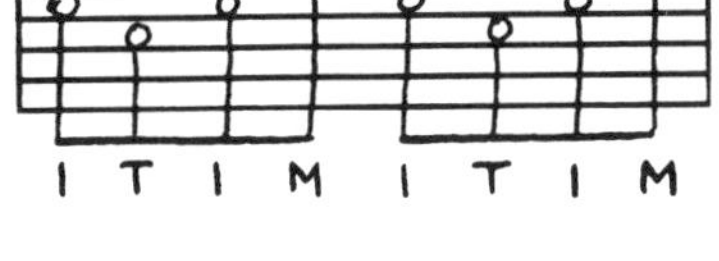

Next, three licks using a new right hand variation: the middle finger hitting the second string. These licks all sound particularly good if the right hand is far enough from the bridge to create a mellow tone, enabling the notes to blend together nicely.

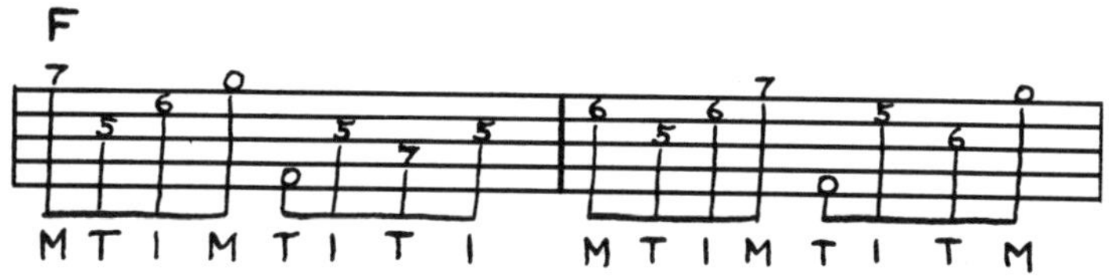

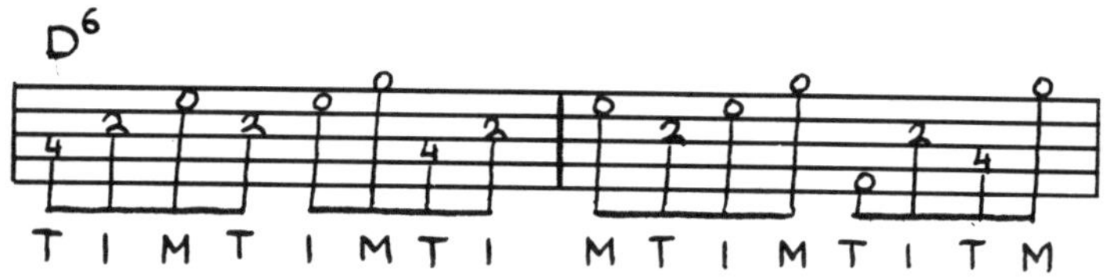

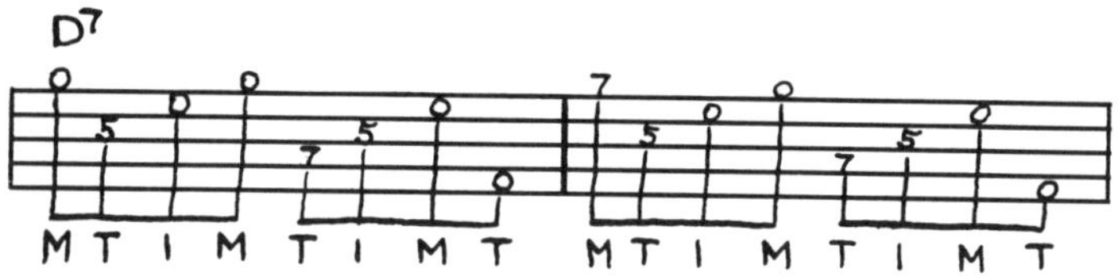

Now here are two arrangements which use some of the right hand ideas you haven't encountered in any of the arrangements I've given to you so far.

In My Mind to Ramble

Peter Wernick

As played by Bill Runkle on Del McCoury's *High On a Mountain* album on Rounder.

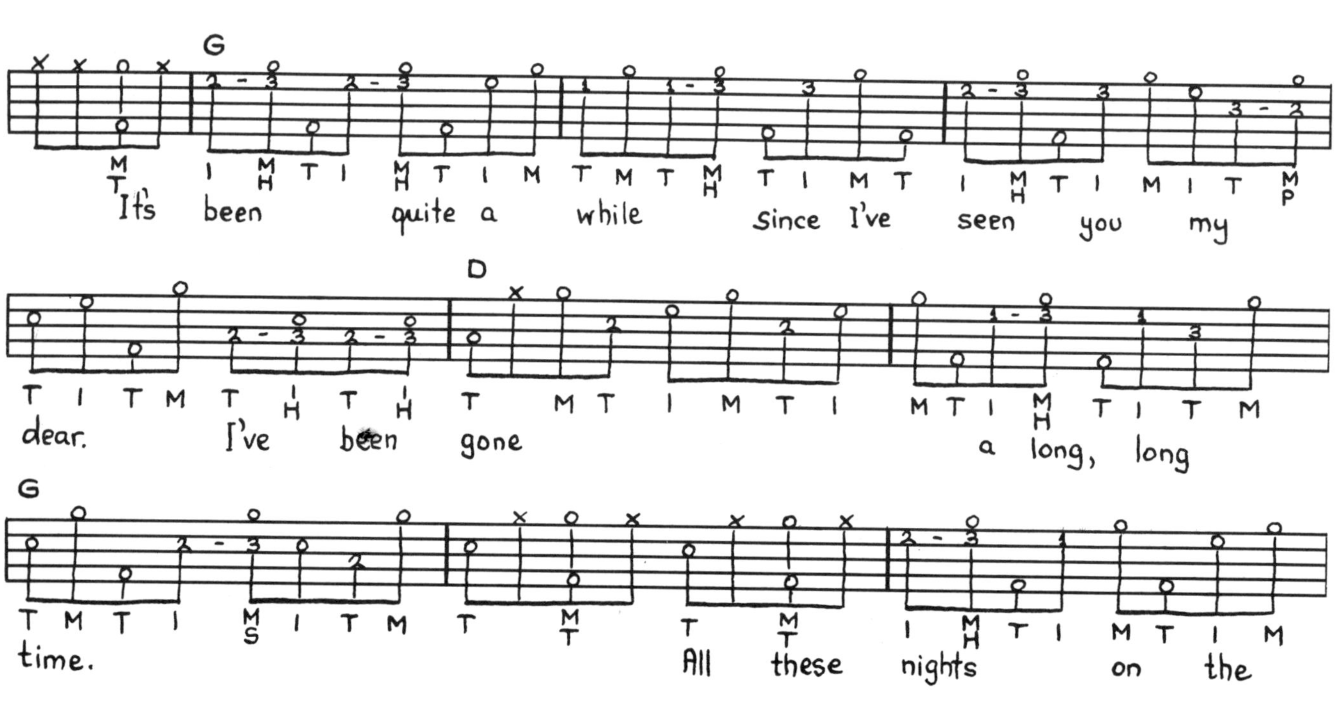

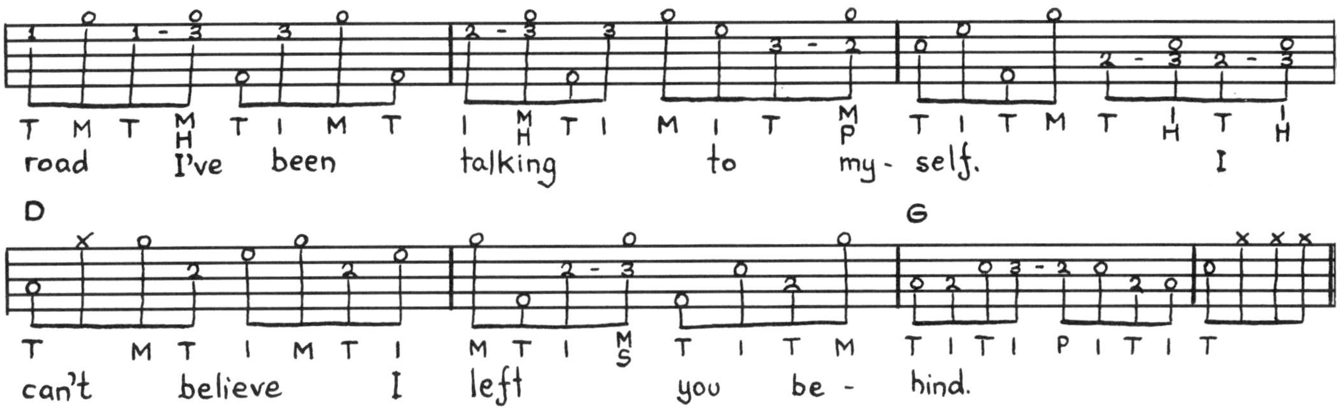

Flatt and Scruggs and the Foggy Mt. Boys

Old Joe Clark

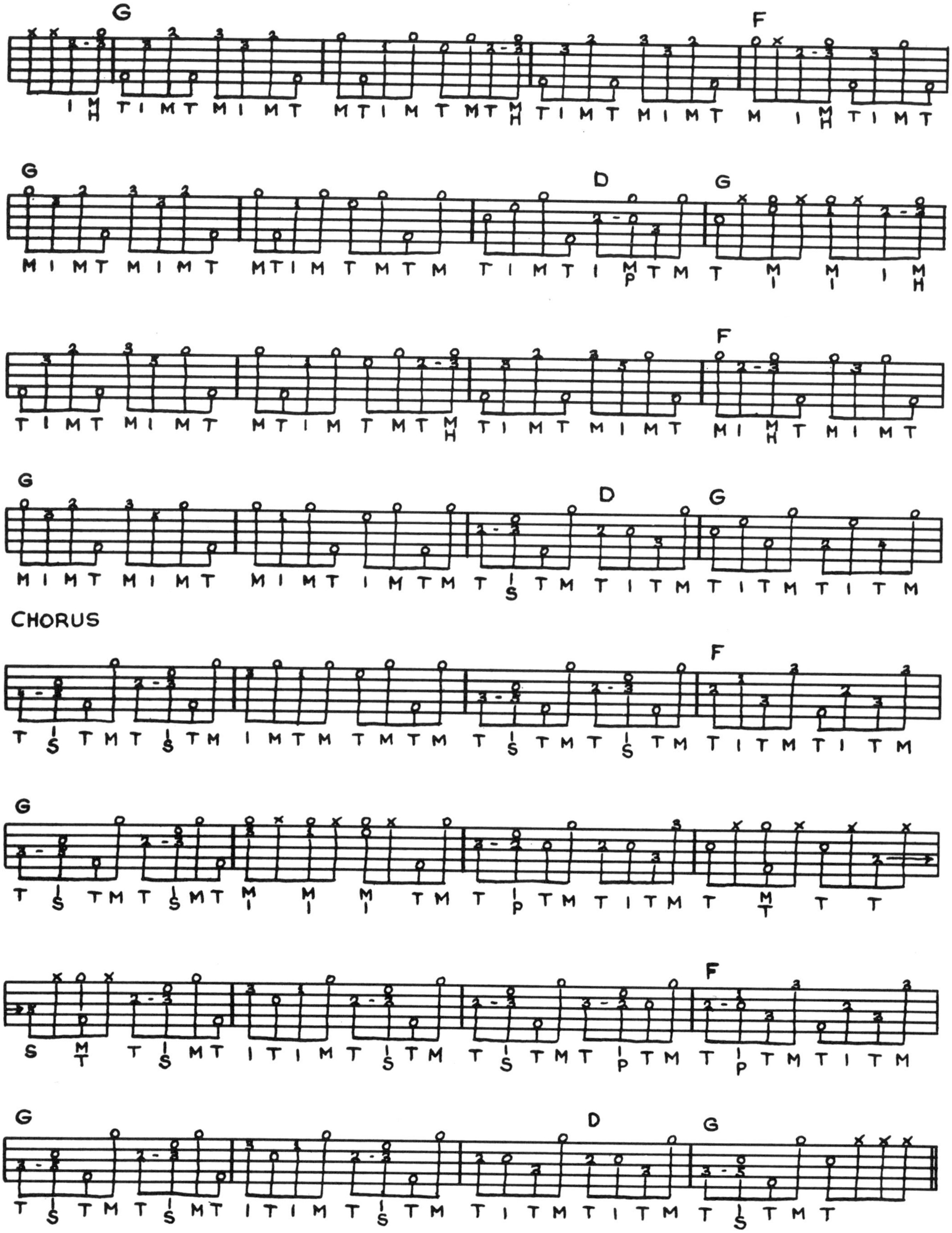

Choking

Choking (or bending) a string means playing a fretted note and then stretching the string with the fretting finger of the left hand to raise the pitch of the note. Here is the way choking is indicated in tablature:

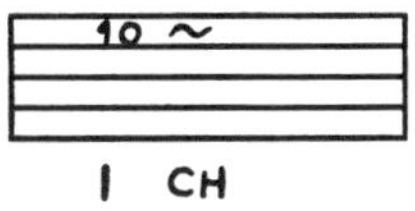

Here is the way it looks:

Choking is a technique not used often on the banjo because it doesn't usually sound good when applied to the sharp, short notes a banjo makes. It sounds great on a guitar or *muted* banjo *(see pages 94-95)*, when the notes are more sustained. In fact, rock, blues, and country style electric guitar all rely a great deal on choking to get the sound of a moving note. Pedal steel works on the same principle of stretching strings. But on a banjo, by the time you choke the note it's practically gone. Nevertheless, it can still sound good; one of Ralph Stanley's favorite and most characteristic licks is this one, based around choking the second string at the tenth fret:

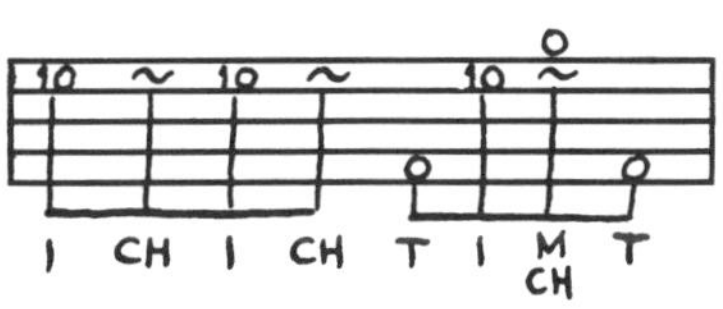

There will be some other examples of choking on pages 62-68, *(Up the Neck)*.

Endings

At the end of an up-tempo bluegrass song there are several licks banjo players often use instead of a straight tag lick, as a sort of final touch. Here is one originated by Scruggs and copied by almost everyone:

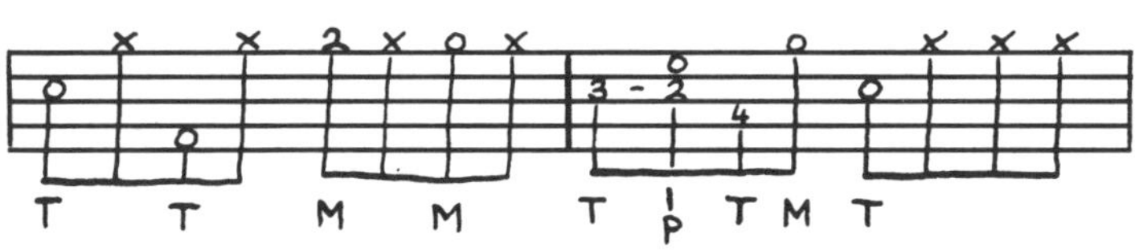

Here are two more:

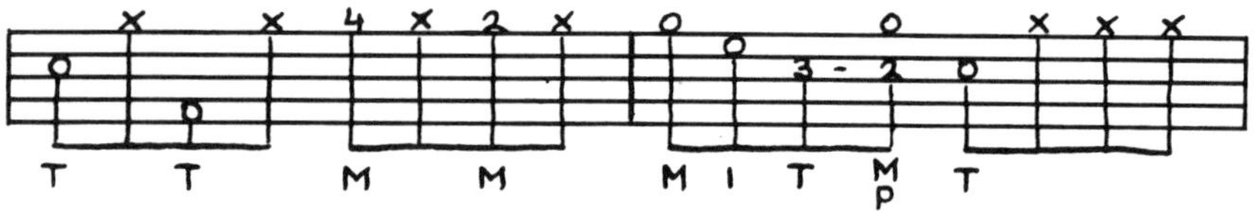

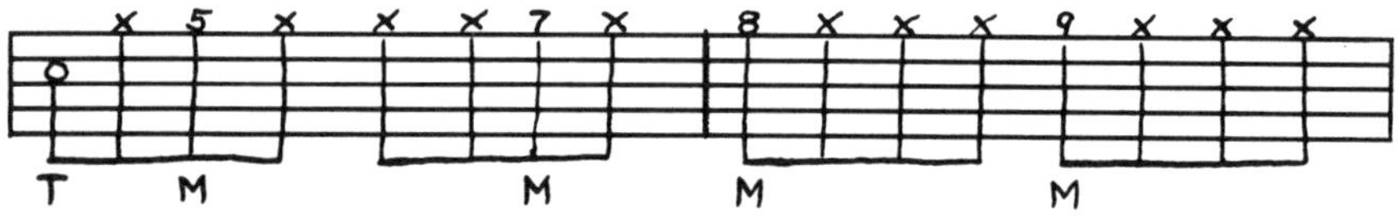

Many instrumentals, especially fiddle tunes, have a characteristic ending sometimes called "shave and a haircut". Most banjo instrumentals use some version of that ending. Here is the basic idea:

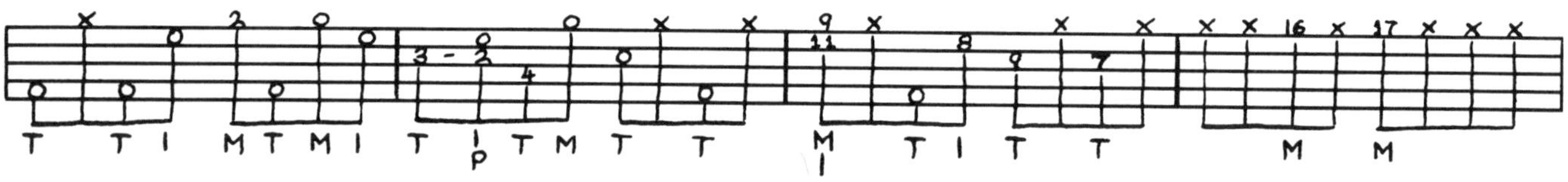

Here is a variation:

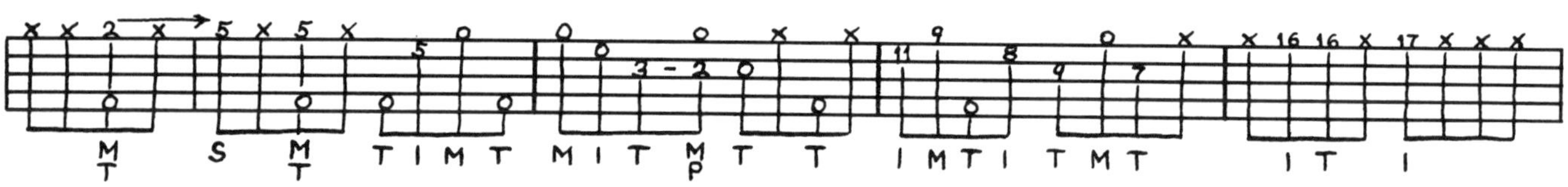

Harmonics

Playing harmonics ("chimes") is a nice little trick which has even had some instrumentals built around it (Scruggs' *Foggy Mt. Chimes* and *Bugle Call Rag* and Osborne's *Sonny's Banjo Boy Chimes*). To play a harmonic the right hand picks-a string while the left hand barely touches the string at a certain point (the best point is over the twelfth fret).

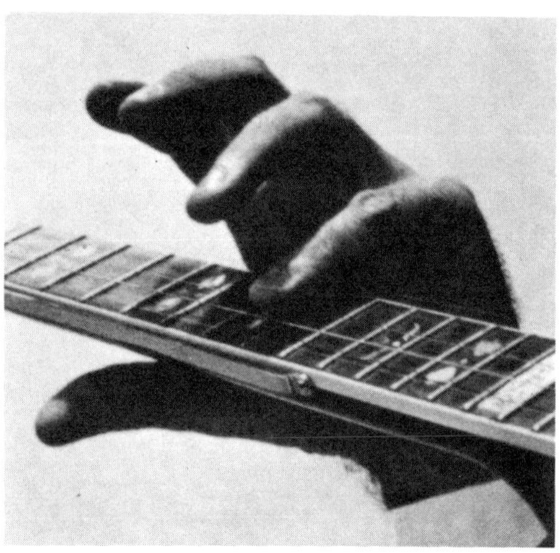

The result is a strange, high-pitched ringing note. The principle behind harmonics is that by touching the string lightly you eliminate the basic tone the string makes. But strings vibrate not only this way· but also this way: and this way:

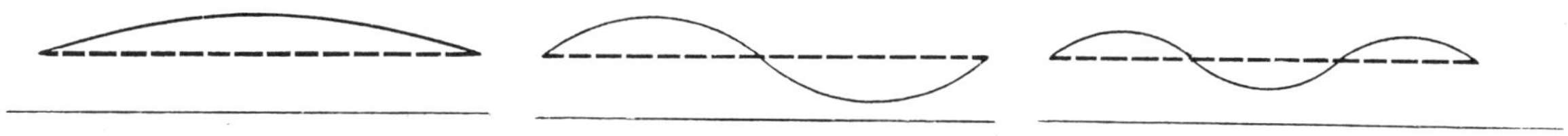

So it's possible to damp one type of vibration and still hear the others. The trick is to touch the string gently in just the right spot: at the halfway point (twelfth fret), the third-way points (seventh and nineteenth frets), the quarter-way points (fifth fret and a point just past the frets), and so on. Harmonics are located at different points of the fifth string because of its different length.

Harmonics are almost always used as a gimmick: the music stops, the banjo hits a few harmonics and the music starts again, to the wild cheers of the crowd. Harmonics go well at the end of slow songs. They can also sound very good in soft or strange-sounding songs, but people don't often think of using them. Just before Country Cooking recorded *Plumber's Nightmare* it struck me that harmonics might fit in well. Listen for some high G harmonics sprinkled through the choruses and then for a whole variety of them at the end.

Scruggs and Keith Tuners

There are several devices which make it possible to change the pitch of a string quickly and accurately from one note to another and back again.

The idea originated with an effect used by Earl Scruggs in several of his most popular instrumentals of the 1950's–*Earl's Breakdown, Flint Hill Special, Randy Lynn Rag*–the sliding sound of *tuning* the string as he picked them. At first he got this effect by quickly tuning the strings by ear, but this method was unreliable. His solution was to mount on the banjo two peg operated cam-type devices to stretch and unstretch the second and third strings by certain intervals (B to A and G to F#, respectively). Many different varieties of these tuners, such as *Scruggs pegs* or *D-tuners*, all based on the cam idea, were introduced over the next decade.

In 1963 Bill Keith invented what are now known as *Keith pegs*. A Keith peg is much like a very good normal peg except it has mechanisms which enable it to be set so it can't be turned downward past a certain (adjustable) point or upward past a certain (adjustable) point. This permits the same tuning action as *Scruggs pegs*, but without adding extra apparatus to the banjo peghead–Keith pegs simply replace the conventional tuning pegs. Their quick adjustability to any intervals and their ability to replace any or all of the standard pegs offer many musical possibilities. A good example is Keith's arrangement of *Auld Lang Syne*, which is played using much turning of four Keith pegs but no fretting whatsoever!

In general, though, the possibilities are still greatly unexplored and most people who have Scruggs or Keith pegs on their banjos rarely use them. I would recommend thinking carefully before investing in them (usually over $60 per pair, 1975 prices).

Music theory

There are plenty of fine musicians who have no knowledge of formal musical terms and principles. It's quite possible to play well without knowing these terms and principles, but they can be a big help in expanding your musical abilities. They can help you learn your way around the neck. They make transposing songs easy. They can point the way to many musical ideas which can improve your playing. And so here is a short section on music theory. If you try to skim it you may just get confused. Spend some time with this section and in a short time you will learn a good deal about banjo playing without even touching your banjo.

Western music has twelve different notes: A, A♯ (called A sharp and also known as B♭ or B flat), B, C, C♯ (or D♭), D, D♯ (or E♭), E, F, F♯ (or G♭), G, G♯ (or A♭). That's a total of twelve notes, the letters A through G with a note between each pair of letters except between B and C and between E and F. To find the twelve notes on your banjo start with the A at the second fret of the third string and move up the neck one fret at a time. The distance from each note to the next is called a half step. Each fret is one half step. This type of sequence, twelve consecutive notes separated by half steps, is called a *chromatic* scale.

Most Western music is built around what is called a major scale, which has eight notes. You're probably familiar with what a major scaled sounds like: do, re, mi, fa, so, la, ti, do. The scale can start with any of the twelve notes named in the last paragraph. That note will then be *do.* The second note in the major scale, *re,* is two half steps (one whole step) above *do.* The third note in the scale is another two half steps higher. The fourth note is only *one* half step higher. To find the fifth, sixth, and seventh notes go up two half steps at a time. Between the seventh and eighth notes, again there is only one half step.

Here are some examples of major scales picked out from the chromatic sequence:

A	do		re		mi	fa		so		la		ti	do			
scale	A	A♯	B	C	C♯	D	D♯	E	F	F♯	G	G♯	A	A♯	B	C

C	A	A♯	B	C	C♯	D	D♯	E	F	F♯	G	G♯	A	A♯	B	C
scale				do		re		mi	fa		so		la		ti	do

You can find the notes for any scale by starting with the proper note and going up *two* half steps at a time except for the *one* half step space between the third and fourth notes and the seventh and eighth notes of the scale. It would be good practice for you to add to the following list of scales by figuring a few out yourself. Try C♯ or G♯ , or try one of the scales written here on a separate sheet of paper and then check to see if you're right. The first note of the scale has to match the last note (they're both *do,* one octave apart).

	(do)	(re)	(mi)	(fa)	(so)	(la)	(ti)	(do)
Key	1	2	3	4	5	6	7	8
A	A	B	C♯	D	E	F♯	G♯	A
B	B	C♯	D♯	E	F♯	G♯	A♯	B
C	C	D	E	F	G	A	B	C
D	D	E	F♯	G	A	B	C♯	D
E	E	F♯	G♯	A	B	C♯	D♯	E
F	F	G	A	A♯	C	D	E	F
G	G	A	B	C	D	E	F♯	G
A♯	A♯							A♯
C♯	C♯							C♯
D♯	D♯							D♯
F♯	F♯							F♯
G♯	G♯							G♯

A major chord (like G, A or C) is made up of a 1, a 3, and a 5 note. Look on the chart of scales for the key of G. The first, third, and fifth notes are G, B and D. A G chord on a banjo (or any other instrument) consists of G's, B's, and D's and nothing else. Another example: An A chord consists of A, C♯ and E – the first third and fifth notes of the A scale.

To form a *minor* chord take the 1 note, the *flatted* 3 note (the note one half step lower than the 3), and the 5. G minor consists of G, B♭, D. A minor contains A, C, E. As you can see, the only difference between a major and a minor chord is one note in the chord – a major chord uses a regular 3 and a minor chord uses a flatted 3. To illustrate this difference, look at the difference between the way you would play an A and an A minor chord, or E and E minor, or D and D minor. In each case the major chord is "minored" by lowering the 3 note (the "third") in the chord.

A seventh chord (like D7 or A7) is simply a major chord with one note added on: a *flatted* 7 note. The flatted 7 note in G, for example, is F, so that G7 has the notes G, B, D, and F. As with all the chords I'm giving as examples, you can play this on the banjo. A G7 chord is played on the banjo by picking two G notes (third and fifth strings), a B (second string), a D (fourth string), and an F (first string). Another 7th chord: C, E, G, B♭ (C7 chord).

If you were to use the regular 7 note instead of the flatted 7, the resulting chord would be called a major 7th chord. Gmaj7 is G, B, D, F♯. Cmaj7 is C, E, G, B.

Another commonly used type of chord is the 6th chord: a major chord plus a 6 note. Examples: G, B, D, E (G6); A, C♯, E, F♯ (A6).

An augmented chord (like G+ or A+) has a 1, 3, and *sharped 5.*

A ninth chord is the same as a seventh chord but also includes a 9 note. A 9 note is the same as a 2 but an octave (one full scale) higher. In other words, it's one full note higher than an 8. When playing a ninth chord, though, you needn't use a high note for the 9. You can use a 2 instead. In fact, you needn't play all five notes: 1, 3, 5, 7♭ and 9. If you leave out one or two it can still sound like a ninth chord.

A diminished seventh chord has a 1, 3♭, 5♭, and 7♭♭. As with the major 7 chord there is almost never a use for this in bluegrass. The same is true of a suspended chord (1, 4, 5) and a minor seventh chord (1, 3♭, 5, 7♭). There are also eleventh and thirteenth chords and many more which I doubt you'll ever use, so I won't go into them here.

Here is a shorthand chart of the types of chords and tips on how to use them:

Type	**Symbol**	**Composition**	**Uses and characteristics**
major	G, A, etc.	1, 3, 5	
minor	Gm, Am	1, 3♭, 5	"Sad" Sound
6th	G6, A6	1, 3, 5, 6	Add a 6 into a chord for a soft, sometimes jazzy sound
7th	G7, A7	1, 3, 5, 7♭	Add a 7♭ into a chord for a bluesy, harsh sound. When going from any chord to its IV chord, it often sounds good to add a 7♭ to the first chord.
major 7th	A maj7	1, 3, 5, 7	Soft, jazzy sound
augmented	G+, A+	1, 3, 5♯	When going from any chord to its IV chord, augment the fifth in the first chord as a transition.
9th	G9, A9	1, 3, 5, 7♭ 9	Exhangeable for a 7th chord. A softer, more complex sound.

Chord progressions

In the preceding chart there is a reference to a IV chord. Hopefully you've kept the idea of chord numbers in mind since it was first presented on pages 9-12, *(Getting ready to play).*

Every tune has a musical structure which can be used in any key. It is convenient to have a way of referring to the musical structure of a piece without having to refer to any particular key. When musicians think or talk about the structure of a piece, often the simplest way to do it is with numbers. The numbers are based on the notes of the scale. Roman numerals are used to indicate the chords.

The basic chord of a piece is the I chord (sometimes called the *tonic*). The chord name of the tonic is the same as the name of the key you're playing in. As you should remember from transposing chords a while back, the most common chords are the I, the IV (sub-dominant) and V (dominant). These are the chords based on the first, fourth and fifth notes of the scale of whatever key you're in. An example: If you're in the key of C, C is the I chord, F (the fourth note of the C scale) is the IV chord, and G (the fifth note of the C scale) is the V. Extending the principle, D is the II, A is the VI, and so forth.

Musicians familiar with this numbering system often use it when they want to refer to chord progressions without having to specify any key. Bill Monroe's *Rawhide,* played in C, has the progression I, IV, I, IV, I, V, I (repeat), III, VI, II, V (repeat). The second part of *Rawhide* has a chord structure almost identical to the second part of *Big Ben,* played in G on Country Cooking's first record. *Big Ben*'s progression is I, VII♭, IV, I, V, I, VII♭, IV, I, V, I / III, VI, II, V, III, VI, II, V, I. Both tunes use the III, VI, II, V sequence which happens to be a progression often found in ragtime and jugband music. In bluegrass, such common songs as *Salty Dog* and *Don't Let Your Deal Go Down* use the VI, II, V, I sequence.

Another common progression is the standard blues progression: I, I7, IV, I, V, IV, I (with V sometimes coming at the end of each verse to lead into the next). This progression and variants of it come up pretty often in bluegrass: in *Muleskinner Blues, Doin' My Time, Rocky Road Blues, Foggy Mt. Special* and in many more.

Some other useful bits of information about chord structure: In bluegrass, sacred songs often include a II to V change. In general, a II chord is most always followed by a V. Tunes with a "mountain flavor" often use VII♭ chords (such as F in the key of G).

As is indicated in the chart summarizing chord structures and their uses, an augmented chord or a seventh chord can be used as a transition between a chord and *its* IV chord. That is, regardless of what key you're in, if there is a sequence where one chord is the IV of the one before it, the first chord can be augmented or seventhed just before the change to the next chord. This can happen when changing from a I to a IV, a V to a I, a II to a V, a III to a VI (to a II to a V to a I), etc.

Vocal harmonizing

Harmonies with three (or more) parts are an important part of bluegrass. Now that you have some knowledge of chord theory under your belt it will be easy to work out three part harmonies. The harmony consists of three voices which form a chord, usually with the middle voice carrying the melody.

To figure out a vocal trio, start by working out the high harmony to the melody. Some people have a natural ability to find these harmonies. Most vocal duets in bluegrass (and in other kinds of music) consist of the melody of the song plus a harmony consisting of notes above, but as close as possible to, the melody. In bluegrass this harmony is called the tenor, regardless of whether it is actually sung in the part of the male vocal range formally referred to as tenor.

The third part of the harmony, sung below the melody line, is called the baritone (again, notwithstanding the formal definition). Baritone parts are harder to figure out than tenor parts, though after a while they too start to come instinctively. A baritone vocal line consists of whatever notes fill out the three-part chords with the melody and the tenor. Some groups sing this third part as the highest part in the harmony, an octave above the usual baritone line. Then the part is called either high tenor or high baritone.

The best way to get the hang of harmonizing is to try it. Here is an example of a typical vocal trio, applied to the chorus of *Jesse James.* It's in tablature for your convenience and also because you may find it easy, as I do, to work out harmony lines as chords on a banjo. For each melody note (the middle note in each group of three notes) there is the tenor's note above and the baritone's note below.

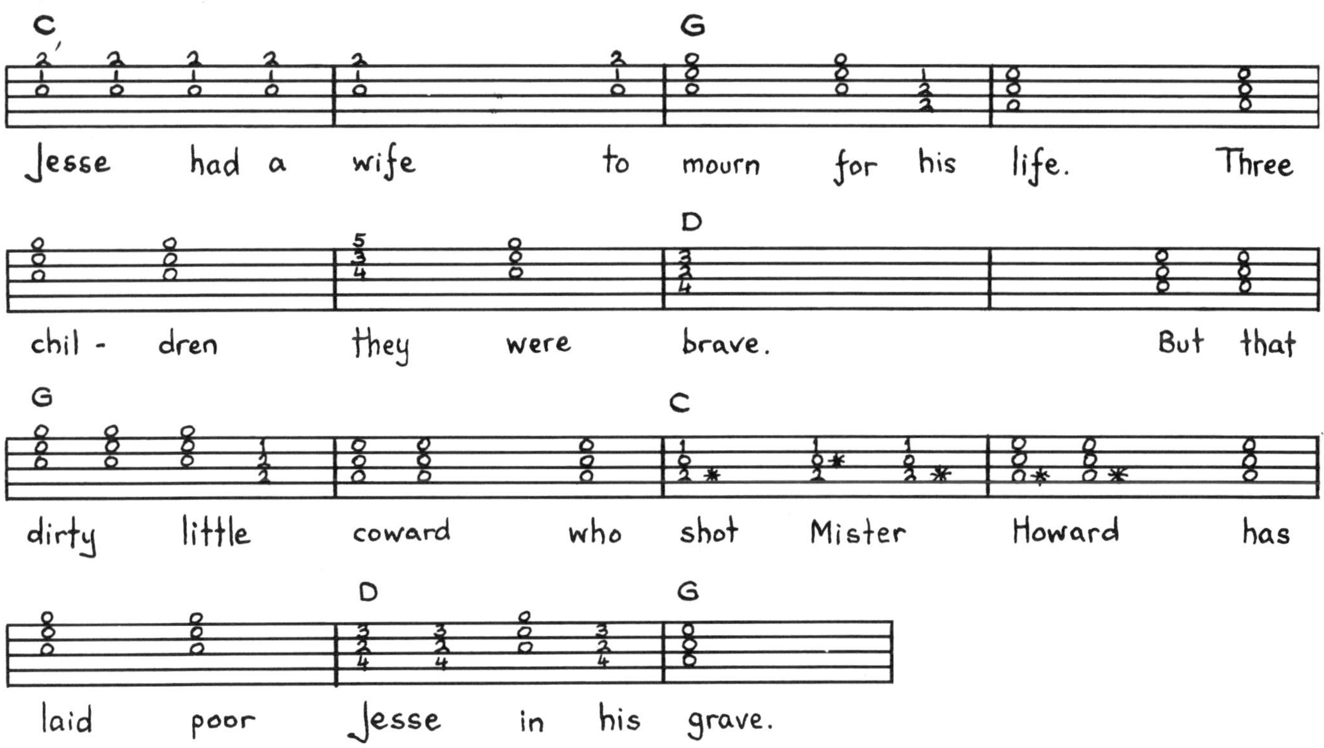

*Melody note. If the melody note is the lowest note in the group, the baritone sings the note above it.

Up the neck

So far your left hand has had to deal only with the part of the neck up to the fifth fret or so. There's obviously a lot of territory still to be covered. The best way to start is to get acquainted with the chord positions in different places around the neck. Fortunately, the basic chords are ones you've already learned, moved up the neck. The trick is to learn exactly where on the neck they go.

There are three chord formations used for playing major chords: a straight barred chord, the F formation and the D formation. Here they are in diagram form:

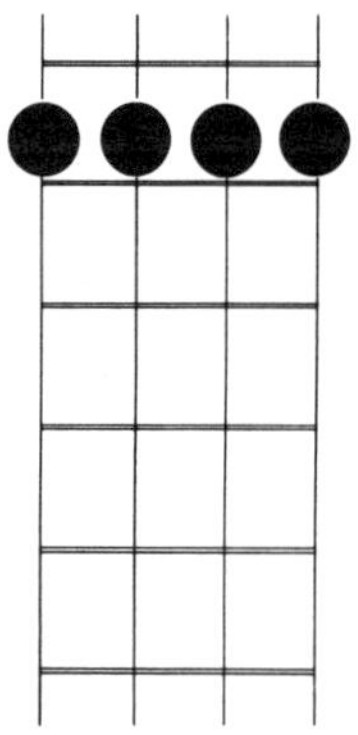

Bar formation

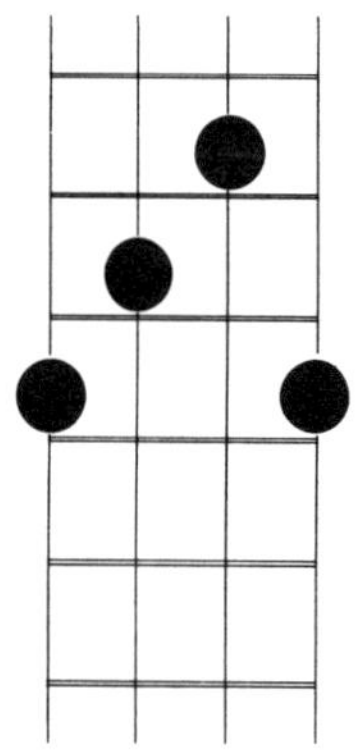

F formation

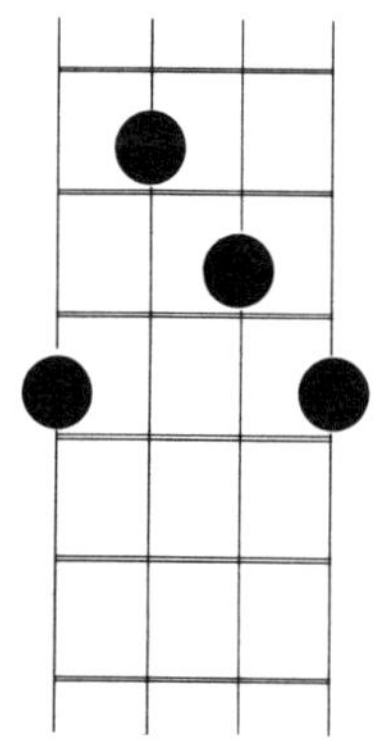

D formation

As you can see, these formations keep all four strings closed, which is what allows them to be used anywhere on the neck.

For example, make the F formation with your ring finger and pinky on the fourth fret (in other words, an F chord raised 1/2 step).

F♯

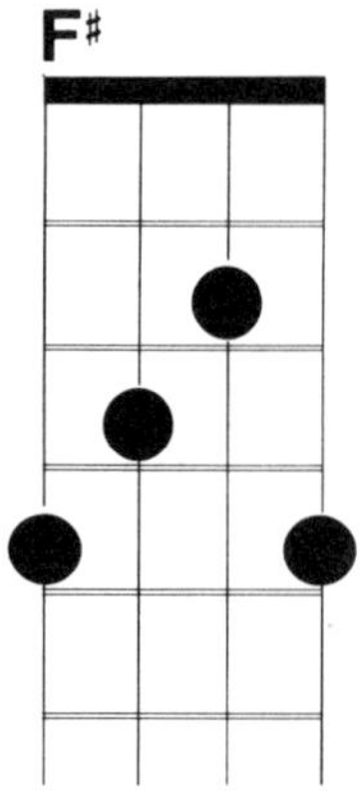

This gives you an F♯ chord. One more fret up and you have a G. Two more up and you have an A, two more and you have B, and so on. Remember, each fret raises the chord a half step, and remember there is only one half step between B and C and between E and F. You can consult the chromatic scale at the beginning of the chord theory section.

The other two formations work the same way. Just start counting from a point you're familiar with: for the barred formation you can start from the A chord at the second fret, and for the D formation you can start with the basic D chord.

I suggest that you memorize the different positions of the chords you'll be using most (G, C, D, A, etc.). Try practicing chording through a few songs using nothing but up-the-neck positions. In fact, chording through a song using these positions is something you'll often have to do in playing situations. When the banjo is supposed to sound percussive, or quiet (as in a slow song), the standard technique is to *choonk* on the offbeats, using up-the-neck chord formations. To *choonk* means to pick the first three strings of the chord simultaneously and quickly damp the strings with the left hand by lifting the chording fingers slightly. If you pick hard with the right hand and damp the sound quickly, you'll get a sharp percussive sound.

In learning your way around the neck it helps to remember that there are three ways of playing any major chord – using the three basic formations – and each formation can be repeated twelve frets up the neck if there's room, to duplicate the chord an octave higher. To illustrate, here in tablature form is a list of all the G chords:

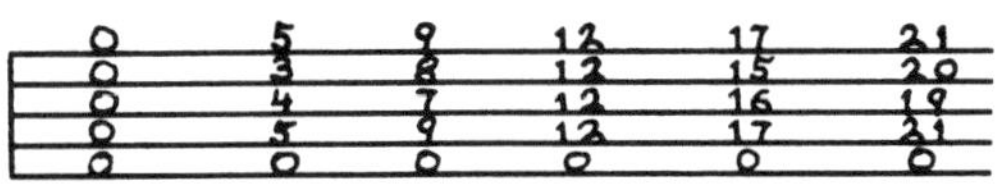

To get further acquainted with the neck, try to find the melody notes for several familiar tunes and then work out the tunes with rolls. In the key of G you'll probably find it easiest to work with the formations of G, C, and D between the seventh and the twelfth frets.

Once you've found your way through a few basic up-the-neck arrangements, you're ready for some licks. Here is a group of some of the most popular up-the-neck licks, again presented according to the chord progression for *Coming Round the Mountain.* Remember, this isn't to be thought of as a real break, just a way of presenting licks so you'll know where they go.

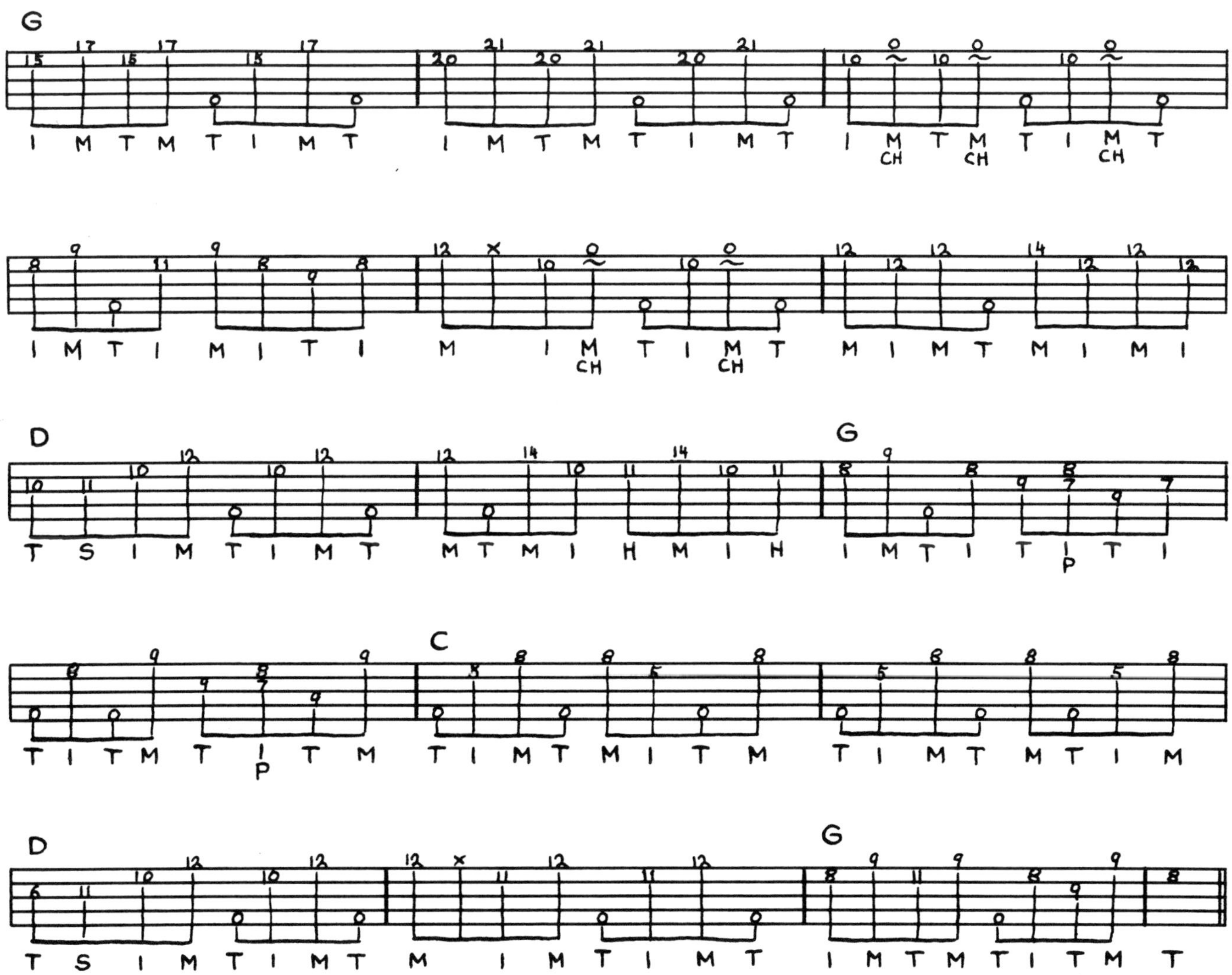

The application of a little chord theory from the last chapter will open the door to many nice sounds. For instance, some of the prettiest sounds you can make on a banjo come from the use of a certain chord progression in situations in which you are going from a chord to *its* IV chord (such as G to C, D to G, A to D). The progression is I, VII♭, VI minor, V minor, IV. An example using actual chords is G, F, Em, Dm, C. The chords should be played descending down the neck. Two examples in tablature form:

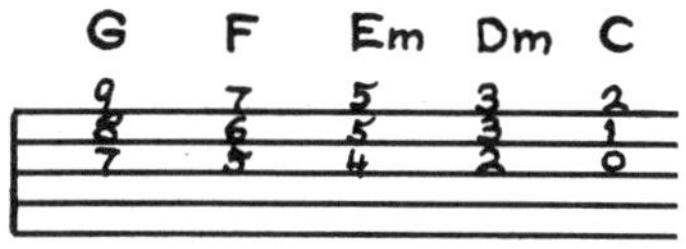

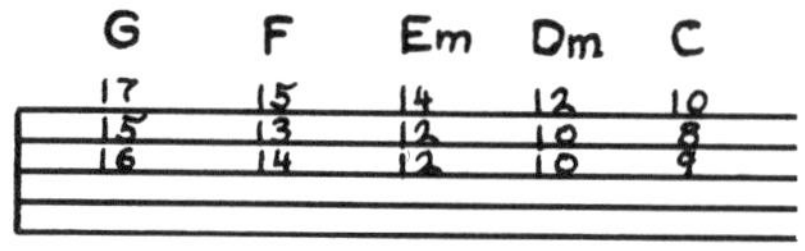

You can get added variety with either of these two sets of chords according to the way you roll the progressions out with the right hand. The four chords leading into the IV chord take one half-measure (four notes) each. Here are two different ways of playing the first of the two series diagrammed above, using two different right hand patterns. Notice that the second right hand pattern, using a middle finger lead, plays only the first and second strings of the chord.

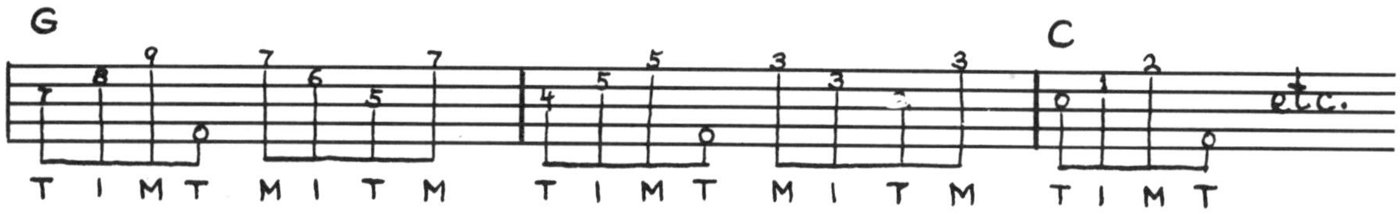

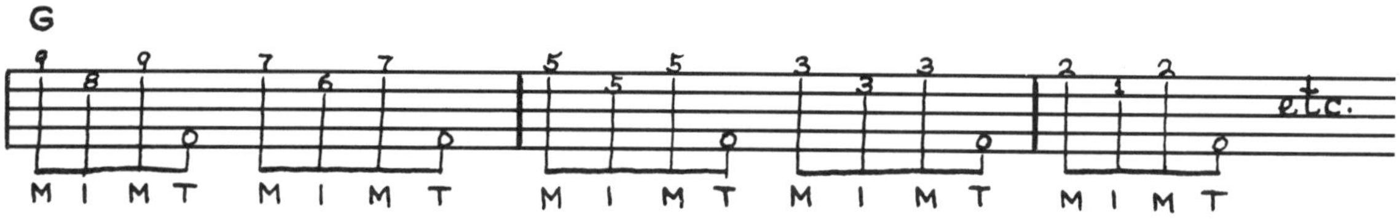

Another nice set of up-the-neck chord positions is used by Don Reno in his tunes *Dixie Breakdown* and *Banjo Special.* The progression, which can be used for two measures of any chord, is I, I7, IV, I. An example using actual chords is G, G7, C, G. Here are the chords the way Reno usually does them:

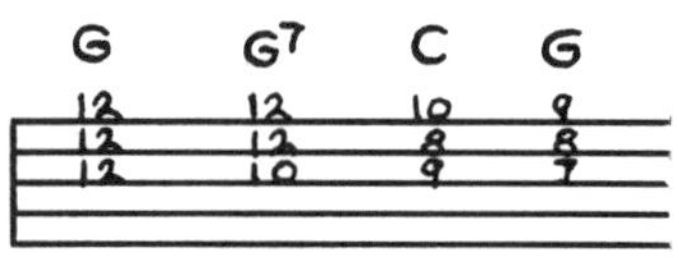

As with the progression we went through before, each chord change usually gets one half-measure (four notes). Now for an exercise based on the Reno progression. The first two measures are for a G chord and use the roll Reno usually plays for it. The second two measures are for C and use a different roll, one that's easier to play rapidly.

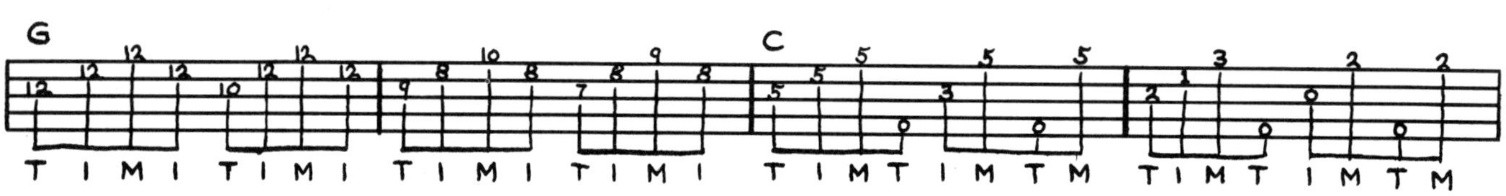

To achieve fluency in playing up-the-neck, work out some arrangements and practice them a lot. Work hard for clarity and smoothness. Playing up the neck can be harder than playing down-the-neck for several reasons:

1. You can't afford to play many open strings – it usually sounds strange to hear notes an octave or more apart as part of the same roll.

2. There's simply more area of the neck to relate to, and therefore more to familiarize yourself with.

3. The frets are closer together and yet there are sometimes fairly long distances to be covered quickly, so it's easier to miss notes or to play them unclearly.

Fretting the fifth string

Until now the fifth string has been used only as a drone string, repeatedly hitting the high G note which gives some of the sparkle to the sound of the banjo.

But playing up-the-neck puts your left hand in position to hook the thumb over the top of the neck and fret the fifth string. This will enable you to get some very nice effects. When playing chords such as C and D using the F formation, your thumb can fret a sixth, seventh, or major seventh note which will change the complexion of the sound when you roll the notes together. When using the D formation (as with a G chord around the seventh and ninth frets) your thumb can get a ninth note or a sharped ninth which can sound quite good in certain contexts. Hooking your thumb over the neck two frets down from a barred chord adds a fourth into the chord, which sometimes fits nicely.

Every chord position has a few variations which, if used correctly, can make your music more interesting and individualistic. Here are three chord diagrams based on the three major chord positions, with indications of how the variations can be played.

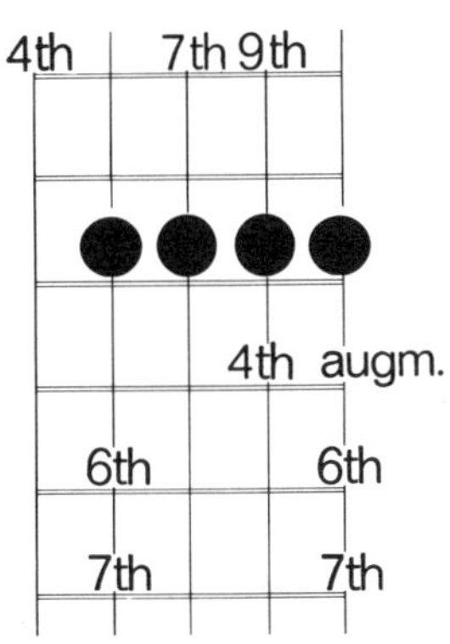

Variants on
Bar formation

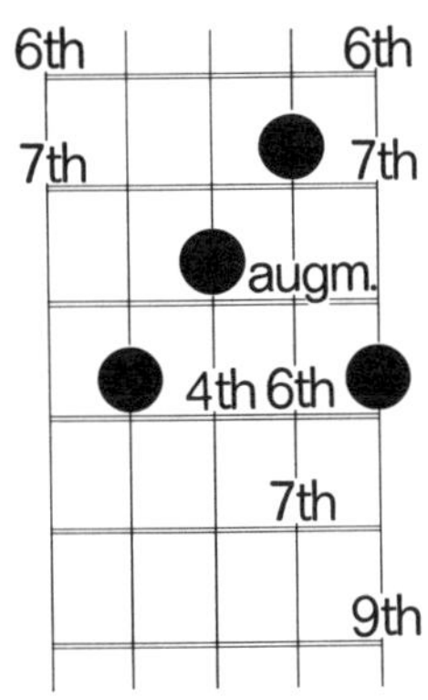

Variants on
F formation

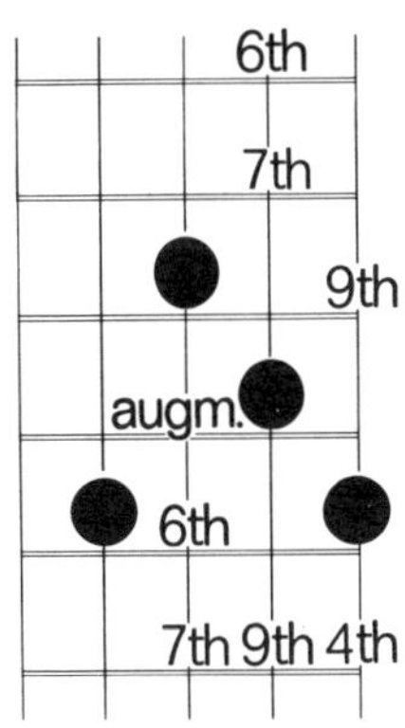

Variants on
D formation

This is my arrangement of David Grisman's tune *Cedar Hill* as I played it on Country Cooking's first record. You'll notice I fret the fifth string quite a bit and use a number of the other ideas explained in this chapter.

Cedar Hill

David Grisman

As played by Peter Wernick on Country Cooking's first album. Key of A.

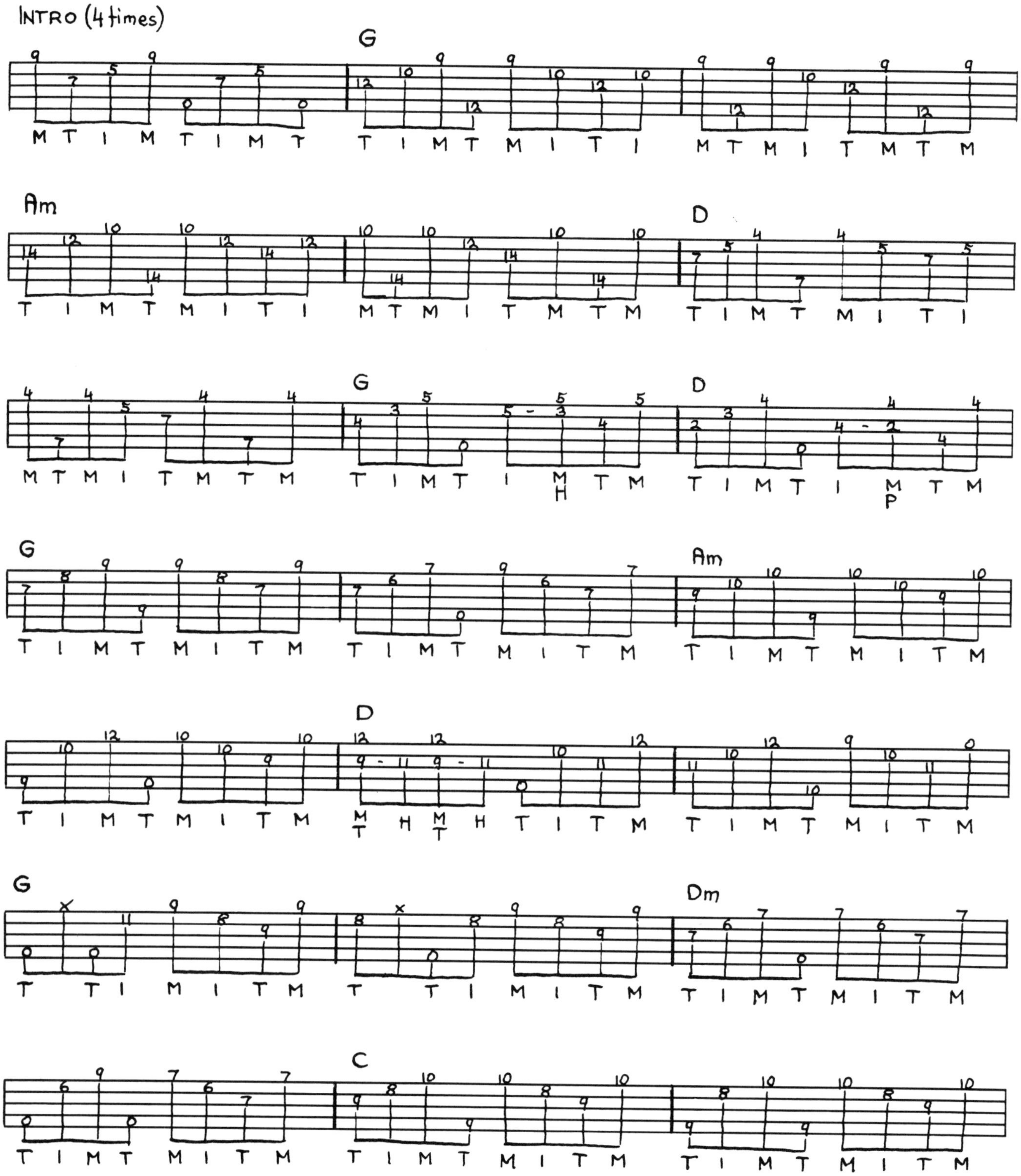

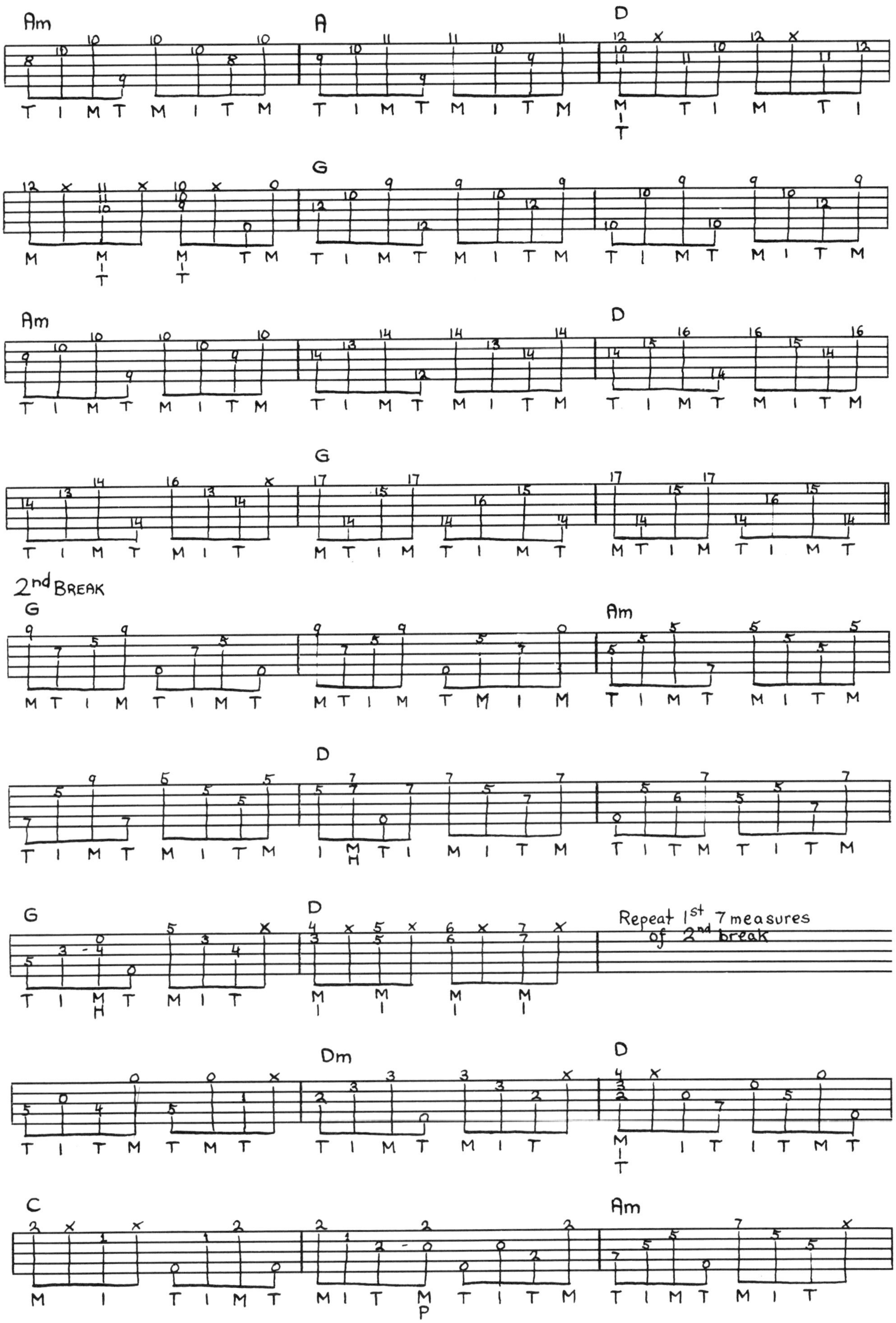
2nd BREAK
Repeat 1st 7 measures of 2nd break

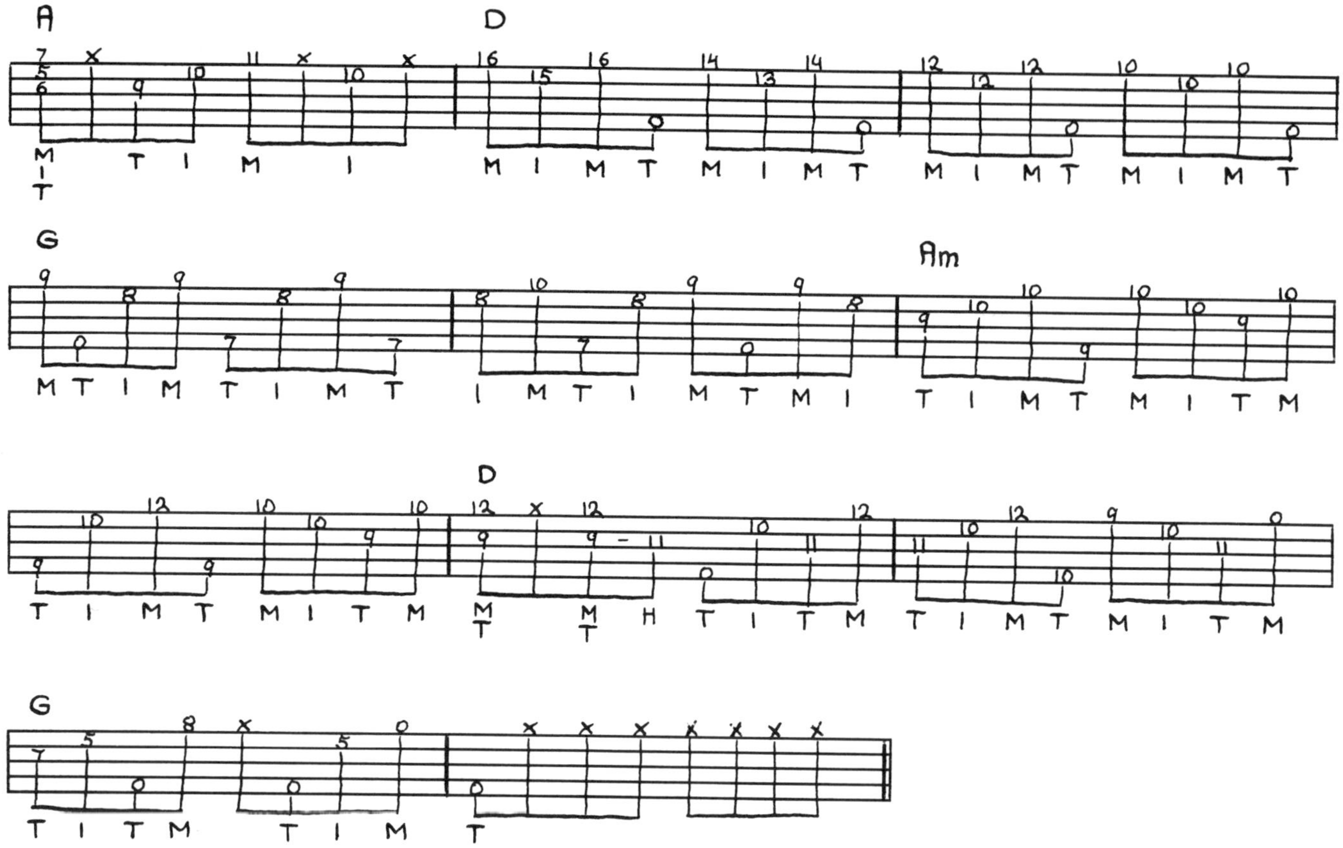

Remember that any up-the-neck chord position or lick you do is probably movable to fit many chords and musical situations. That means each discovery you make is more like several discoveries. If you work through all the possibilities you'll learn much more about playing up-the-neck. To really take advantage of what you've picked up you must practice a lot. Try putting your new ideas into different contexts; go over them again and again until they sound just right and they've ingrained themselves into your musical consciousness.

The early Country Gentlemen, with Eddie Adcock

Mike Lilly and Wendy Miller

Playing in different keys

Most up-tempo bluegrass songs and instrumentals are in keys between G and C. These tunes cause no difficulty for the banjo player who can get around in the key of G. All you have to do is play as you would in G but with the capo and the fifth string adjusted to the key you're in *(see pages 46-47)*.

Adjusting the capo and the fifth string is fine for keys between G and C but above the key of C it gets harder – some capos aren't made for the thickness of the neck past the fifth fret, and if you use nails in the neck to raise the pitch of the fifth string they probably don't go high enough to get the pitch you would need without a lot of extra tightening of the fifth string. In addition, the sound of a banjo capoed up more than five frets is then so high it's likely to sound out of proportion to the sound of the rest of the band.

One alternative to these problems is to learn how to play comfortably using frameworks other than the G, C, D framework you've been using. Many banjo players know how to get around in the key of C (using C, F, and G chords) or D (using D, G, and A chords). These abilities plus a capo makes it easy to play in any key, whether it be E, F or even F♯ (use D formations with the capo on the fourth fret). These situations don't come up often but they do come up. Some examples are songs like *Little Birdie, Footprints in the Snow, Rabbit in the Log, Can't You Hear Me Calling,* which are usually played in keys D, E, or F, depending on the range of the singers' voices.

Playing in C or D is sometimes required for some instrumentals. Many fiddle tunes, for example, are in the key of D (*Soldier's Joy, Lost Indian, Ragtime Annie*). And even some banjo tunes are written to be played with C (Bill Emerson's *Sweet Dixie*) or D (Eddie Adcock's *Turkey Knob*) positions.

There are some commonly used special banjo tunings for the keys of C and D, and I'll get to them shortly. Before I do, though, a few more words on playing in C and D formations with G tuning.

There is no big secret to playing well in C or D while tuned to G. You must familiarize yourself with the main positions and with the kinds of sounds you can make in these keys, and then spend a lot of time practicing in order to get a comfortable feel.

Here are two arrangements of songs usually played out of C positions on the banjo:

Little Birdie

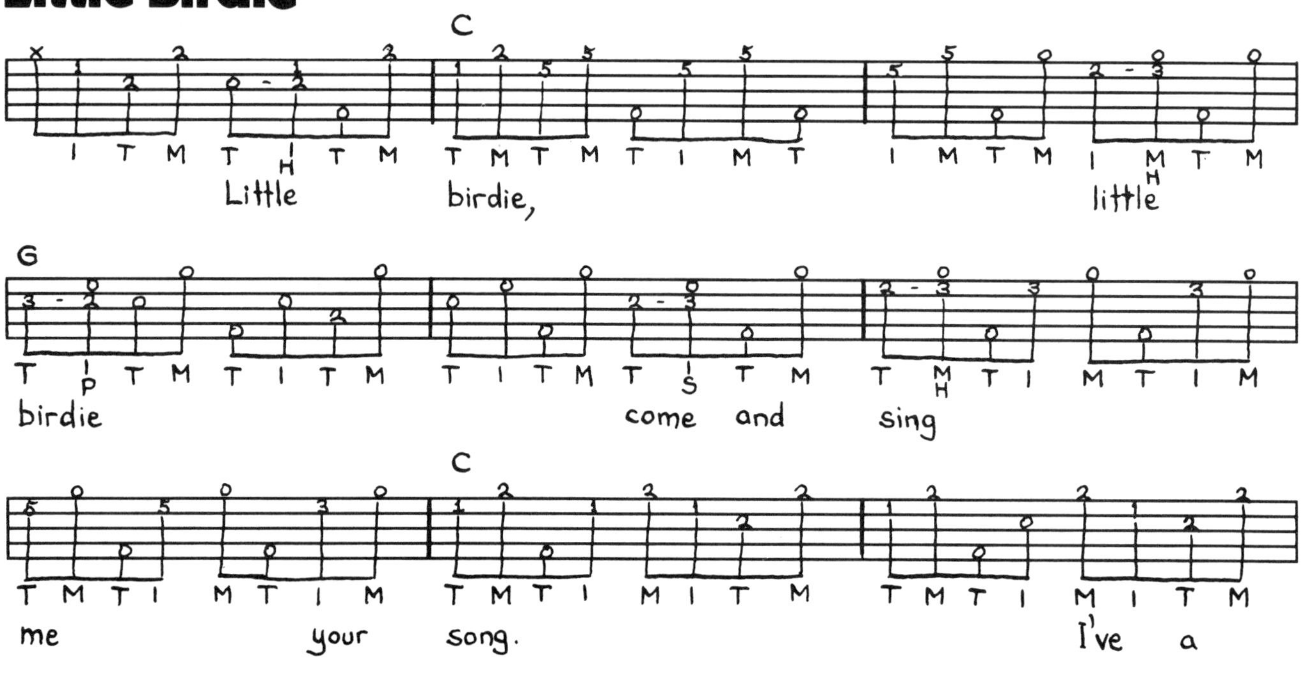

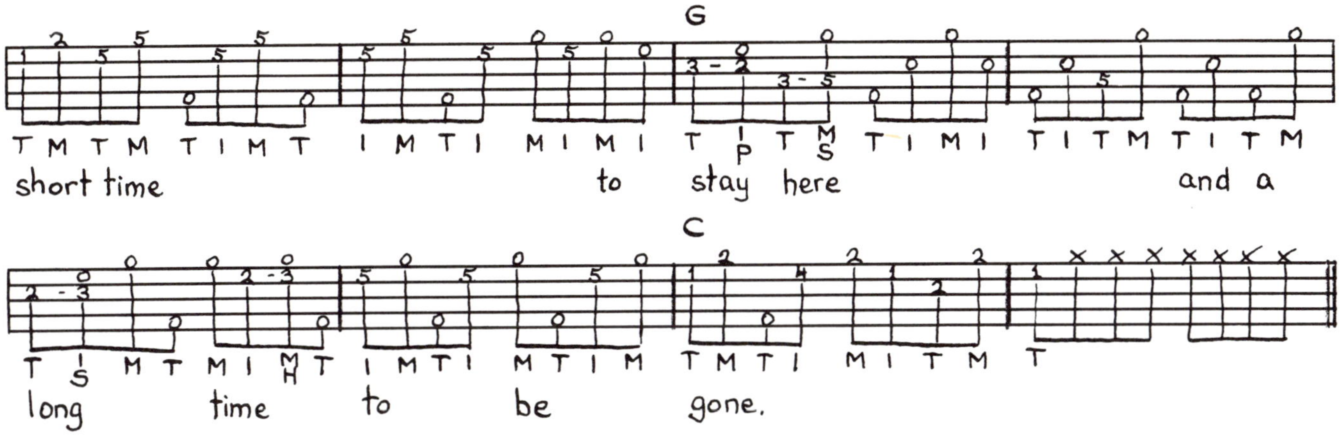

Rabbit in the Log

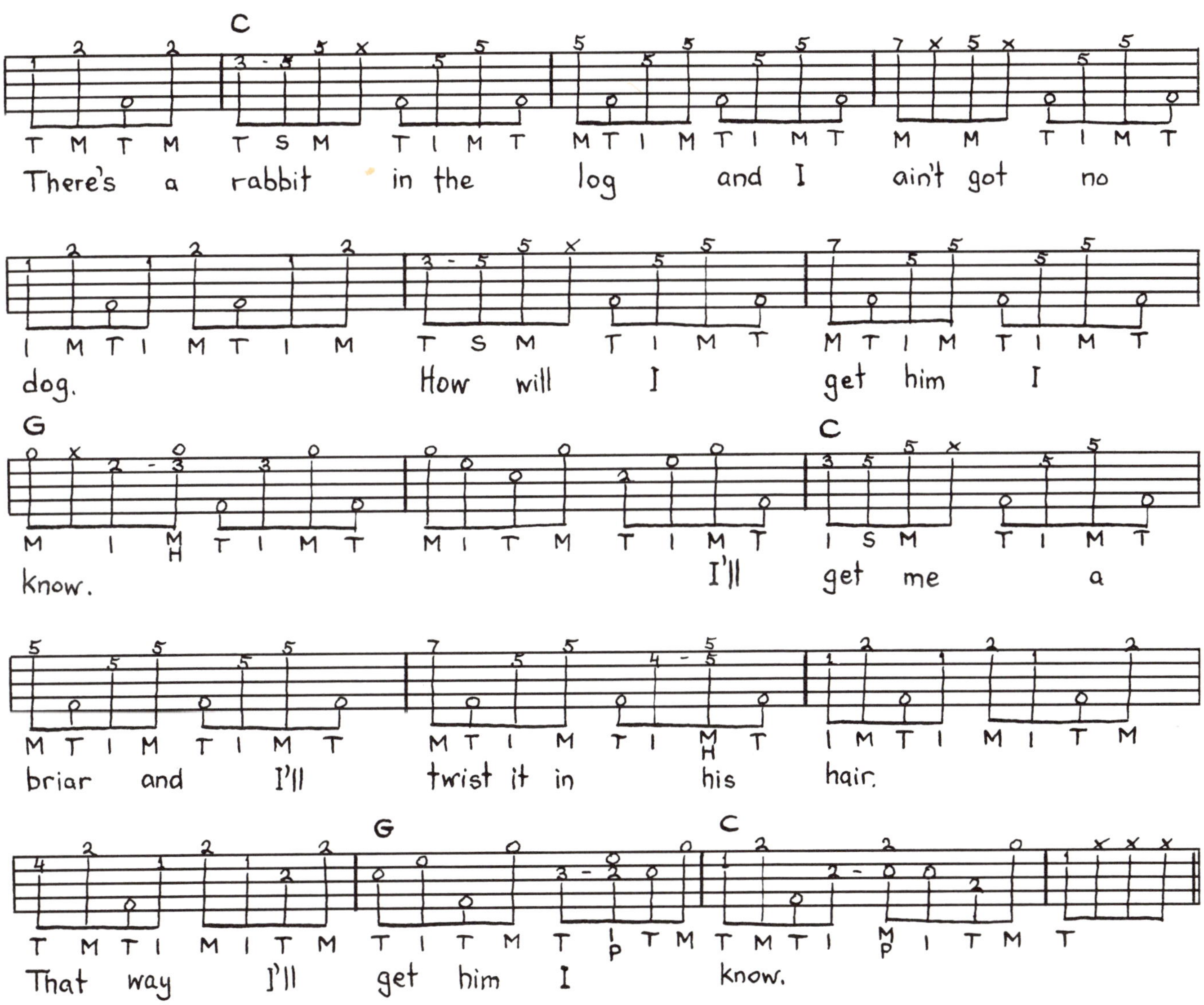

Playing in D positions offers you a choice of how to tune the fifth string. You can leave it as it normally is – tuned to G – where it will sound good with the G and A chords, but a little in the way on a D chord (a solution to the problem is to avoid hitting the fifth string on a D chord whenever possible). You can also tune the fifth string down to F♯, where it can contribute to a very nice sound as part of a D chord (the third in a D chord). The F♯ also sounds good with an A (it makes an A6 chord). The problem with the F♯ is that with a G chord it makes Gmaj7, which is likely to sound out of place. Otherwise, tuning the fifth string to F♯ makes for a full and mellow sound. The last alternative is to tune the fifth string to A. That note harmonizes with the D, G, and A chords, but you might like some of the sounds you can get with the other tunings better.

There are some situations in which playing in the key of F (with the banjo tuned to G) can work nicely. Scruggs plays in F in the song *Don't Let Your Deal Go Down,* which has a I, VI, II, V progression. The chords come out: F, D, G, C, F, and Scruggs makes good use of them. To play the same song in G positions would mean playing G, E, A, D, G, which for most banjo players would probably not be as easy to handle as the F position changes.

Sometimes banjo players use tunings other than G. First, the most popular – C tuning.

C tuning

C tuning is the same as G tuning except that the fourth string is lowered from D to C. The main advantage of this is that it makes a C chord sound better by adding a low C to the bottom of the chord (instead of E, which the fourth string on a C chord in G tuning plays). The result is a full and resonant C chord which, when the banjo is in tune, is one of the nicest sounds you can make on the instrument.

When I am going to play a song using C positions, sometimes I lower the fourth string and sometimes I don't. It depends on whether I want to hear that low C note in the C chord enough to put up with the inconvenience of having to alter some of the chord positions or fingerings I might otherwise use. For instance, playing melody notes on the fourth string tuned down to C means having to play notes on that string two frets higher than usual, and that can be both confusing and physically difficult.

Here are the three main chords used in C tuning. You can figure out the rest using what you know about chord theory *(see pages 58-60).*

C

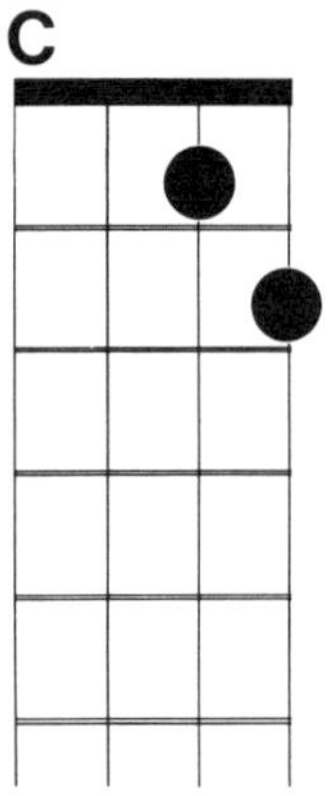

F

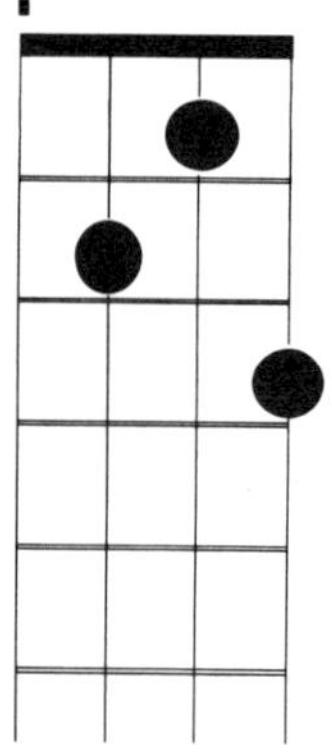

G7

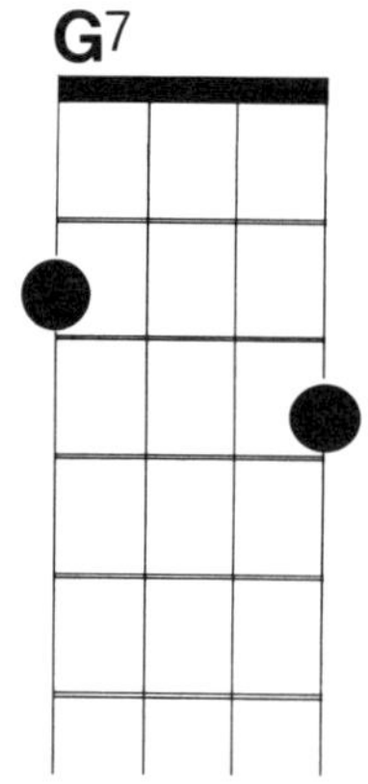

Here are two licks in C tuning, which take advantage of the fourth string being tuned down.

C

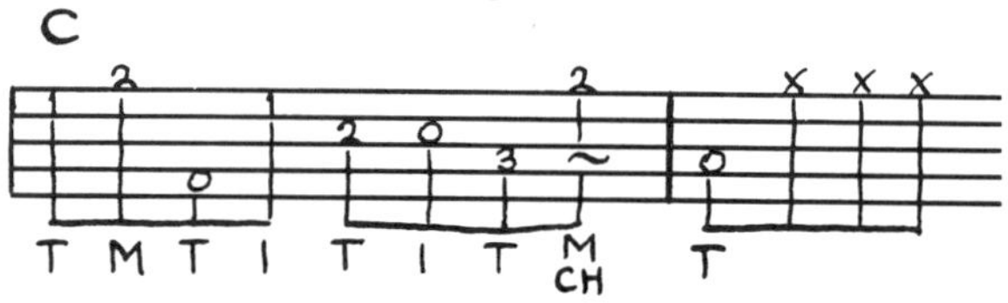

G7

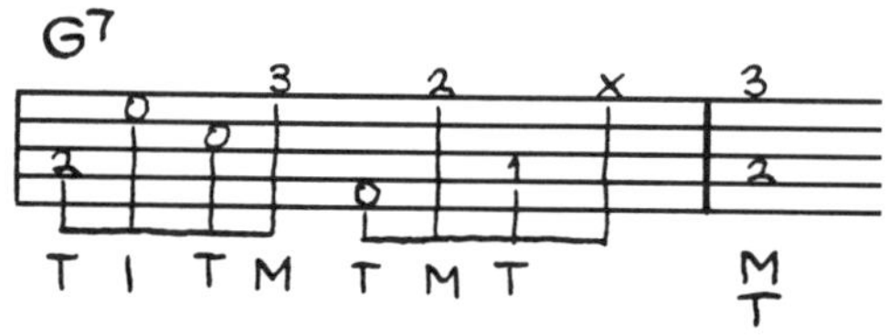

Scruggs uses C tuning fairly often. Some of his instrumentals in C tuning are *Home Sweet Home, Farewell Blues,* and *Old Folks* (*Bill Cheatham*). J.D. Crowe's *Bear Tracks* is in a variant of standard C tuning (the first two strings are tuned to E and C, to give an open C chord).

Pete Seeger uses mostly C tuning on the banjo, and comes up with lovely accompaniments for all kinds of songs, including some from other countries. Seeger's influential banjo instruction book (an Oak Publication) has most of its arrangements in C, and, largely as a result of this, many folk-style banjo players think of C tuning as standard.

It's interesting to note that standard tuning for a plectrum banjo (a four string banjo with a neck as long as a five string, normally played with a pick – "plectrum") is the same as the tuning of the first four strings of a five string banjo in C tuning.

D tuning and other tunings

D tuning involves lowering the third string to F♯ and the second string to A. These, incidentally, are the notes which Scruggs-Keith pegs, set the standard way, enable you to tune down to instantly. In D tuning the fifth string is tuned down to either F♯, as in Scruggs' *Reuben* or to A, as in almost everything else in D tuning, such as in various instrumentals by Don Reno and Ralph Stanley.

D tuning enables you to get some unusual sounds you otherwise couldn't, so it's natural that some instrumentals would be written using it. But the fingerings and chord positions are somewhat limiting, which is probably why few people use it for songs in D.

Here are the three main chords in D tuning:

D

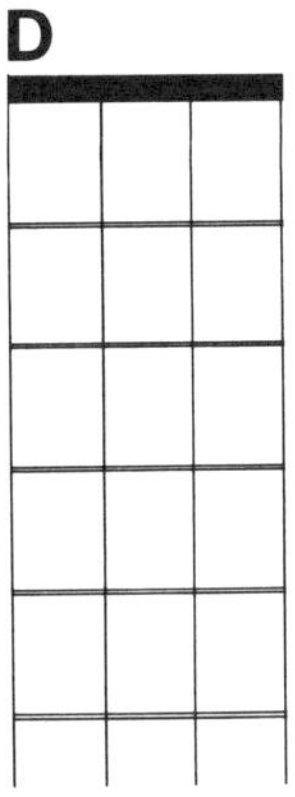

(open)

G

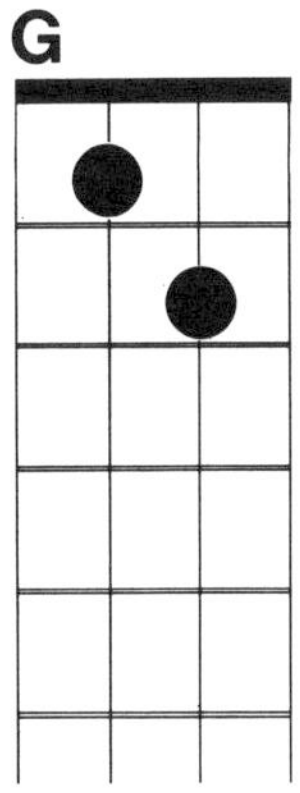

A7

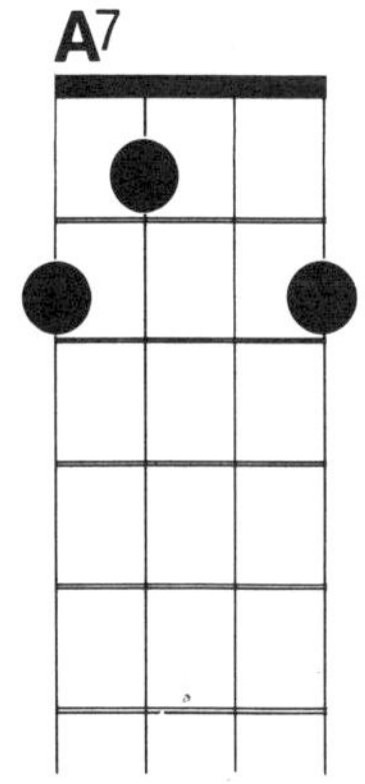

Another tuning some banjo players use is called "mountain" or "modal" tuning. This tuning is the same as G, except that the second string is raised one fret, to a C. People who play old-time styles such as frailing sometimes use this tuning, and occasionally so do bluegrass pickers, when they want to sound a little "old-timey" on songs such as *Pretty Polly.* The tuning lends itself to this type of sound because in the version of the G scale that some old time melodies are based on, C is used and B isn't.

I never use this tuning because it's possible to get the same effect without having to retune. When I want to have that C note added into the sound I'm making I just put my index finger on the first fret of the second string and leave it there as long as I need it.

There are other tunings which are known to have been used on the banjo, but bluegrass pickers have used only the ones I've mentioned, with a few isolated exceptions. Among the exceptions are Scruggs' *Nashville Blues* (A, D, F, A, D), Eric Weissberg's *900 Miles* (A, D, G, A, D), and Tony Trischka's *Kentucky Bullfight* (G, D, G, B, C). Tablature for *Kentucky Bullfight* appears later in this book.

Slow stuff

This is one area which receives very little attention from most people teaching or learning bluegrass banjo. After all, the banjo has to do a great deal on fast songs, and fast songs make up the bulk of bluegrass. Slow songs and the banjo's role in making them sound good are often lost in the shuffle. Some banjo players never think about learning to play slow bluegrass until they get into a playing situation with other people and find themselves not knowing what to do.

The banjo receives less emphasis in slow bluegrass than the other instruments. Mandolin and fiddle are better suited to playing at slow tempos since unlike the banjo, they can sustain single notes. But the banjo can make sensitive and pretty music when given a chance.

In playing a slow break, the melody notes are far enough apart to allow you time to make a real selection of what notes you want to hear and how to put them across. This kind of playing is a lot different from up-tempo bluegrass, in which you're playing eight or ten notes a second and rely a great deal on patterns or pre-planned moves. The relative lack of structure in slow playing opens up new possibilities: there are many different rhythmic and phrasing ideas you can use; you have the choice of playing single notes or chords; and there is plenty of room for melodic variation. You can go as far as your musical imagination and your knowledge of the neck allow you to.

As usual, *practice* is the key. The more time you spend doing it, the better will be the results. It also helps to listen closely to what other banjo players do with slow material. Eddie Adcock, Sonny Osborne and Don Reno are all especially good. They are always coming up with new ideas, some of them borrowed from other instruments such as guitar or pedal steel.

Here are two arrangements of breaks for slow songs. Because they're relatively unstructured, you might find them a little harder to make sense of than the arrangements for up-tempo breaks you've worked out so far. Both arrangements use counter-melodies, not the strict melody of the song. Watch for symbols in the tablature that indicate tricky groupings of notes in a few places: the grouping of two notes to take the rhythmic space of one note, and the grouping of three notes ("triplets") to take the rhythmic space of two notes.

Dark Hollow

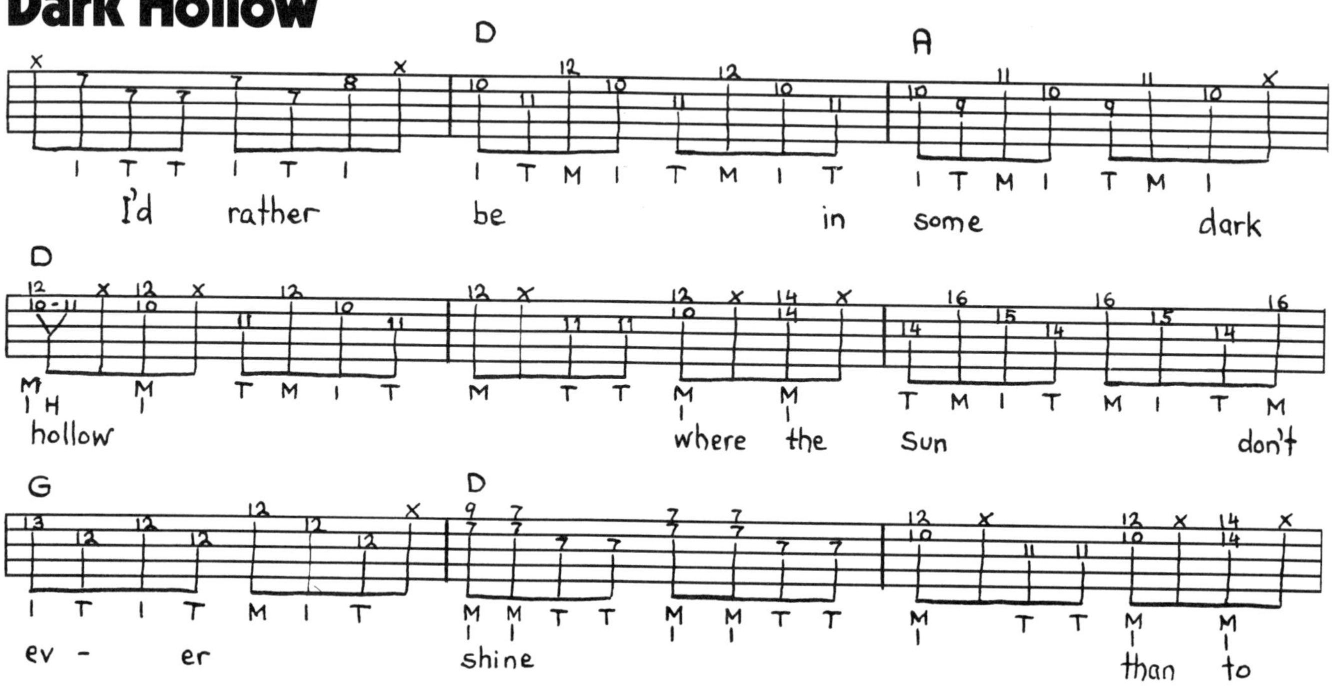

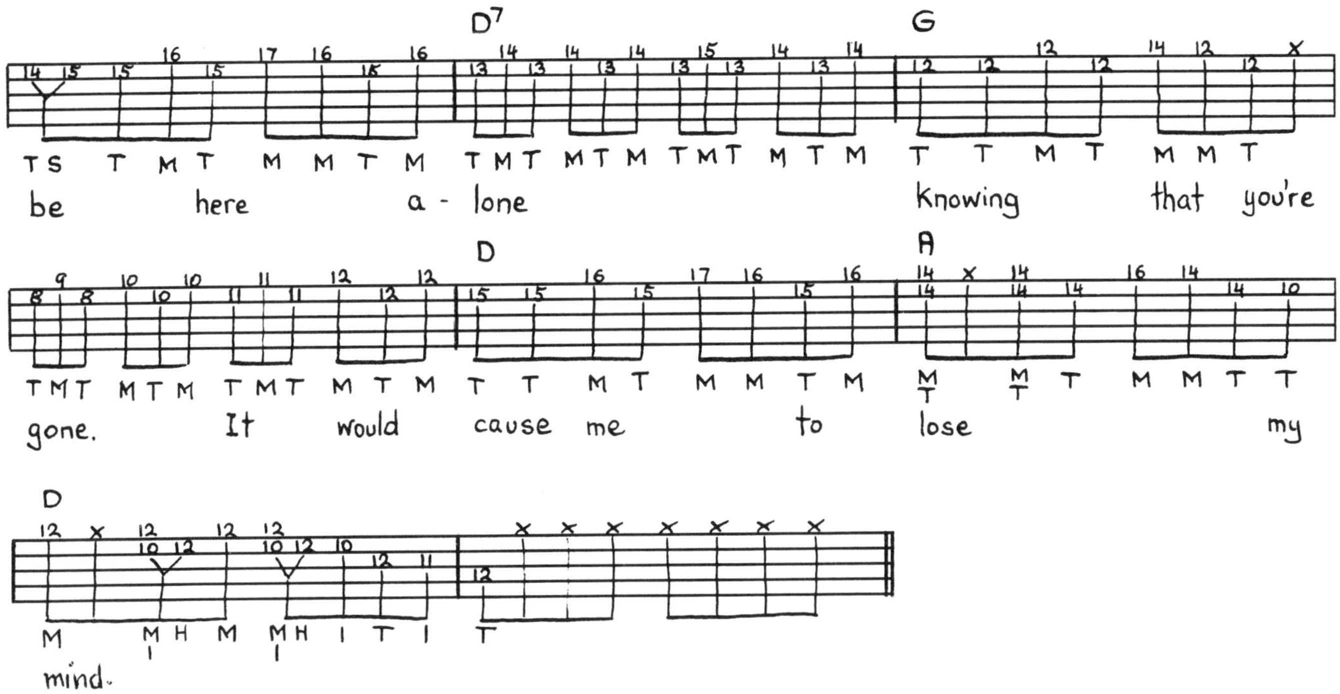

Don Reno with Carleton Haney

Banks of the Ohio

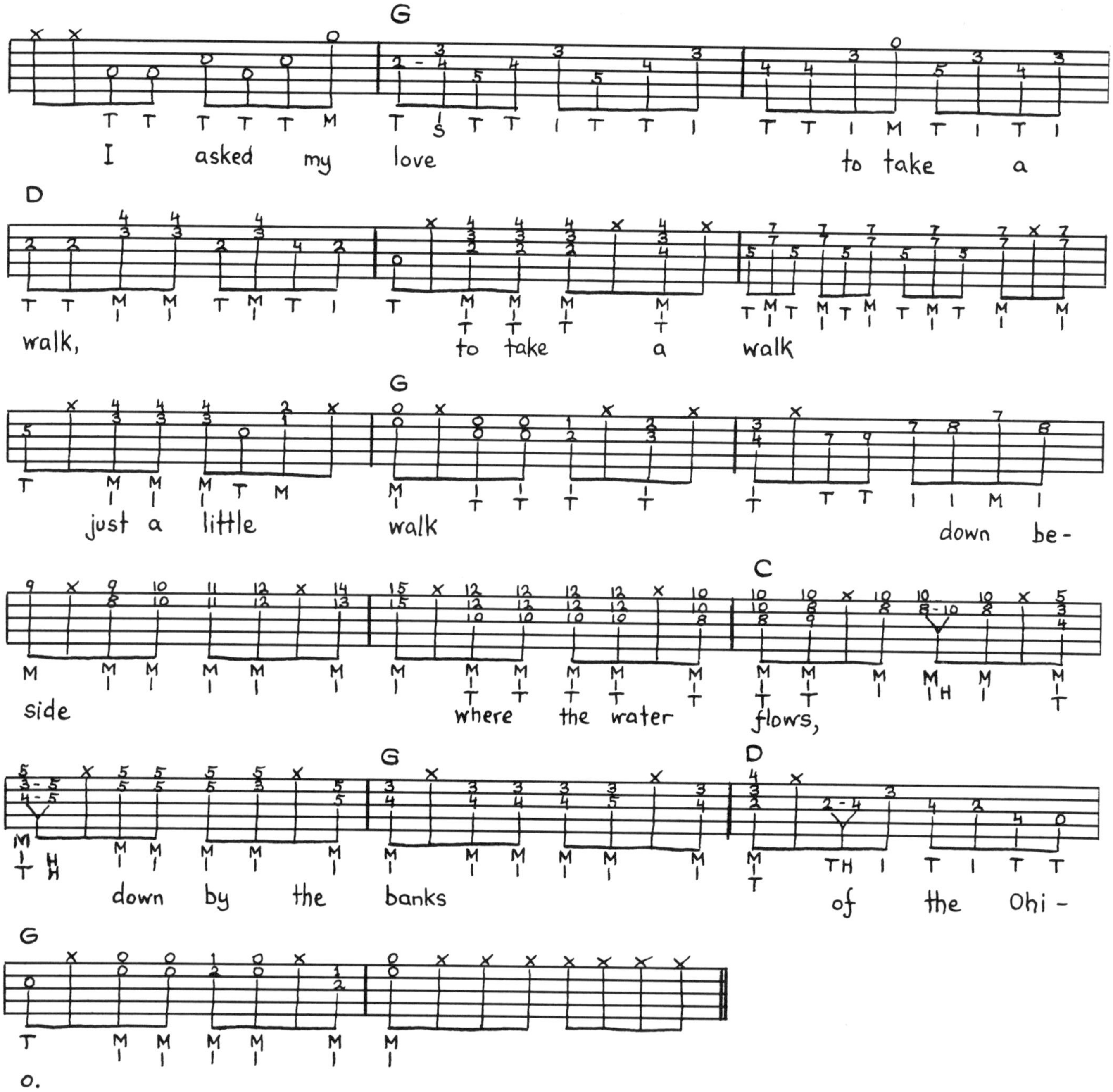

Playing backup behind slow songs involves the same principle as playing backup in general: try to find the best way you can play to help the overall sound of the group. On slow songs it's usually important to have a steady rhythm and a full sound. Since the words are usually more important on a slow song than on a fast one, backup should be more subdued than usual to allow the singing to stand out.

One popular right hand pattern which produces a steady rhythm and a full sound is the triplet pattern used briefly in both of the song arrangements presented so far in this chapter:

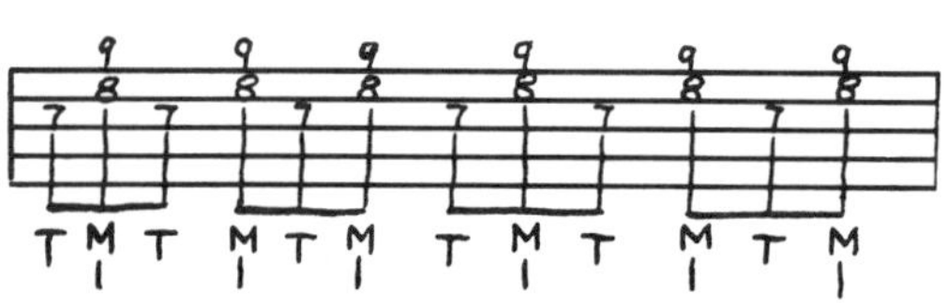

The right hand can be varied this way:

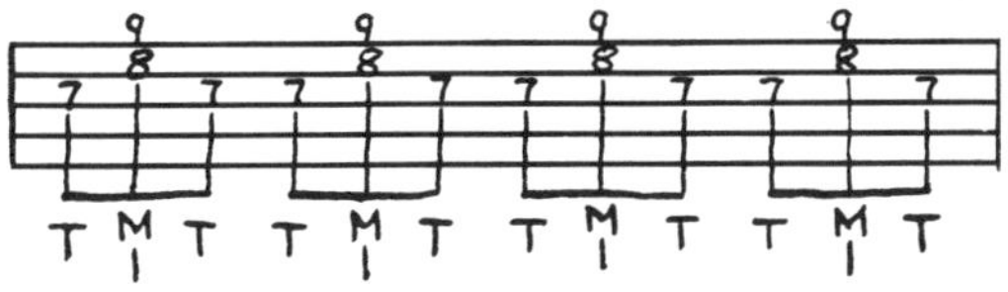

The rhythm of this pattern, instead of fitting the usual "*one* and *two* and *three* and *four* and", is felt as "*one*-and-a *two*-and-a *three*-and-a *four*-and-a". This triplet pattern has twelve notes to a measure of standard 4/4 time. Each of the twelve notes has the same time value, but the first note of each triplet is accented a little.

A good general hint for your left hand is to try to connect the main chords and notes in your playing with transitional phrases. Instead of switching suddenly between positions there are usually intermediate steps you can go through.

Here are a few measures of chord changes to give you an example of what I mean. Remember, the same basic idea can be used for different chords – just move the positions to different places on the neck.

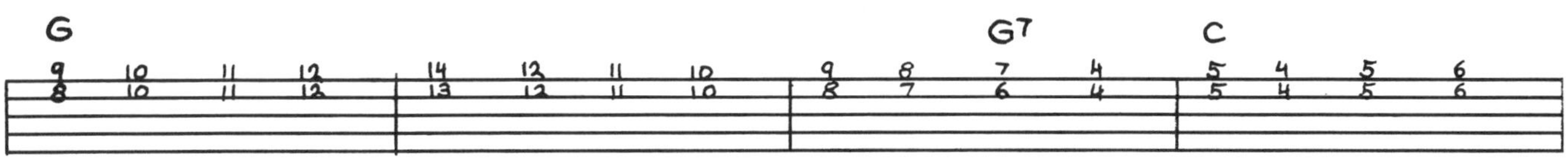

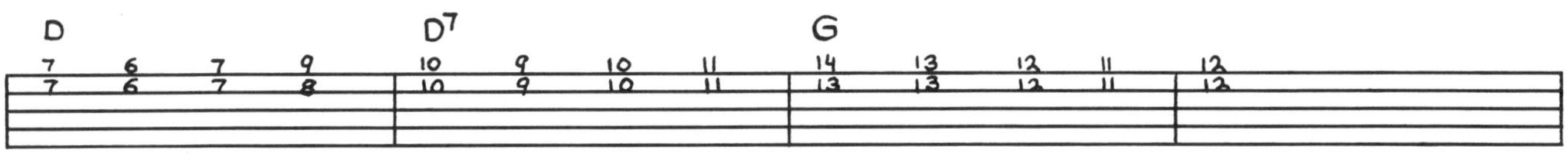

Bill Emerson with Jimmy Martin

Medium tempo

Some songs are too fast to be played easily in the unstructured style used for slow songs, and yet they're not quite fast enough to feel entirely comfortable using conventional rolls. Some examples of well-known bluegrass songs in this tempo are *Footprints in the Snow, Jimmy Brown the Newsboy, Can't You Hear Me Calling, You Don't Know My Mind, Man of Constant Sorrow* and *Little Cabin Home on the Hill.* Banjo breaks for these songs can be played with rolls, but for backup, rolls don't give as full a sound as you sometimes need. Scruggs and others have developed a style of playing which sounds good in situations like this. Since many of Jimmy Martin's songs are in this tempo, his banjo players use it a lot. It's a full and rhythmic style which helps the overall band sound jell. Here is tablature for a few sample measures of that style. Give a strong accent to the first note of each measure, and to the third note of each measure – the first offbeat (usually on the first string).

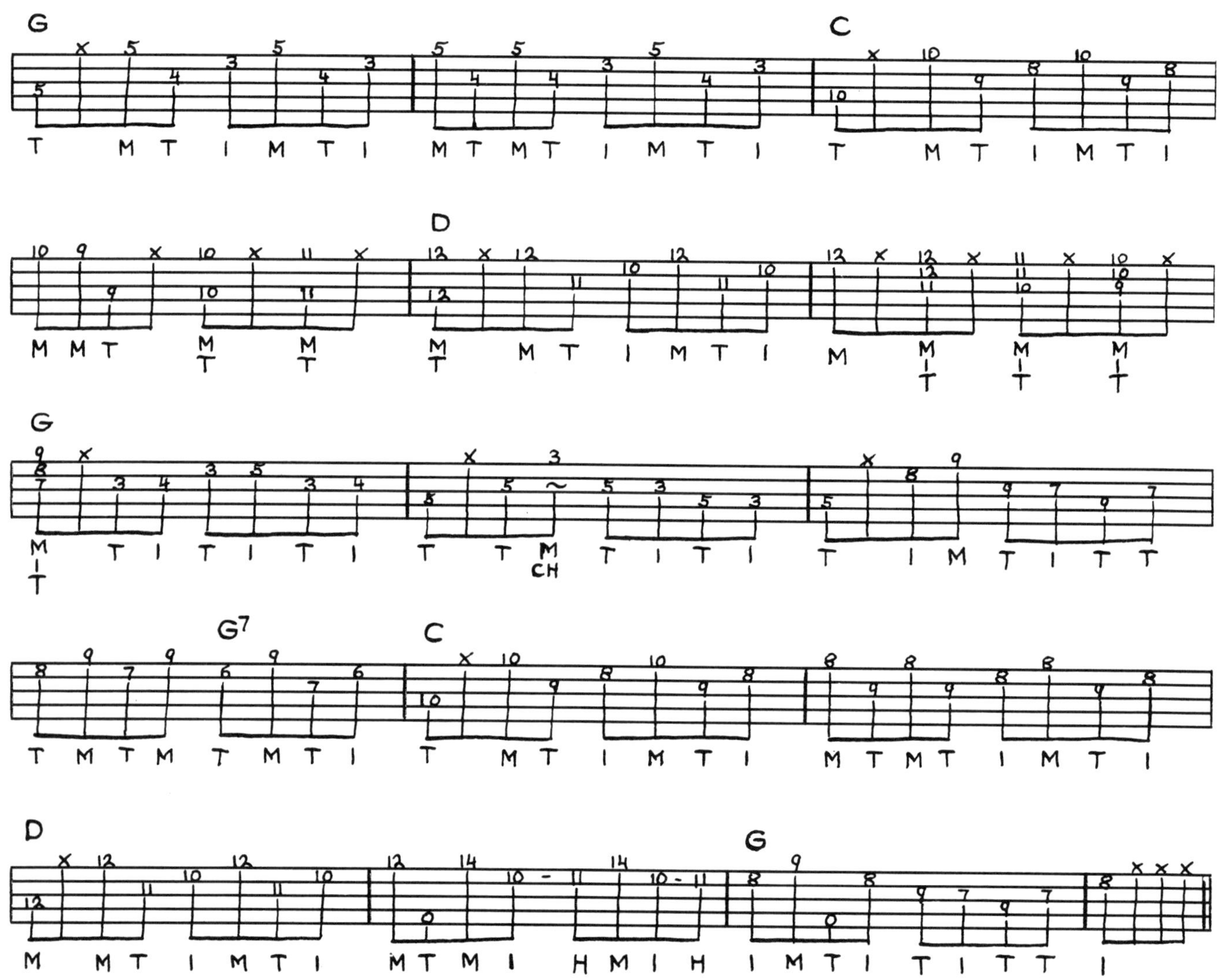

Three-quarter time

A small percentage of bluegrass songs are in 3/4 time. Rarely is 3/4 time used in anything but slow songs, and since banjo is infrequently used for lead on slow songs you will hardly ever have to do a lead in 3/4. But of course you should be prepared for whatever comes along, and playing backup and occasionally lead in 3/4 time will come along.

The phrase 3/4 time means the rhythm goes "boom-chick-chick, boom-chick-chick". Fast bluegrass is in 2/4 time ("boom-chick, boom-chick") and most slow bluegrass is in 4/4 time ("boom-chick-chick-chick, boom-chick-chick-chick"). Sometimes 3/4 time is called waltz rhythm – waltzes are always played in that time because the dance involves one big step and two smaller ones.

Backup for a slow song in 3/4 means following along with the "boom-chick-chick", especially the "boom" which you'll usually find yourself playing with the thumb. As with slow songs in 4/4 time, you don't play rolls, just go at it in an open-ended way with the aim of doing what you can to contribute to a good overall band sound.

Here is the basic right hand pattern for 3/4 time:

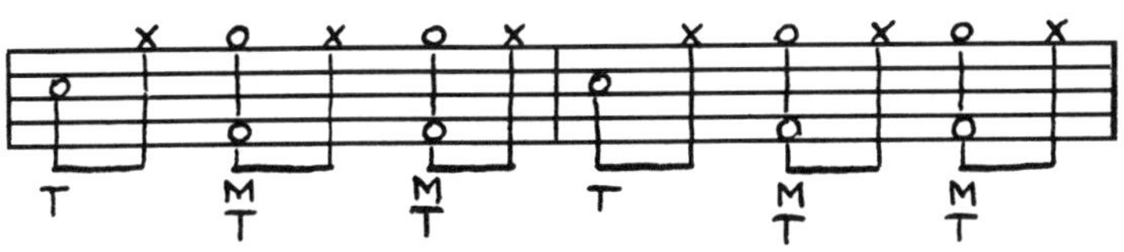

Or to fill up more spaces, any of these three patterns:

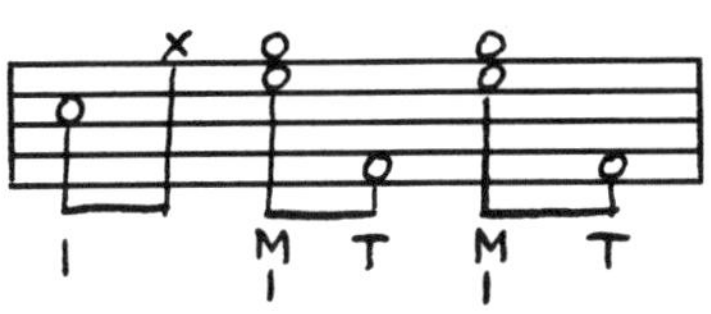

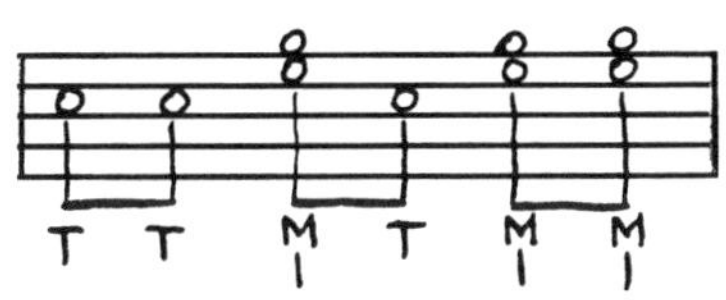

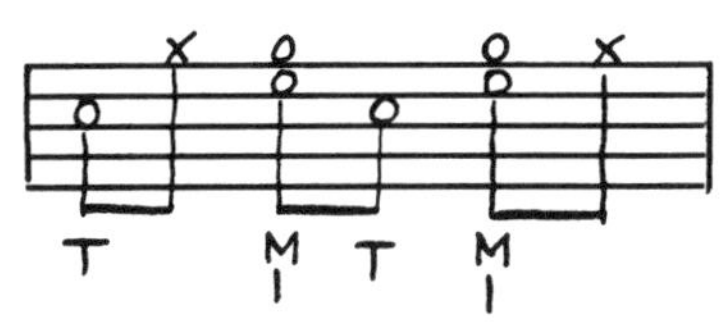

The main thing to keep in mind is that you now have six spaces, not eight, to fill up a measure. If you play along with records in 3/4 time, you'll probably fall into simple ideas after a while. Some examples of well-known songs in 3/4 are *Tennessee Waltz, Shenendoah Waltz* (or any other waltz), *All the Good Times Are Past and Gone, White Dove, Ocean of Diamonds, That Was Before I Met You,* and the first half of *Blue Moon of Kentucky* (which then speeds up into a brisk 2/4).

Every now and then a song in 3/4 is fast enough to make it worthwhile for the banjo to play rolls. Playing rolls in 3/4 is weird at first because the rolls have to be six notes long and not eight. Here are some sample six-note rolls:

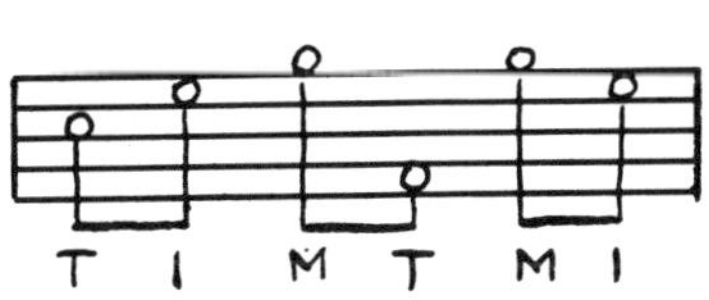

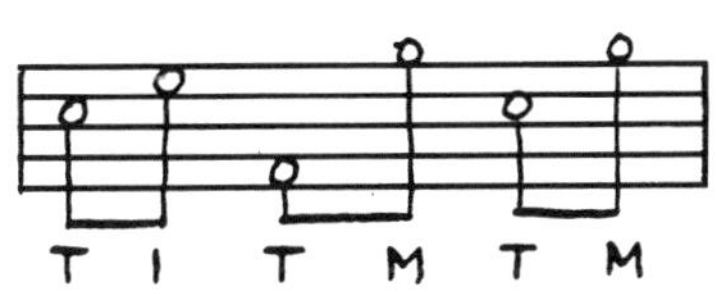

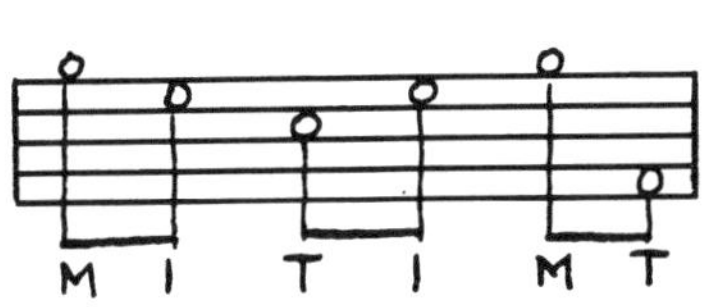

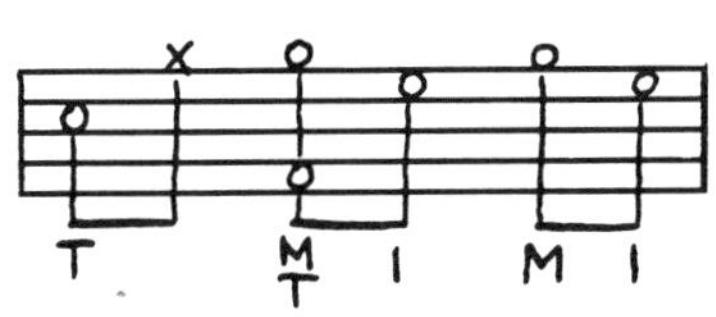

The most popular 3/4 song suited to playing rolls is *All the Good Times Are Past and Gone* which is not only a standard, but one in which the banjo is often given a chance to play lead. Here is an arrangement of this song:

All the Good Times Are Past and Gone

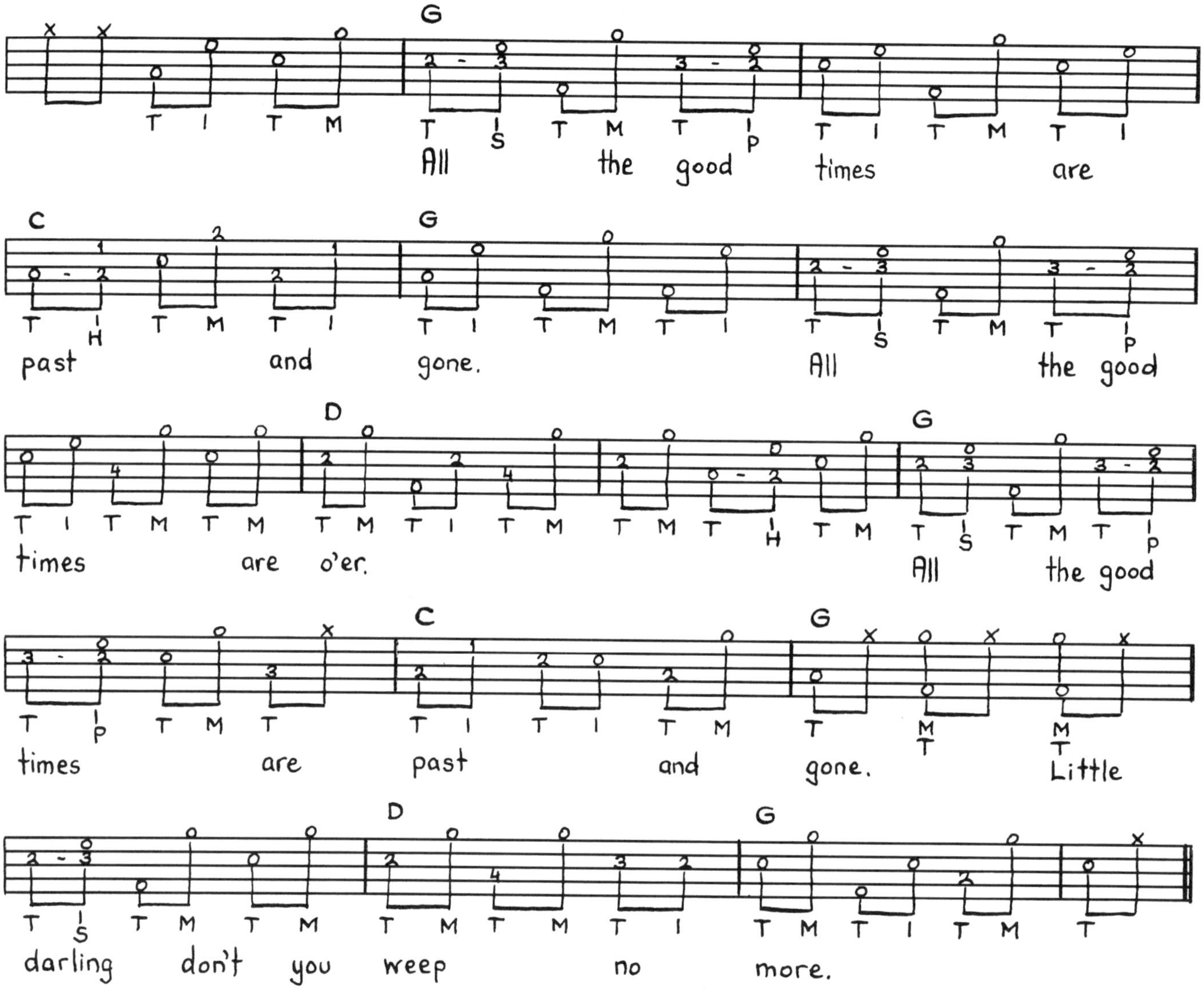

Melodic style ("Keith style," "Chromatic style")

This style was originally known as "Keith style" or "Keith picking." However, Bill Keith's independent discovery of the style came some years after Bobby Thompson used melodic runs in several tunes he recorded with Jim and Jesse and Carl Story in the '50's. It wasn't until the early '60's that Keith brought it into wide attention, mostly through public appearances and a couple of records during his stint with Bill Monroe. At about the same time, Marshall Brickman and Eric Weissberg of New York were experimenting with the style, and recorded an album later to be repackaged as the Deliverance theme, *Dueling Banjos* album, which featured a lot of melodic banjo playing (including Brickman's infamous "bumblebee break" on *Shuckin' the Corn*). Actually, the principles of technique used in melodic-style banjo go back quite some time, both in classical guitar playing and in the styles of banjo playing which were popular around the turn of the century. So it is pretty hard to label any one person as the originator of the style. Suffice it to say that Bill Keith popularized it and that many banjo players, especially in recent years, have used it to make some great music.

The basic principles of the melodic style are pretty simple.

All or almost all of the notes played in this style are melody notes. This is unlike standard bluegrass style, in which the minority of the notes played are used as melody notes (most are used as background, fill-in notes). Sometimes, though not always, melodic sequences are chromatic. That is, the melody notes are separated by half steps. As a result, some people call the style "chromatic," which isn't really accurate.

The idea that the same note can be found on more than one string is basic to the style, which is *to choose the strings your right hand plays so that it never plays the same string twice in a row.*

Instead of playing:

you can play:

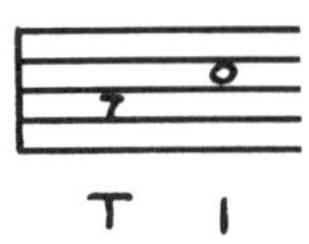

Instead of playing a G scale like this:

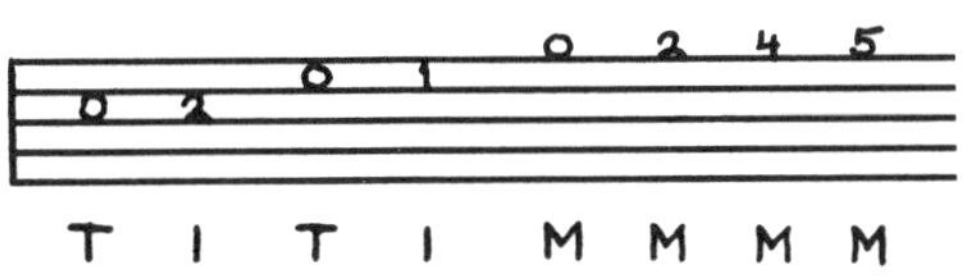

you can play:

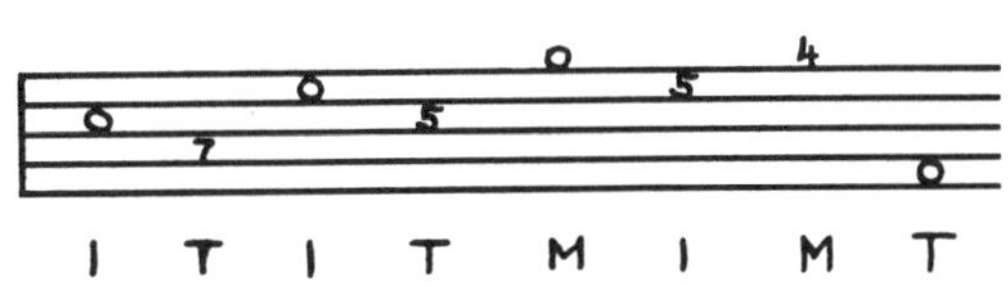

This allows you to play the notes faster and more smoothly. You may have noticed that wherever possible in the last run I used open strings. Using open strings when possible makes it easy on the left hand. However, just to prove that you have a lot of alternatives, here is another way to play that same G scale:

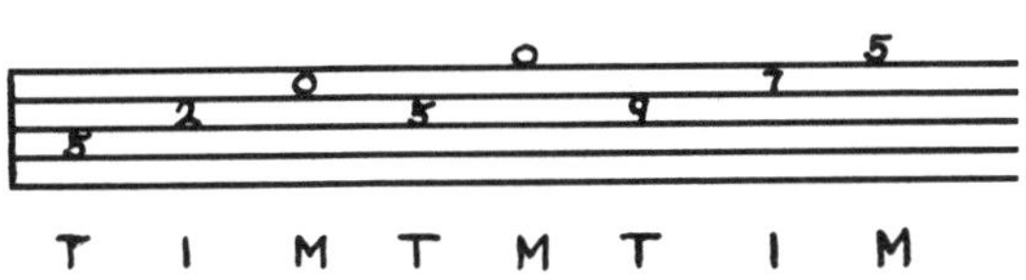

Originally, this style was most commonly used in bluegrass to play accurate versions of fiddle tunes. Fiddle tunes usually have a lot of melody notes (eight per measure) – many more melody notes than can be worked into standard bluegrass style rolls. And so, until the melodic style came along, banjo players had to work hard at playing an arrangement of a fiddle tune that sounded close enough to the tune so as to make it recognizable. Melodic style changed that by making it possible to get every last note in the fiddle tune. Melodic style also went a step further – some banjo players started making up melodic runs that weren't based on a fiddle tune, but just on a musical idea of their own – something that would sound good on a banjo. The styles of Bobby Thompson (the Nashville studio banjo player), Larry McNeely and Carl Jackson, both of whom gained fame as banjo playing sidekicks to Glen Campbell, use a lot of melodic ideas made up specifically for the banjo.

As with standard bluegrass style, you have room for eight notes in a measure. When you play melodically, that's quite a bit. Here, step by step, is how to go about figuring out a melodic arrangement.

Know every note you want to play. For each note, figure out a couple of places you can play it. Then try to select from your alternatives a combination allowing you to play the notes (1) so that your right hand doesn't have to play the same string twice in a row and (2) so that you don't have to contort your left hand too much or move it too quickly from one spot to another.

Just continue in that manner, making sure to remember what you figured out at each step of the way. It makes sense to practice each fragment right after you work it out. When you become comfortable with each one, try running it together with the ones before and after it. Eventually the whole piece will take shape. Then if you're like most banjo players, you'll need quite a bit of practicing to roll the notes together smoothly and play the tune at the speed it deserves *without making mistakes.*

There are several pitfalls in trying to play in the melodic style, and they are serious.

1. Whereas with almost everything you've played before the accents were on thumb notes and thumb notes only, accents can be anywhere and any time in melodic style. Although in earlier styles the first and fifth strings were usually supposed to be relatively quiet, they now have to be loud and sometimes accented. This means much more agility will be demanded of your right hand in the way it hits the notes.

2. Before the notes were supposed to blend together a little to produce a sort of chordal sound. In melodic style that is something of a drawback – each note has to be distinctive enough to allow it to be heard as a melody note. This method of playing involves a different overall right hand "feel" than you would use in normal bluegrass style.

3. In standard bluegrass style you could fall back on convenient patterns and licks and rolls allowing you to play almost mechanically a whole string of notes while hardly having to concentrate. Melodic style is much more demanding. *Every* note has to be decided on and memorized beforehand. When every note counts as a melody note, you can't just let your hand play anything it happens to fall into. Every melody requires its own roll to play it, so a tune with 16 measures could conceivably require 16 different right hand rolls to play it.

4. If by some chance you should make a mistake, and say, play an index finger instead of a middle finger, you're sunk. Because the finger you used was probably the one you should have used for the *next* note, and it can't be used now because it just finished playing the one before. Most likely your hand will keep on rolling and it will end up playing a whole string of wrong notes. In the measure or two it might take to recover, you could have played as many as ten or fifteen wrong notes. In standard bluegrass style using the wrong finger doesn't have to throw you off – just make sure you don't lose the rhythm or break the roll. Since most of the notes you play aren't supposed to be melody notes anyway, it's hard for anyone to tell whether what you're playing is exactly what you intended. You can make mistakes and no one will know, as long as you play them forcefully and clearly.

5. Keeping a tune memorized and in shape to be played is not too difficult in standard bluegrass style. There is leeway for variation and small mistakes. Since melodic style is so precise, a melodic arrangement needs to be practiced periodically to be kept in shape. If you let too long a time slip by without practicing it you're likely to slop it up on your next try.

6. Improvising in this style is also difficult. What makes it so rough is that if you should slip and break up the string of melody notes even for just a short interval, it's likely to sound bad. Improvising in melodic style is more of a gamble than with standard style, in which there's (relatively) much more time to get your bearings between melody notes.

Those are all of the complexities. However, melodic style banjo offers so many advantages that these are worth overcoming. Obviously, it gives you a chance to play things that you couldn't play otherwise. Pure melodic runs are not the only option: straight bluegrass style can be combined with melodic style to weave an altogether new sound. To be convinced of the good points of melodic style, it helps to hear it played well. Some of the leading practitioners today include Alan Munde, Jimmy Arnold, Tony Trischka, Courtney Johnson, Bela Fleck, Pete Schwimmer, Pat Cloud, Larry McNeely, Jack Hicks, Carl Jackson, Ben Eldridge and a host of others who I hope will forgive me for not giving their names here. Although not all of the musicians listed above have been recorded yet, check Appendix 7 for information on how to hear those who have.

One trend in melodic banjo playing is the introduction of notes outside of the major scale, especially the two "blue notes": flatted thirds and flatted sevenths. In addition, chromatic sequences—runs consisting of notes a half-step apart—are sometimes used. With the use of non-major notes, melodic runs can take on sharp edges and create a distinctly different sound of banjo playing. I recommend using non-major notes the way you would use a strong seasoning in cooking: as spice, not as the main dish.

Here are two long melodic sequences, each of which goes through a few chord changes. They'll give you an idea of the two kinds of melodic banjo playing: major scale notes only, and chromatic scale notes includes.

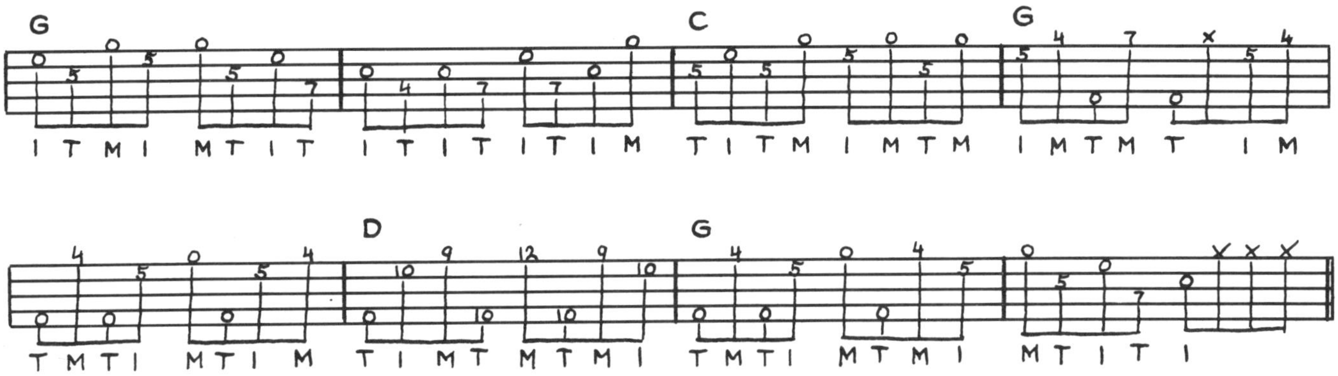

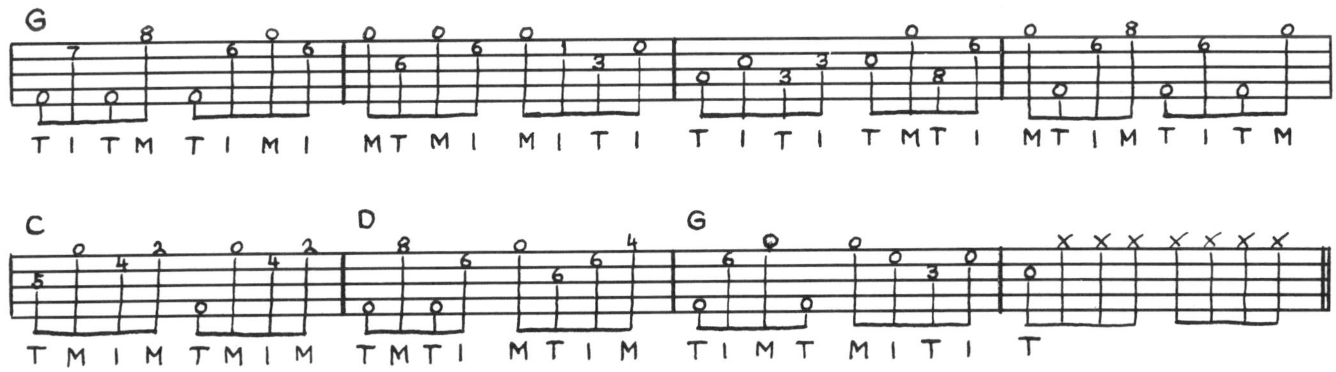

Here are some instrumentals – two fiddle tunes and two banjo tunes – using mostly melodic style.

Devil's Dream

Bill Monroe

As played by Bill Keith with Bill Monroe and the Blue Grass Boys.

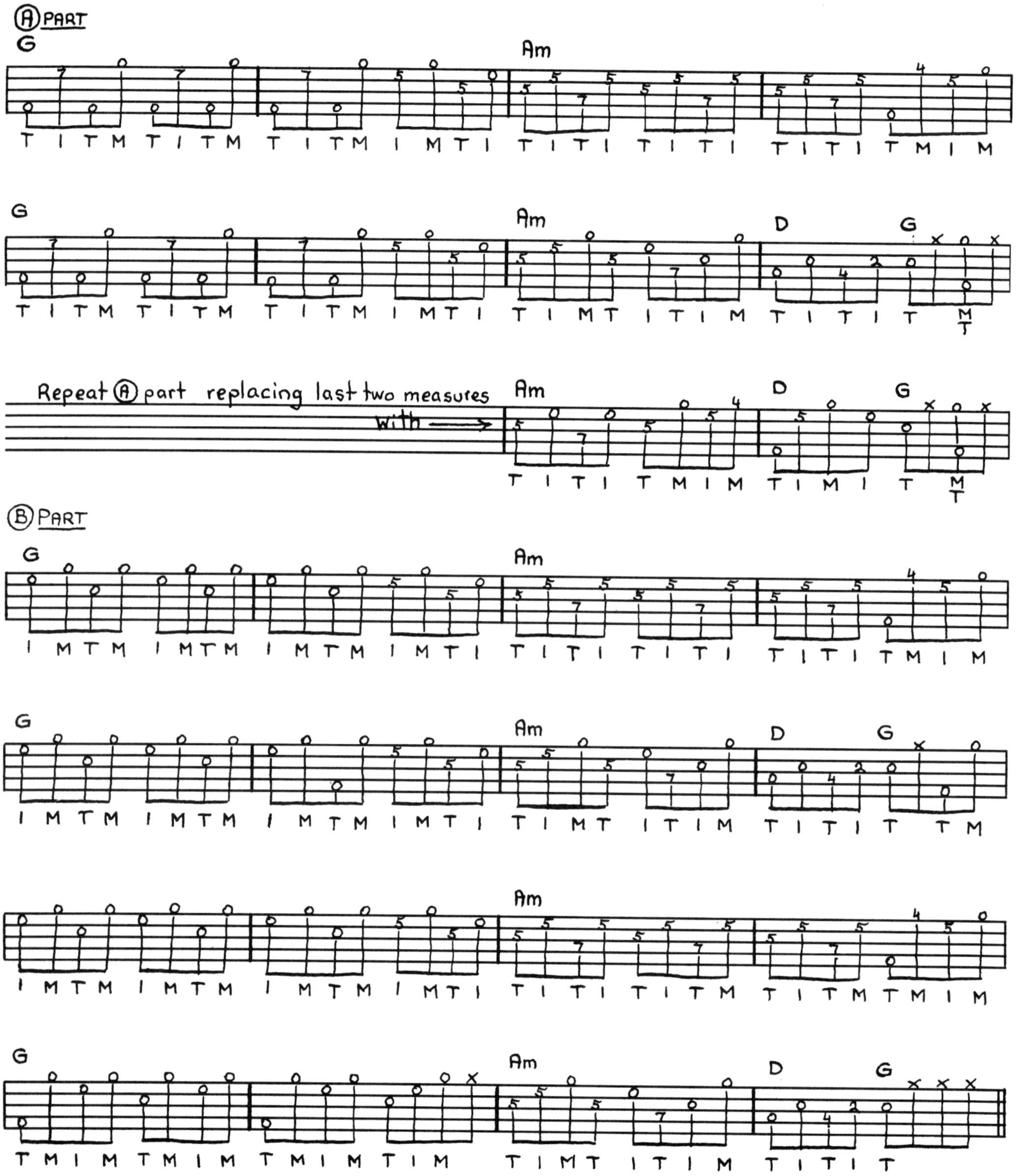

Sailor's Hornpipe

Bill Monroe, Bradford Keith
As played by Bill Keith with Bill Monroe and the Blue Grass Boys.

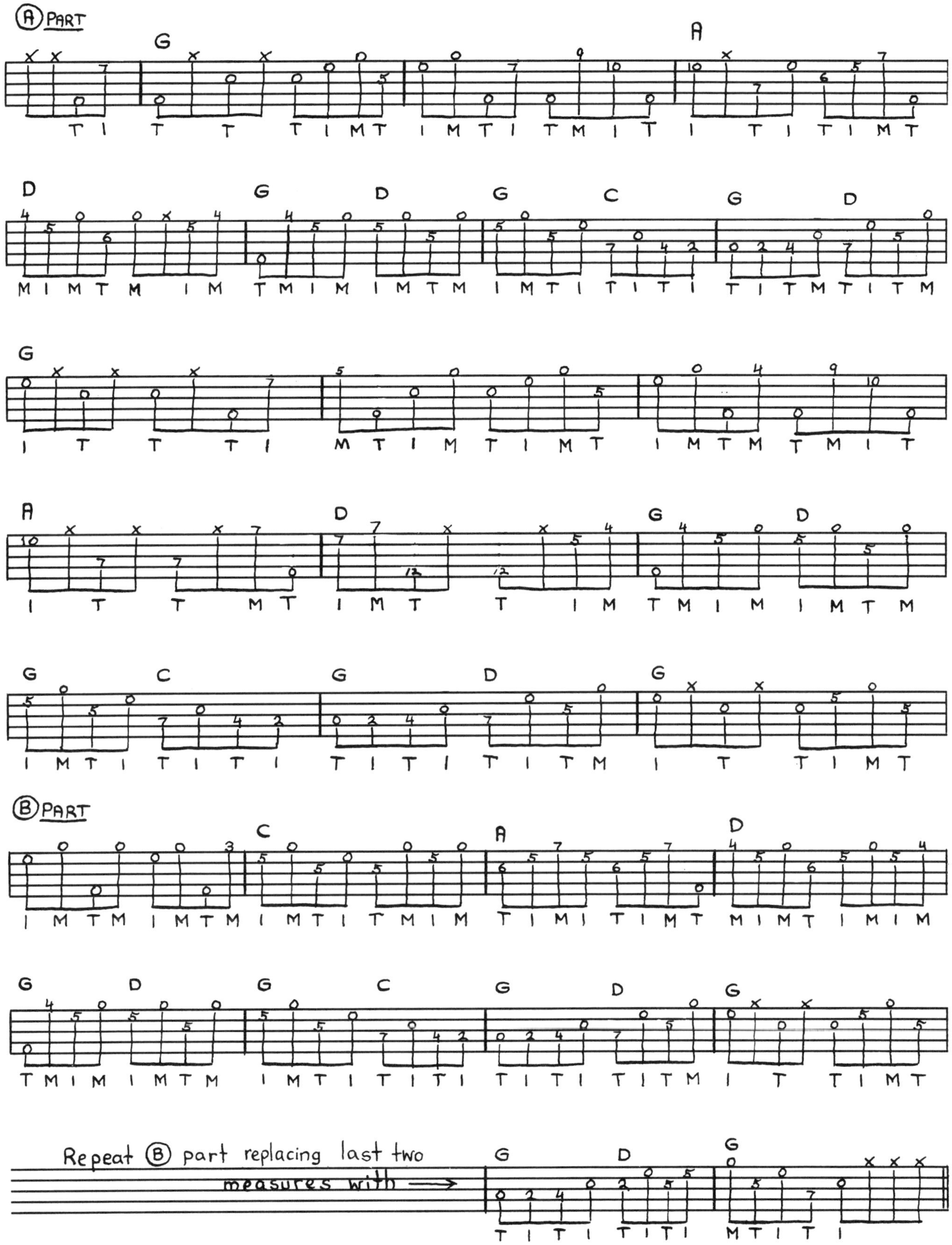

Orange Mountain Special

Peter Wernick
As played on Country Cooking's first album. Key of A.

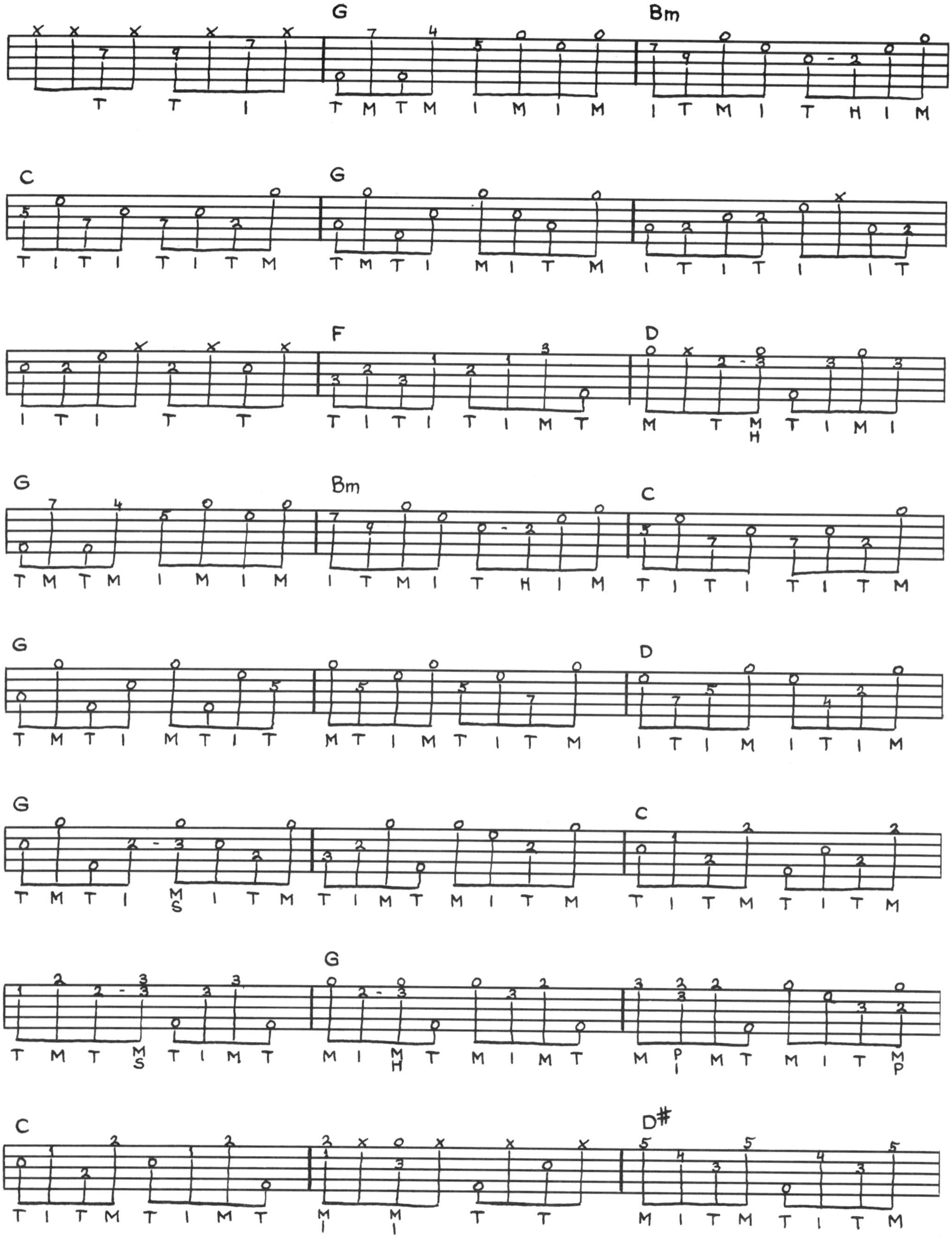

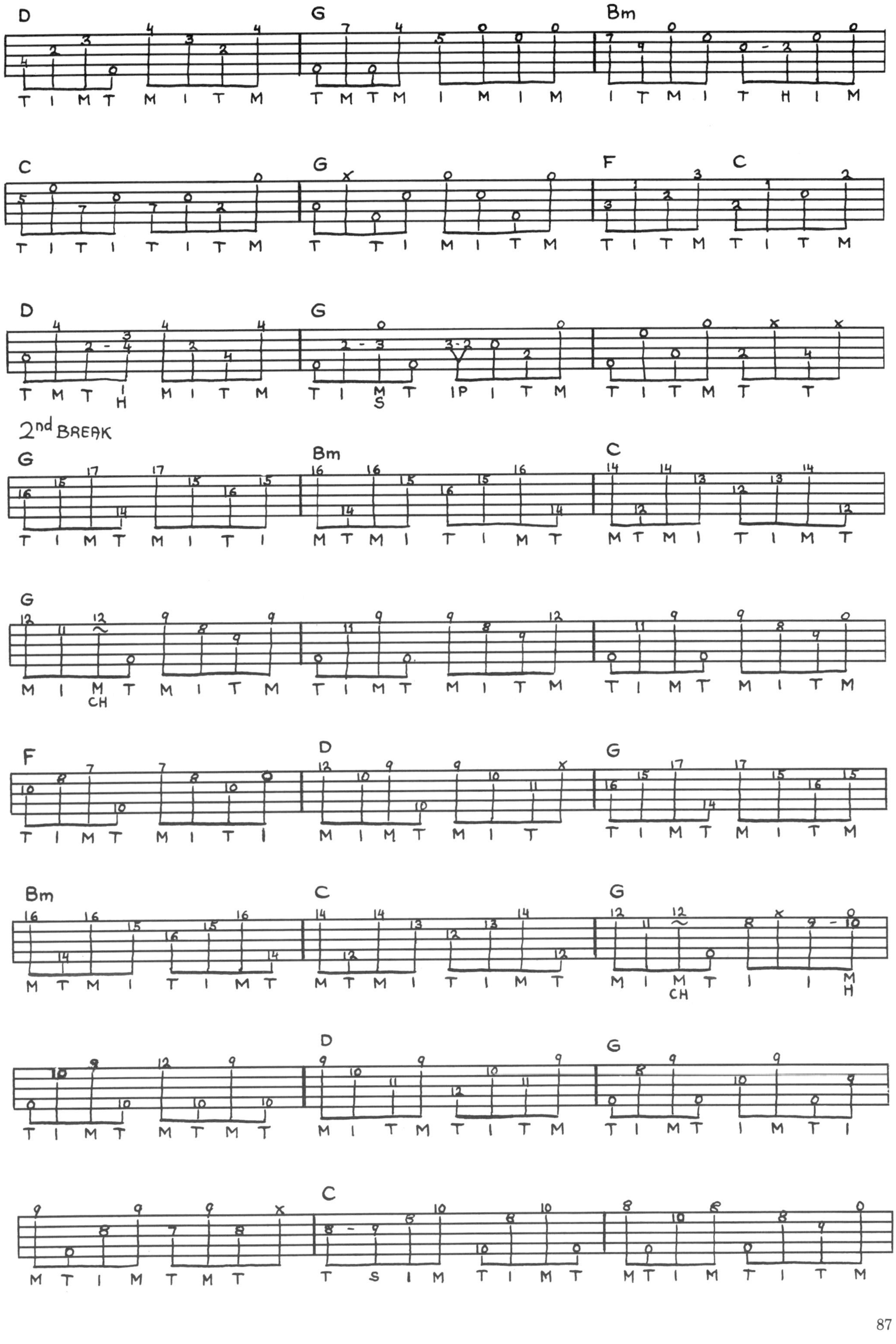
D
G
Bm
C
G
F
C
D
G
2nd BREAK
G
Bm
C
G
F
D
G
Bm
C
G
D
G
C

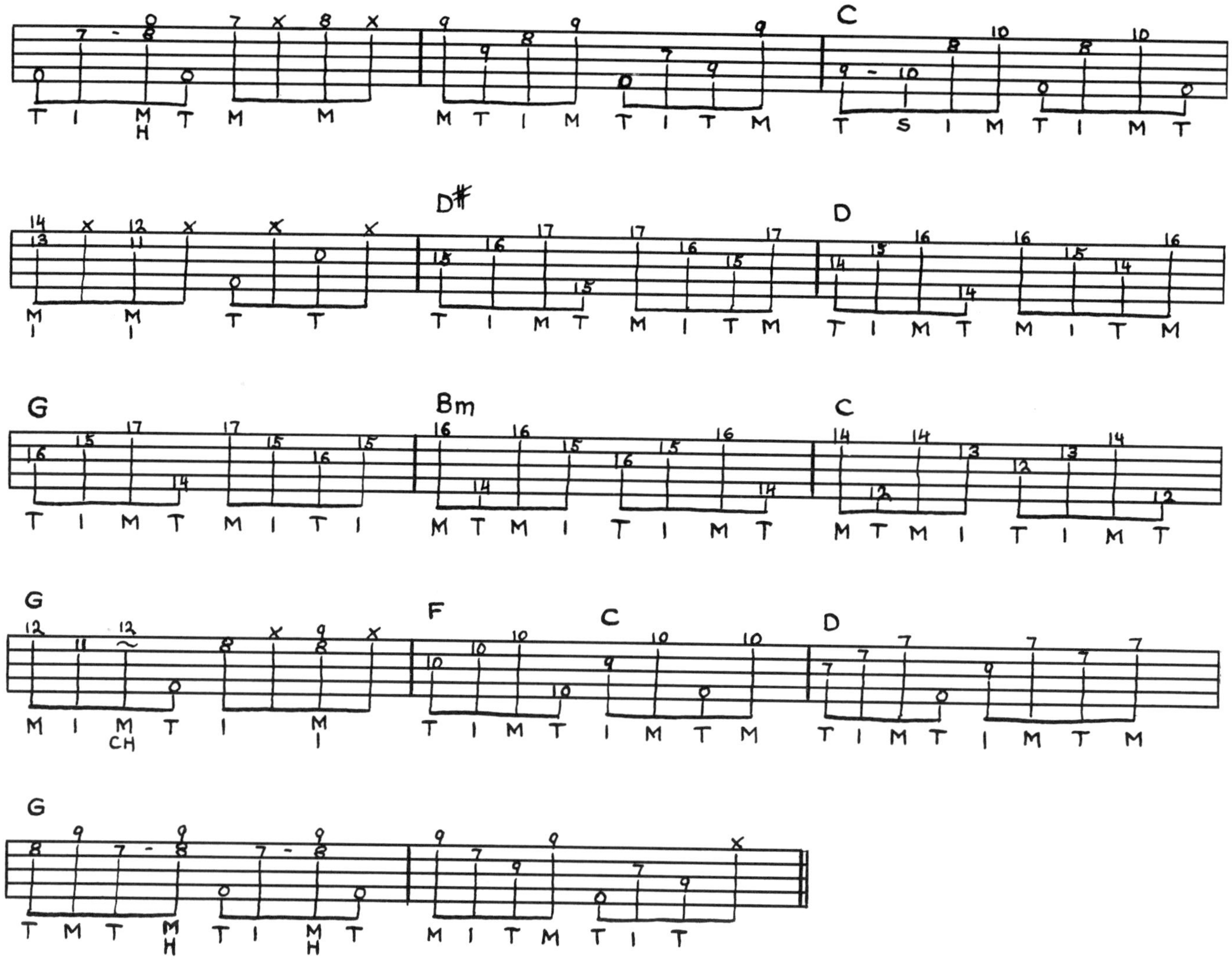
C
D#
D
G
Bm
C
G
F
C
D
G

Chromania

Tony Trischka

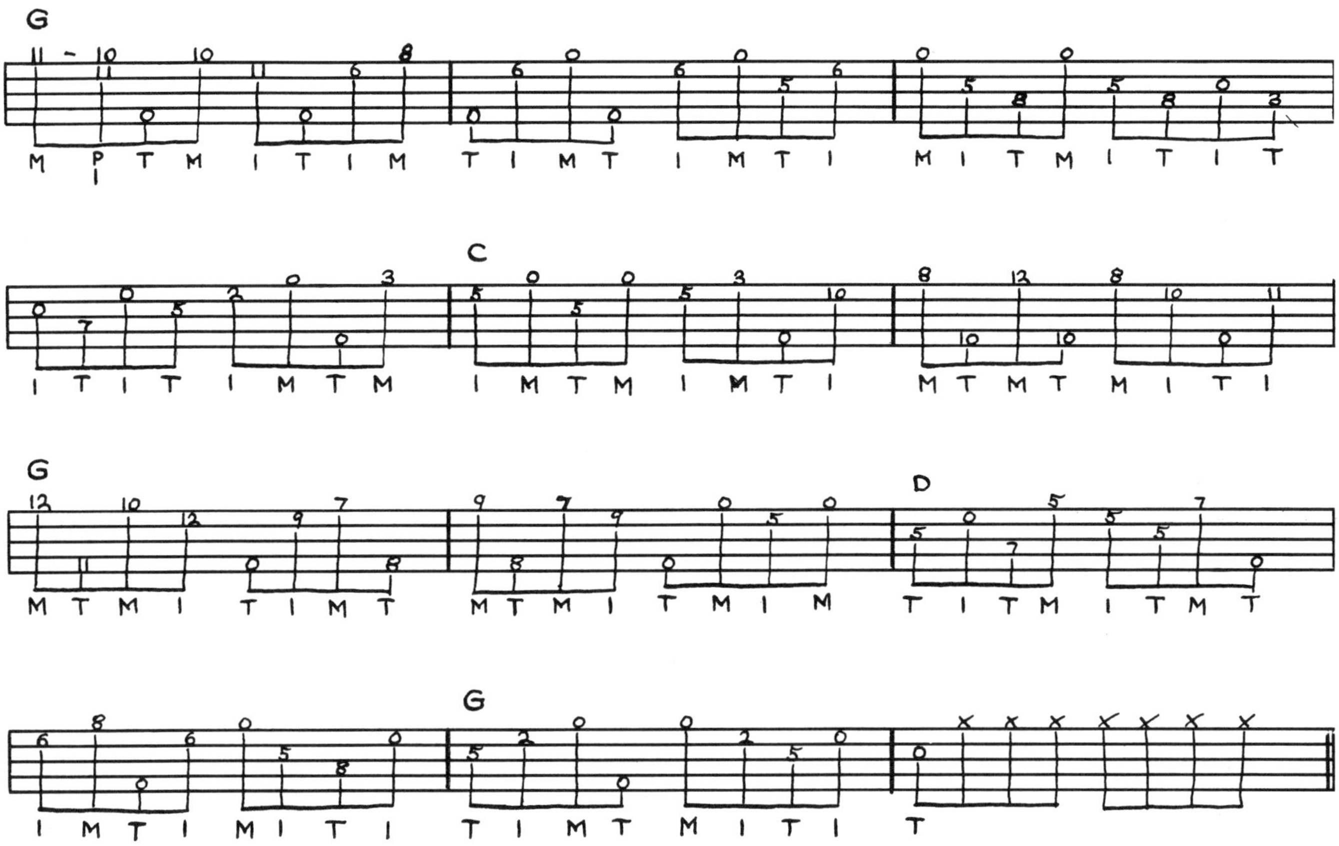

Single string style

In this style, as in melodic style, all the notes played are melody notes. The difference is that in melodic style the notes are played as part of rolls, while in single string style the thumb and index finger alternate, imitating the up and down motion of a flat pick. In melodic style the same string is never played twice in a row – it would interfere with the roll. In single string style the thumb and index finger might alternate playing the same string for several consecutive notes.

Don Reno introduced single string banjo playing to bluegrass. He and Eddie Adcock are the two masters of it. Reno's *Follow the Leader* and Adcock's break for *Sunrise* popularized the style as the main variation to standard Scruggs style in the '50's and early '60's, before melodic style became popular.

Single string work imitates closely what a flat picking guitar player might do on a banjo (Joe Maphis is one guitar player who actually does flat pick single notes on a banjo – and it sounds pretty good). The way Reno and Adcock play, the left hand technique is the same as with guitar flat picking. They both play "freehand" – that is, with the left hand not based in chord positions. All four fingers are used to quickly get single notes and then move elsewhere fast. This makes single string work the style of bluegrass banjo playing which demands most of the left hand, especially when playing up the neck, where open strings can't be used. Technique-wise this style is quite different from standard Scruggs style, in which it's possible to work with connected rolls of notes instead of individual notes and to think more in terms of chord positions.

Here is a single string workout through the chord progression of *She'll Be Coming Round the Mountain:*

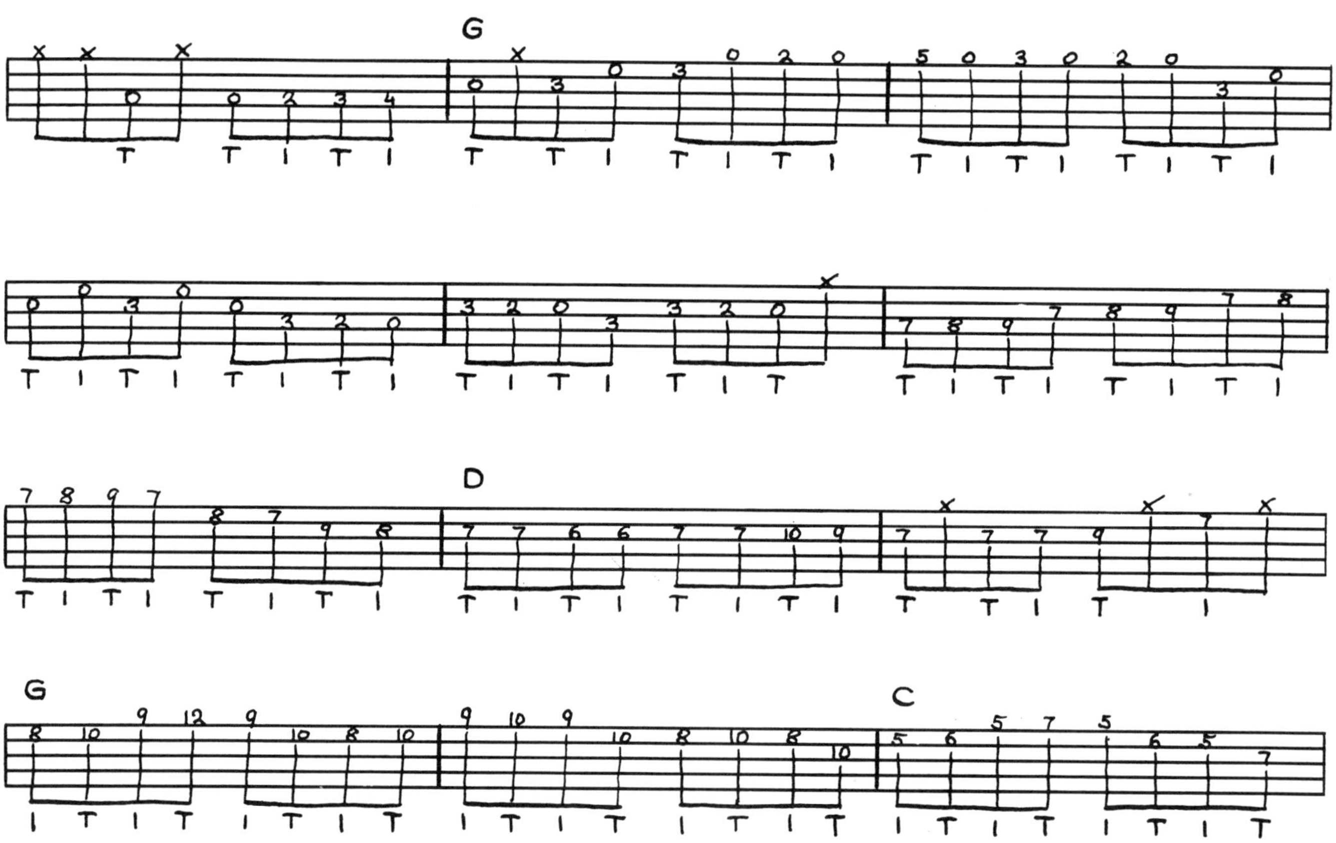

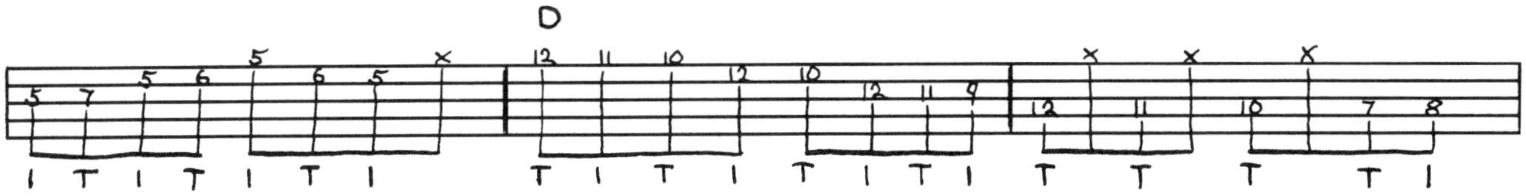

Eddie Adcock and Bill Monroe

Double banjo

Double banjo can be lots of fun and sounds great when it's played right or even sometimes when it isn't. Simultaneous leads by two instruments sound good when they are played together in close harmony and rhythm or when they're contrasted in such a way as to complement each other rather than to get in each other's way.

Bluegrass banjos produce so many notes that it's hard for two of them not to produce a cluttered sound. (This is a common problem for pickup bands – two banjo players who really want to pick wind up in the same group of musicians, and if they're both loud the music turns into a banjo mess.)

Double banjo is usually played the other way, the two instruments working closely together rhythmically and harmonically. In standard double banjo set-up, one instrument plays the melody and the other plays the tenor harmony. The problem with double banjos (as opposed to double fiddles, guitars or mandolins) is that it's not easy to work up an arrangement where the banjos play *every* note in harmony. That's because there are so many notes in an arrangement. To figure out how the two banjos can play *every* pair of notes in harmony would take a long time in most cases. One of the main problems would be the fifth string which, unless you fret it all the time or retune it and occasionally fret it, will be the same note on both banjos, creating a unison sound, not a harmony. The easier and much more popular alternative is to play just the melody notes of the arrangement in harmony and keep the two banjos' right hand rolls as similar to each other as possible. The overall effect is that the banjos produce a big, full, close-knit sound. Here is a sample arrangement of a tenor part for *Jesse James,* a favorite of double banjo players. This part fits well with the simple melody arrangement of the tune in the *Intermediate Tablature Section.*

Jesse James banjo harmony

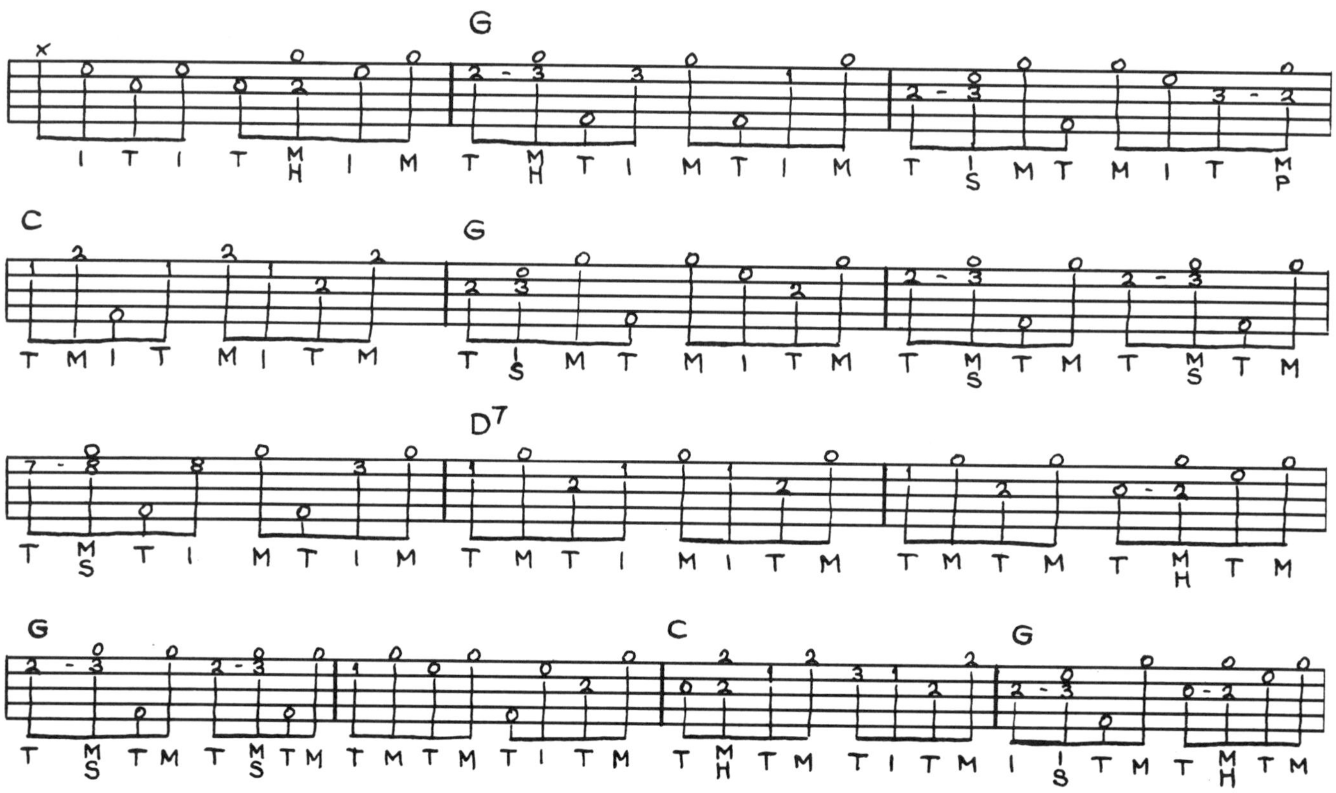

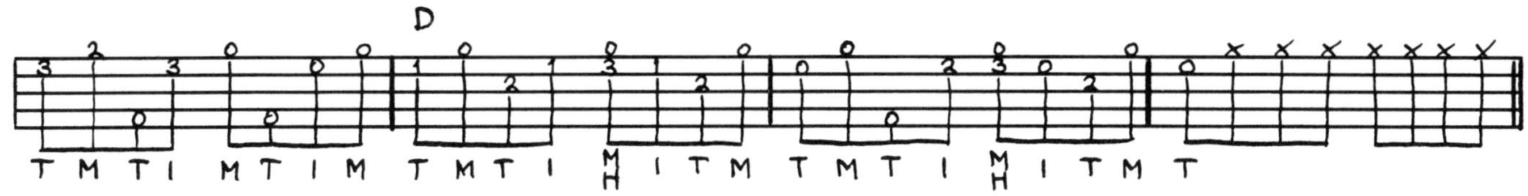

Both parts are recorded on Side I of the record included with this book. Each part is recorded so as to play out of a separate channel in your stereo. By turning down either part and playing that part yourself you can get a taste of what it's like to play twin banjos.

In a few cases it's possible to play all the notes of an arrangement in harmony. The second part of *Big Ben* as Tony Trischka and I play it on the first Country Cooking record is one of those cases. We both play the chords (B, E, A, D) using no open strings (including the fifth). We used two positions for each chord, so that the two first string notes, the two second string notes, etc., harmonized with each other. By playing identical right hand rolls, we got a harmony on every note.

For the B chord in *Big Ben* Tony uses this position (making what is actually a Bmaj7 chord).

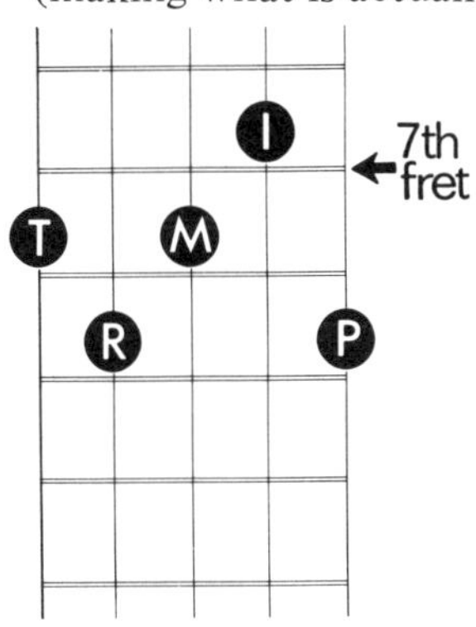

A little later he uses the same position two frets down for the A chord.

For the E chord he uses this position (actually an E7 with a flatted fifth),

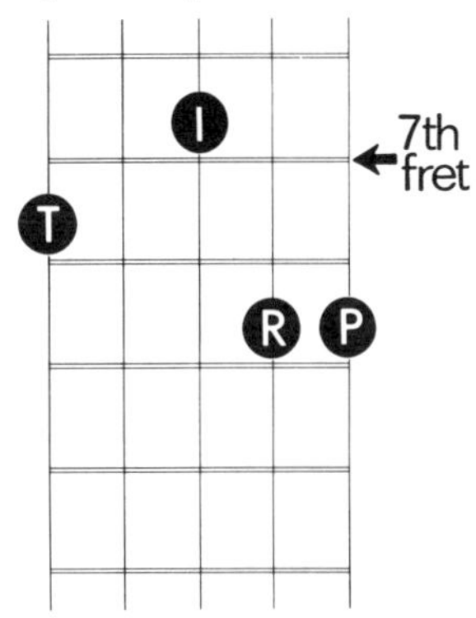

and repeats the position two frets down for the D.

I use a B9 (later moved down to A9):

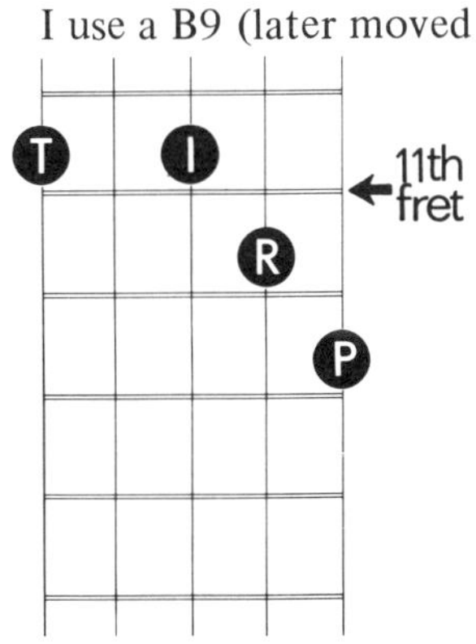

and an E7 (later moved down to D7):

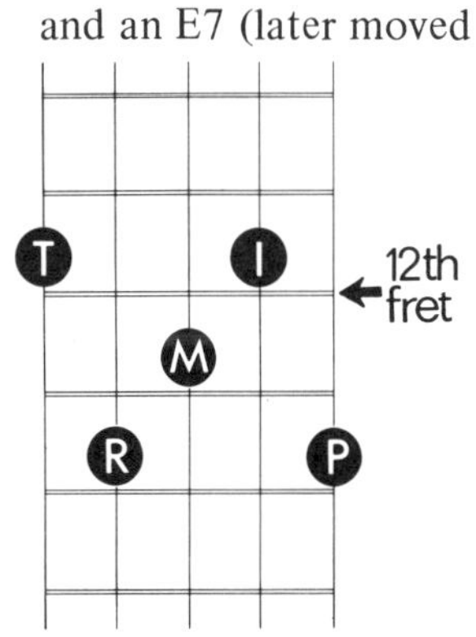

We play these two rolls on each chord position (B, E, A, D)

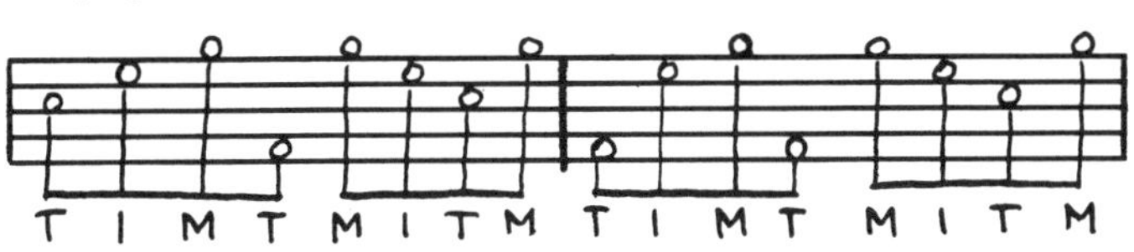

and the effect is what you hear on the record.

Muted banjo

When the banjo strings vibrate, most of the sound passes through the bridge and is transmitted to the head. By preventing the bridge or the head from vibrating normally the sound can be quieted and altered a great deal. The easiest way to set up this different sound is to place a mute on the bridge. The mute is just a clamp which by its weight prevents the bridge from vibrating freely to transmit the normal banjo sound. The result is a quiet, velvety soft, very sustained sound instead of the usual sharp, loud, brief sound. Low notes sound almost like a soft dobro (listen to *Tarry Not* on the Frank Wakefield/Country Cooking album) and high notes sound almost like a soft electric guitar (listen to *Old Old House* on Country Cooking's first album). The thing I like best about muted banjo is that the notes are sustained for such a long time, it's easy to bend them and get other subtle effects on slow songs. It's also fun to try playing normal bluegrass style with the mute on because the notes last so much longer that it produces a full-bodied textural sound instead of the usual rat-a-tat-tat. If you hit the strings gently and play a little more slowly than usual the effect can be really delightful, partly because it sounds so good and partly because it's such a change from what you're used to.

It's not too hard to find a mute that will do these wondrous things. Violin mutes will work and many music stores have them. I use two violin mutes at the same time – one is a little heavy cylinder of metal with three prong-like clamps. The clamps fit between the strings and grab the bridge. Since to mute the strings equally the bridge has to have clamps evenly distributed on it, I also add a different kind of mute on the end of the bridge which the clamps miss. This mute is a little hunk of rubber with a notch in it and I just slip it over the unclamped end of the bridge. Here are my two mutes in action:

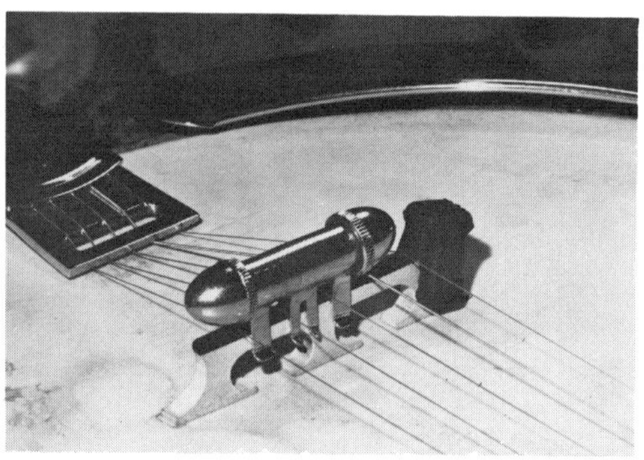

This combination is not the best one I've tried. I used to have an old violin mute that was lighter in weight and longer than the cylinder-type mute. It had five clamps, enabling it to fit over the bridge quite neatly. The lighter weight meant that it did not mute the sound as thoroughly as the cylinder-type mute but the extra volume was quite welcome in most playing situations.

In fact, the main problem with muted banjo is that it's too quiet to be played with many other instruments. I have found that unless everyone else is playing *very* quietly, my muted banjo can't be heard well enough for its subtlety to come through. When making records, I have been able to use it on quiet songs but in every case it's needed a lot of boosting. In these situations and when playing with just one or two guitars it does very well.

If you can find a mute I suggest you try it. They're not very expensive. There's another good reason to get a mute, of course – to use for practicing when your usual volume would disturb others. *I suggest that you experiment with whatever type of mute you come across.* Here is an arrangement of *Dark Hollow*, to be played with a mute:

Dark Hollow

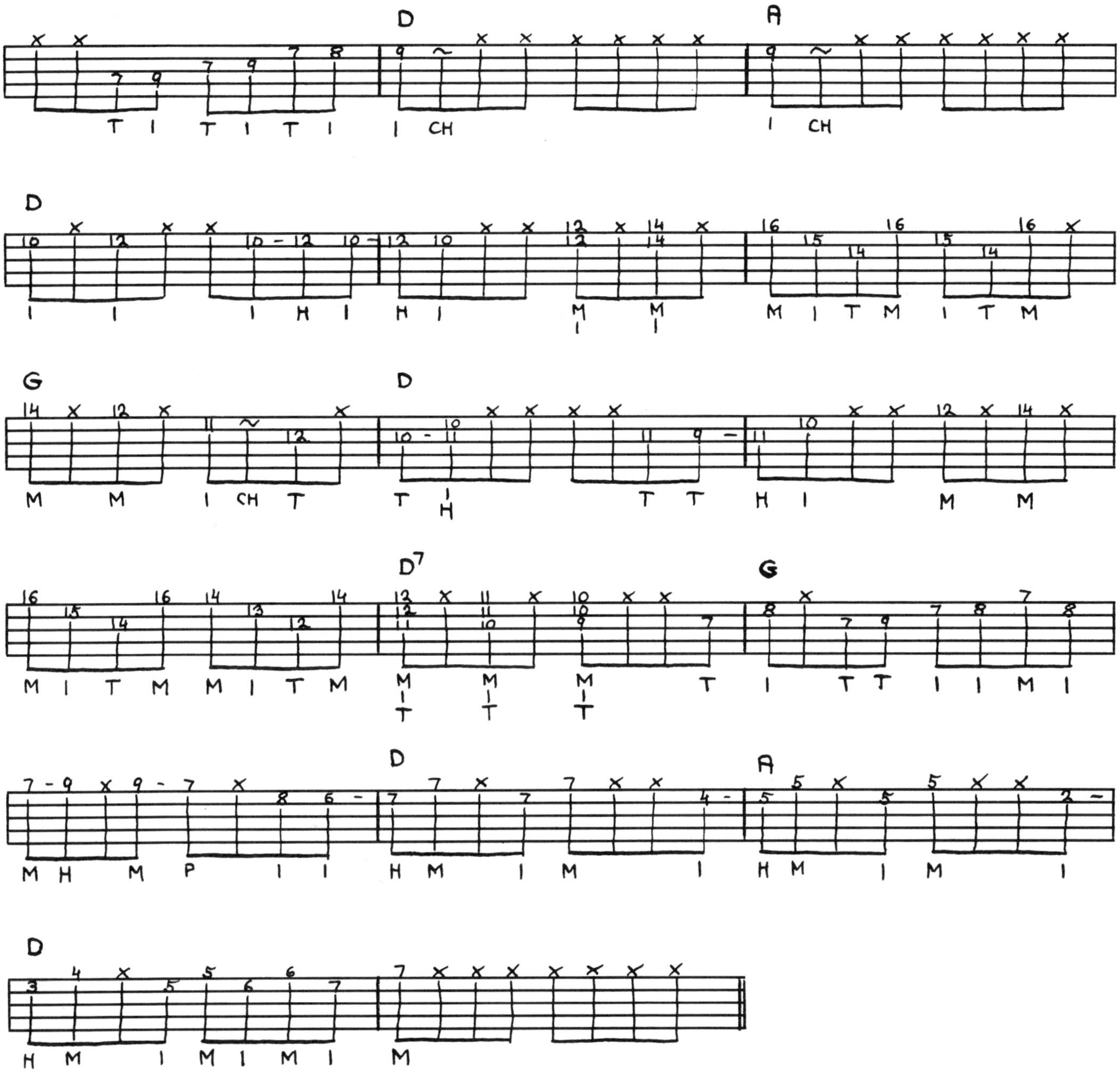

Advanced tablature section

This section contains plenty of advanced arrangements in tablature. There are several breaks for songs included, plus a number of instrumentals. Most of the arrangements in this section are either mine or Tony Trischka's, so look for many rhythmic turns. Often important notes will not fall in the usual places. Normally accents fall on the beats – the first note of each measure, but be ready for them anywhere in the measures of these arrangements. Look for odd techniques such as using the middle finger on the second string (listen to *Kentucky Bull-fight* and *November Cotillion*), the index on the first string right after a middle finger note there (in *John Hardy*), slides that take two beats instead of one, etc.

I hope that anyone who is serious about learning advanced banjo technique will listen to Tony Trischka's playing on records and at personal appearances. His technique is the most advanced I've heard in terms of both rhythmic and melodic creativity, as well as pure sound and execution. Much of what he plays is spontaneous.

The unexpected rhythmic and melodic turns in these arrangements may get confusing, especially for those arrangements which can't be checked against recorded versions. You may be tempted to think a troublesome part of the tablature is the result of a mistake in printing; I can't guarantee absolutely that the tablature is completely free of errors, but you can be sure that a great deal of care went into proofreading them before the final version was printed. If you spot anything you think is a mistake on my part, please let me know.

Lonesome Road Blues

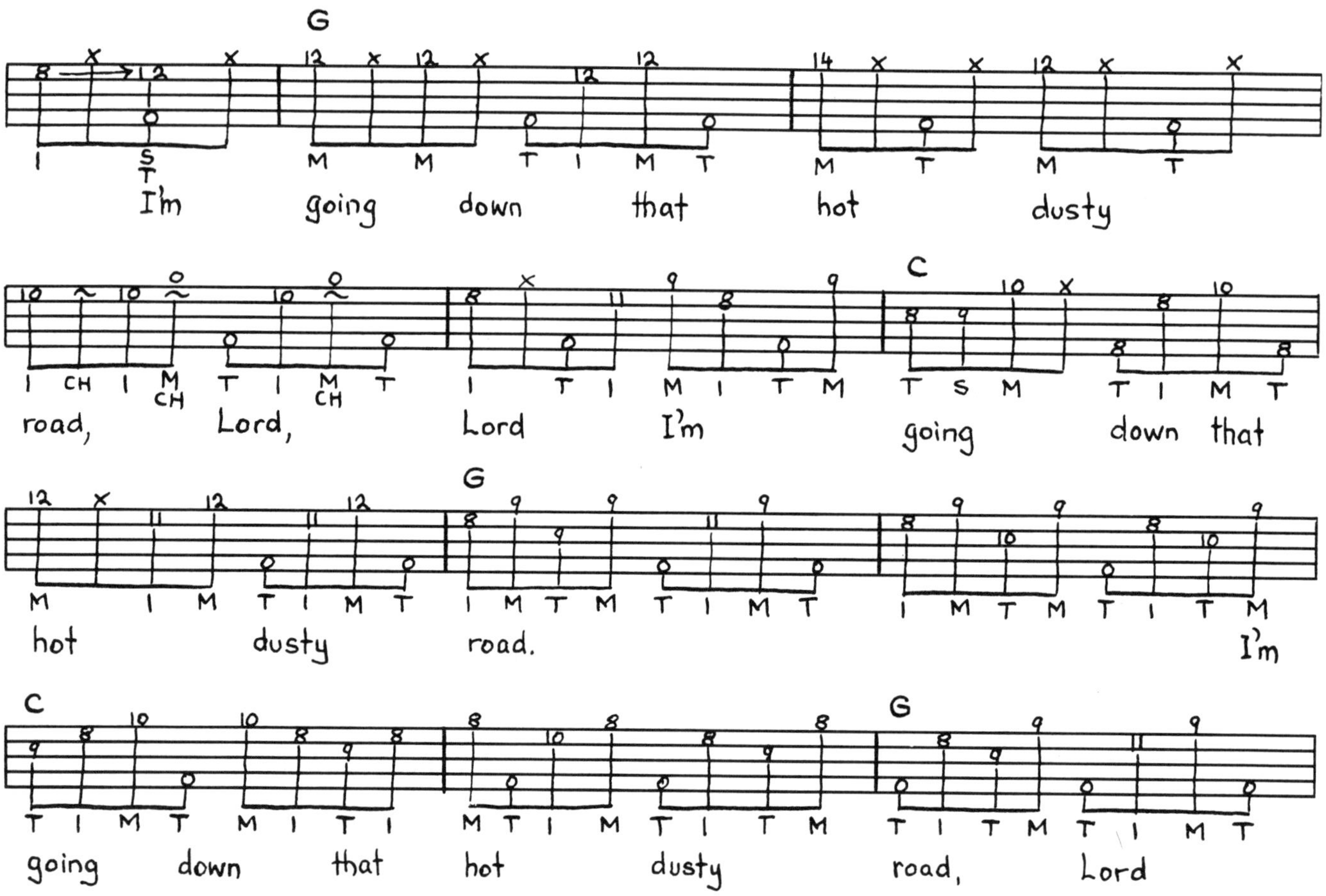

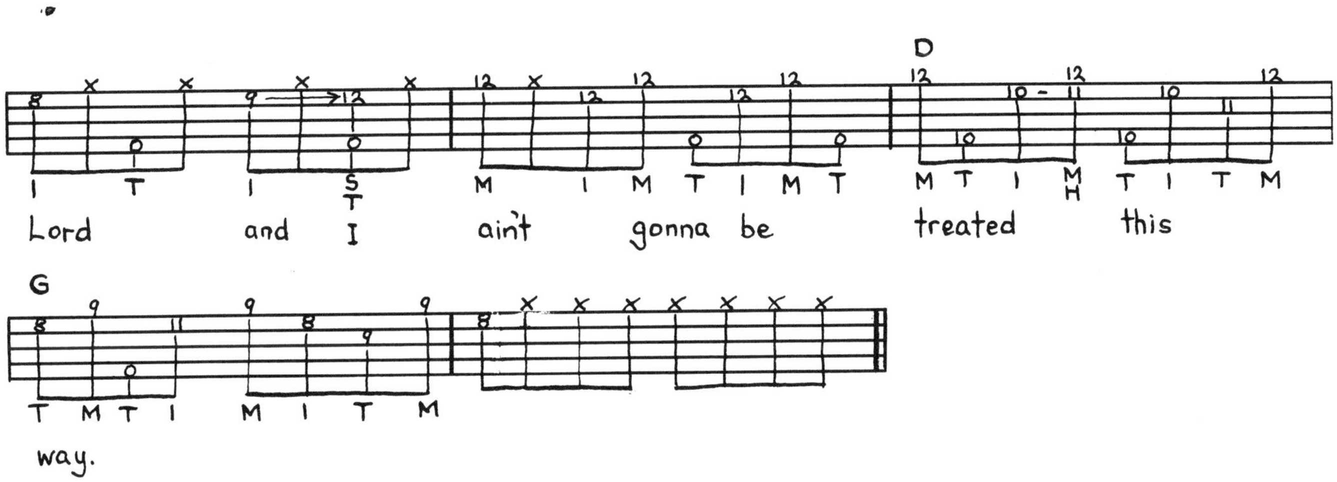

Will the Circle Be Unbroken

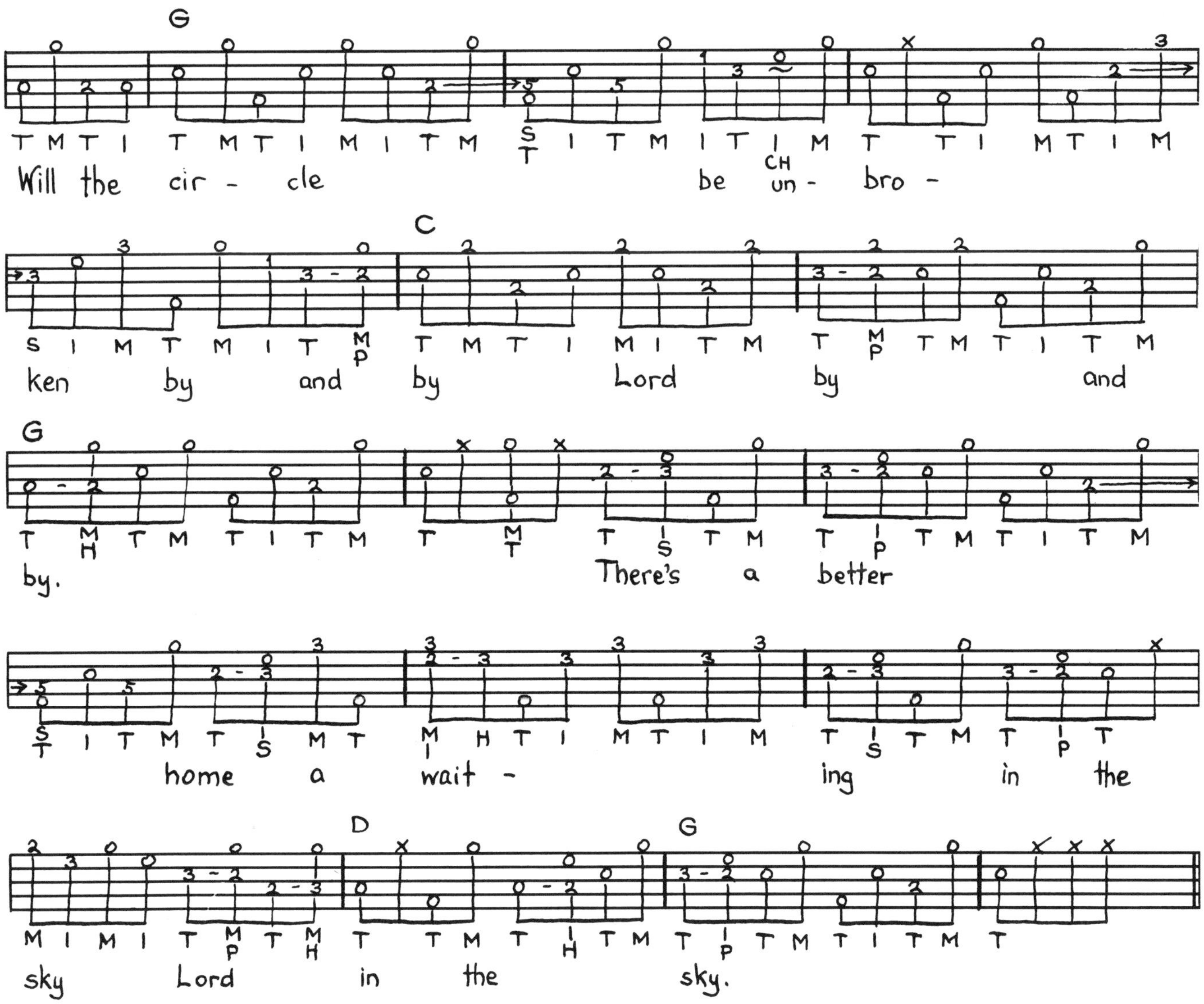

John Hardy

John Hard - y was a
desperate little man. He carried two
guns every day. He
killed him a man on the West Virginia
line. You should have seen John Hardy getting a -
way, oh Lord, should have seen John
Hardy get a - way.

John Henry

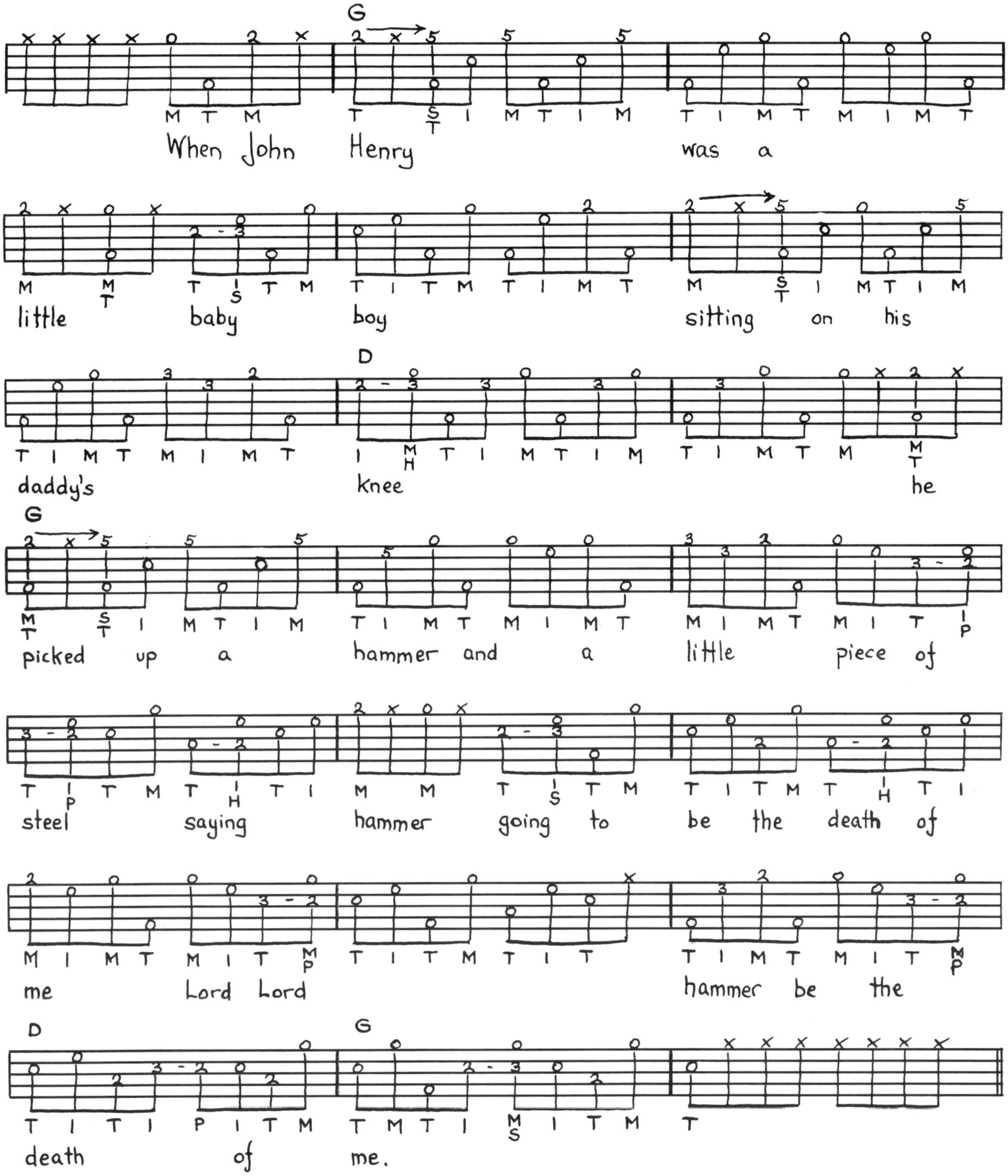
G
When John Henry was a
little baby boy sitting on his
D
daddy's knee he
G
picked up a hammer and a little piece of
steel saying hammer going to be the death of
me Lord Lord hammer be the
D
death of
G
me.

Buffalo Gals

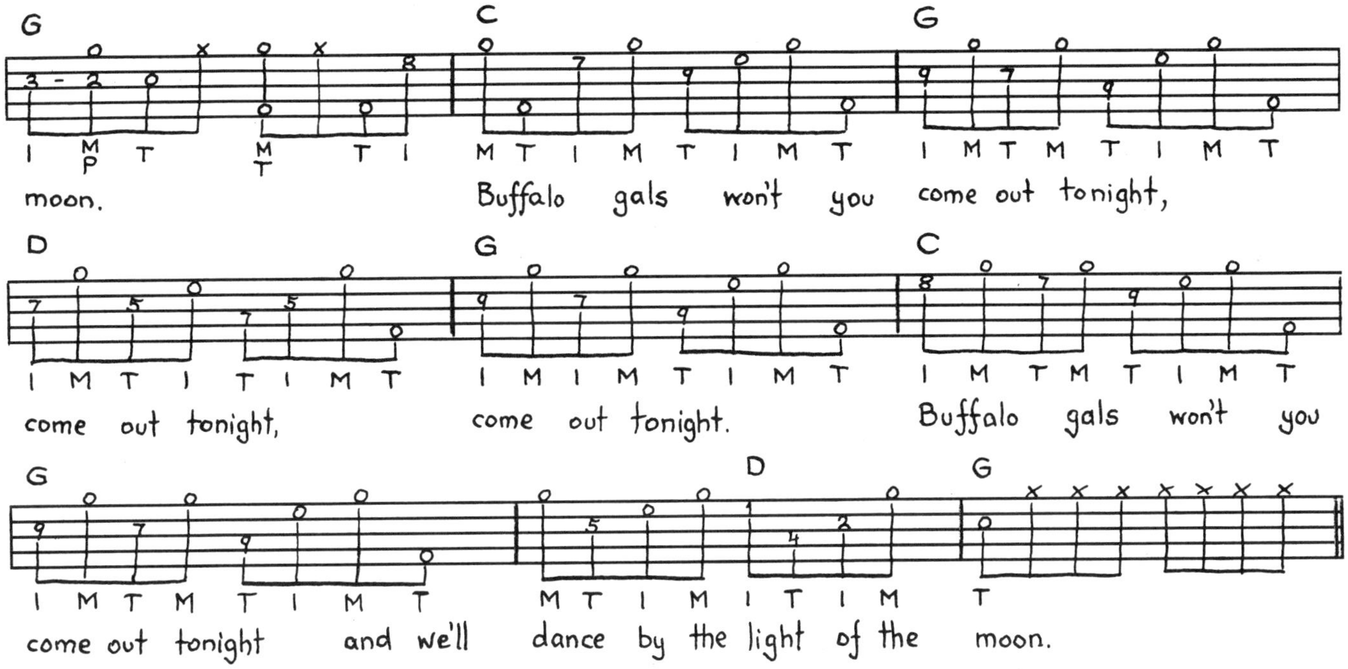

The Tarriers with Eric Weissberg

Cripple Creek

(A) PART

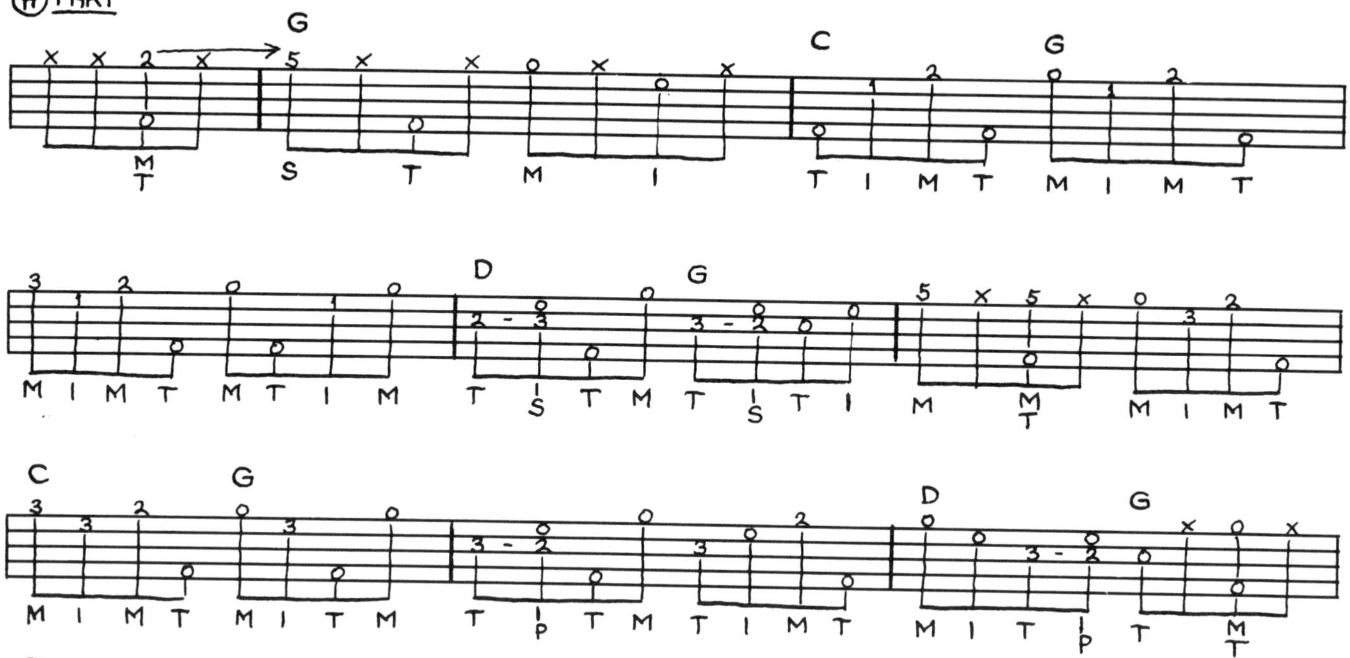

(B) PART

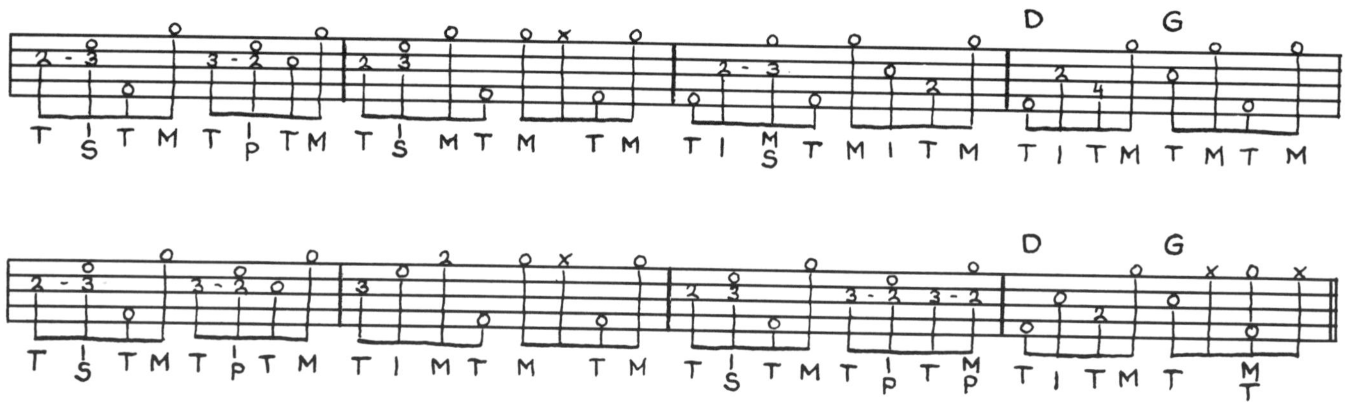

Pow Wow the Indian Boy

Peter Wernick

Recorded in key of A on Country Cooking's first album.

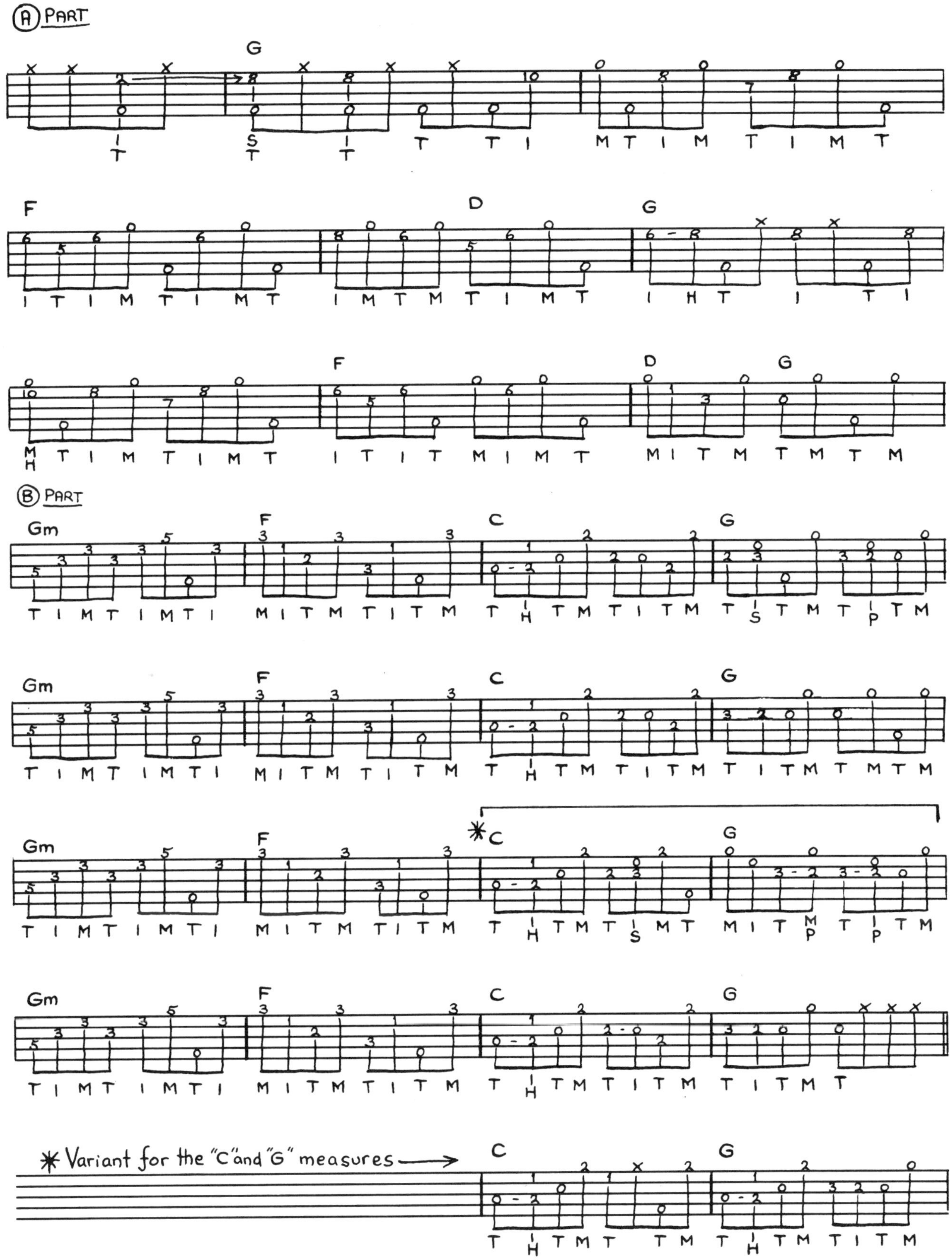

Salt Creek (Salt River)

Bill Monroe, Bradford Keith
As played by Bill Keith with Bill Monroe and the Blue Grass Boys.

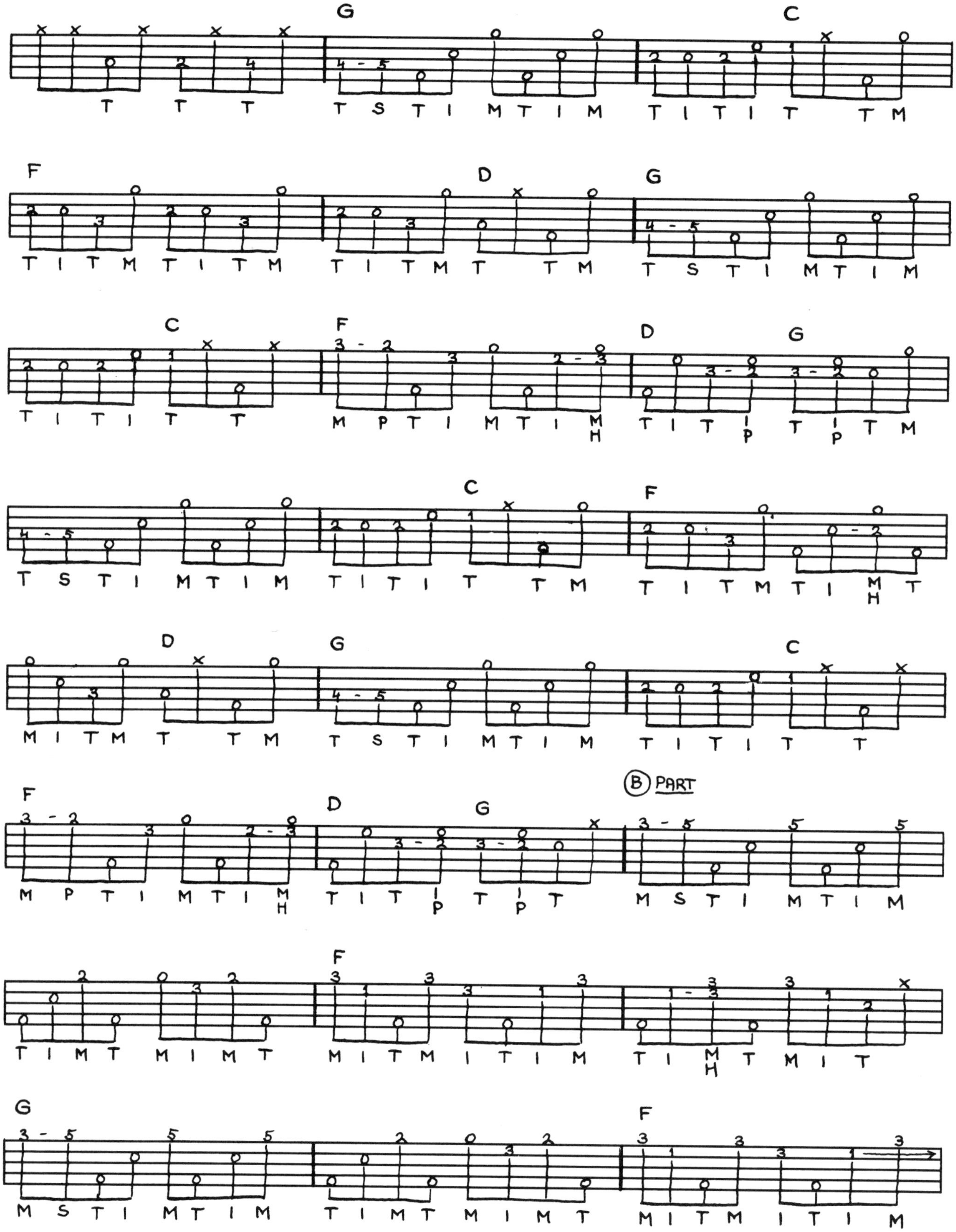

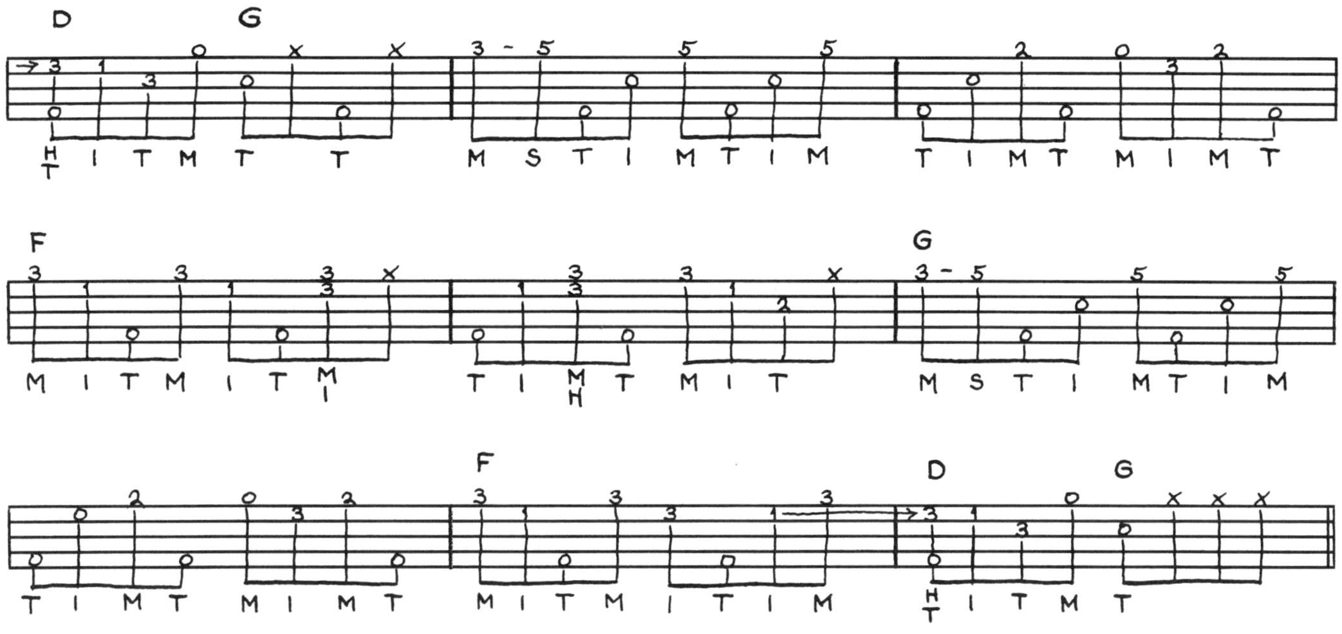

Bill Keith

Huckling the Berries

Peter Wernick

Recorded in key of A on Country Cooking's first album.

November Cotillion

Ken Kosek

As played by Peter Wernick on Country Cooking's *Barrel of Fun* album. Key of G.

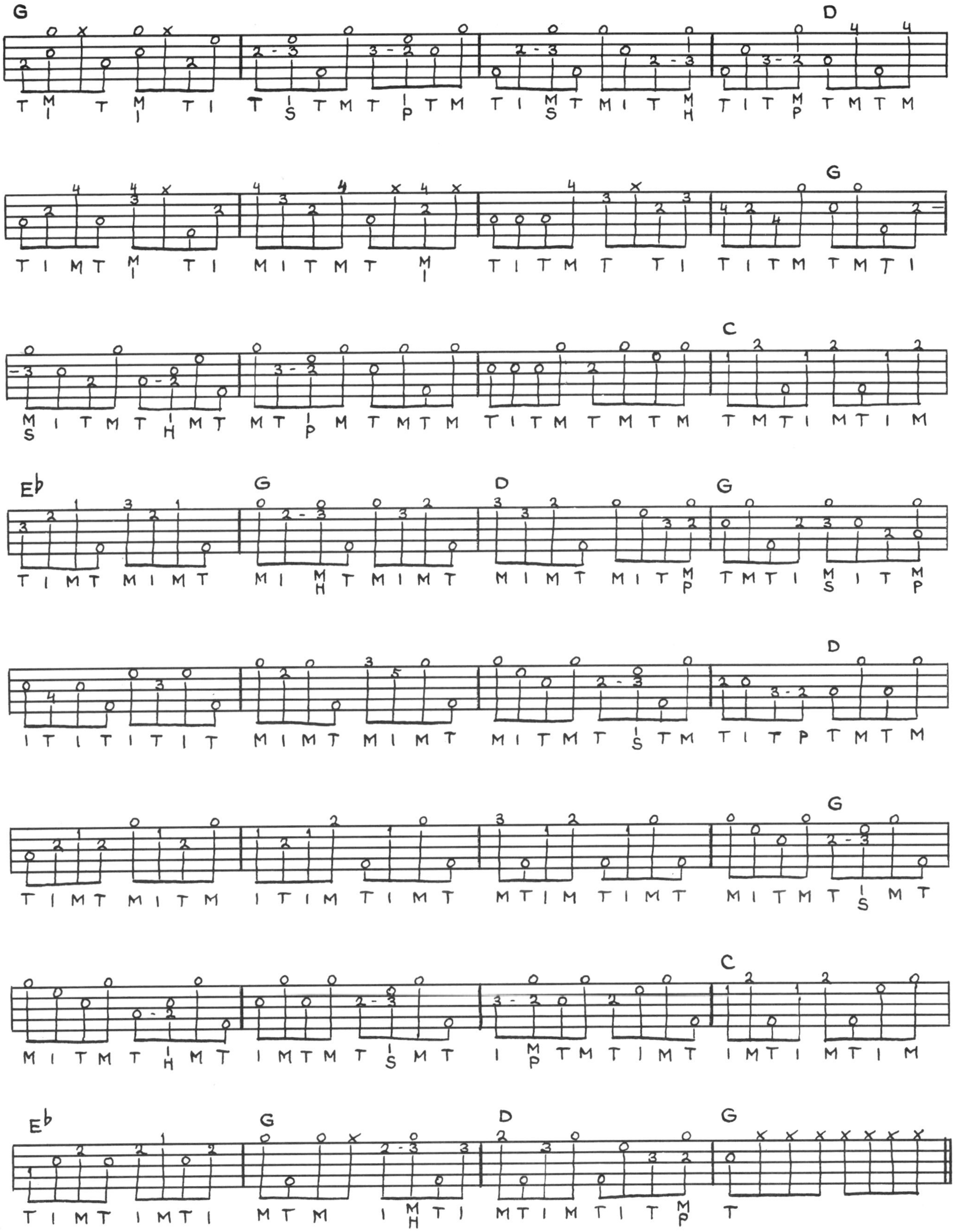

Armadillo Breakdown (first break)

Peter Wernick

Recorded in key of A on Country Cooking's first album.

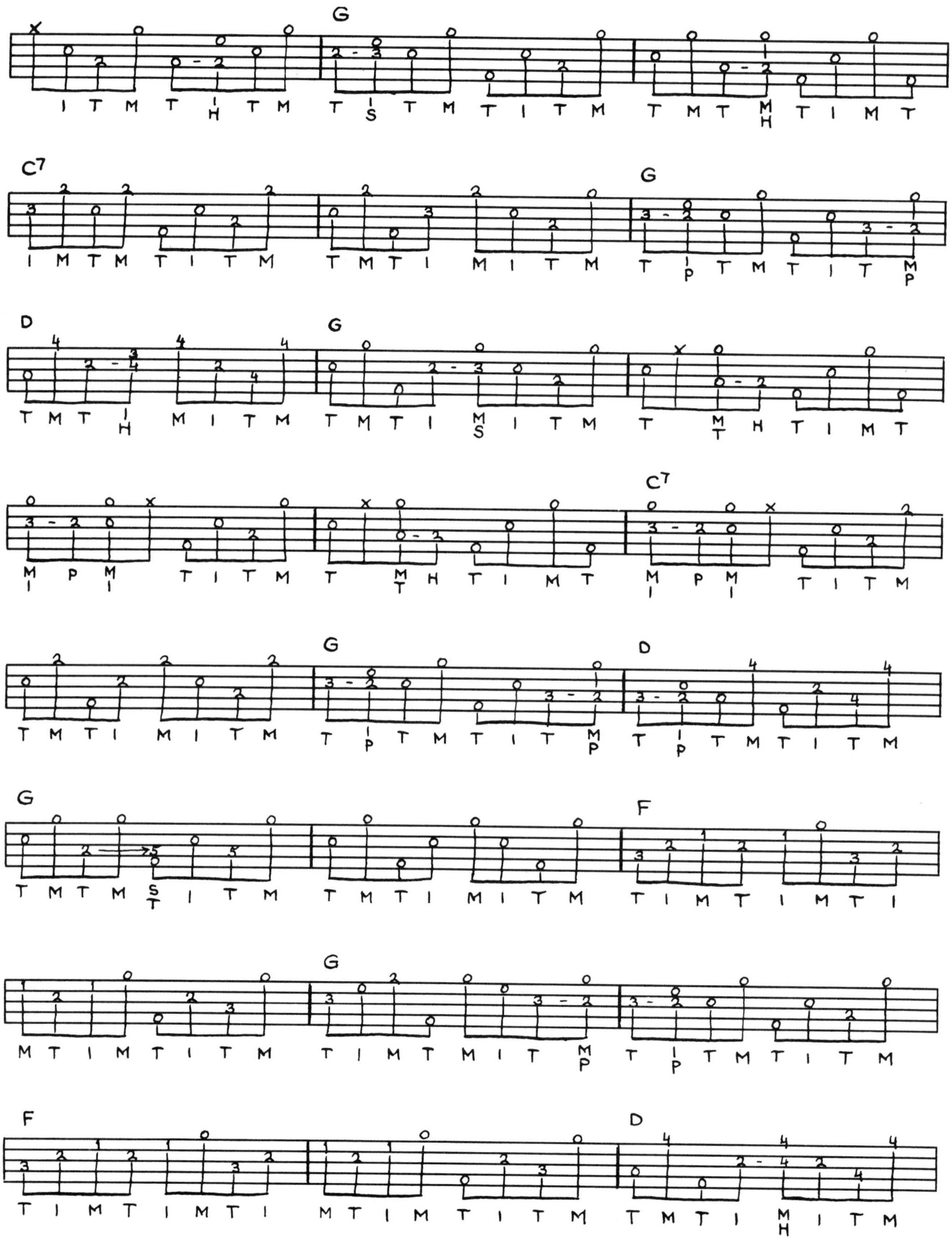

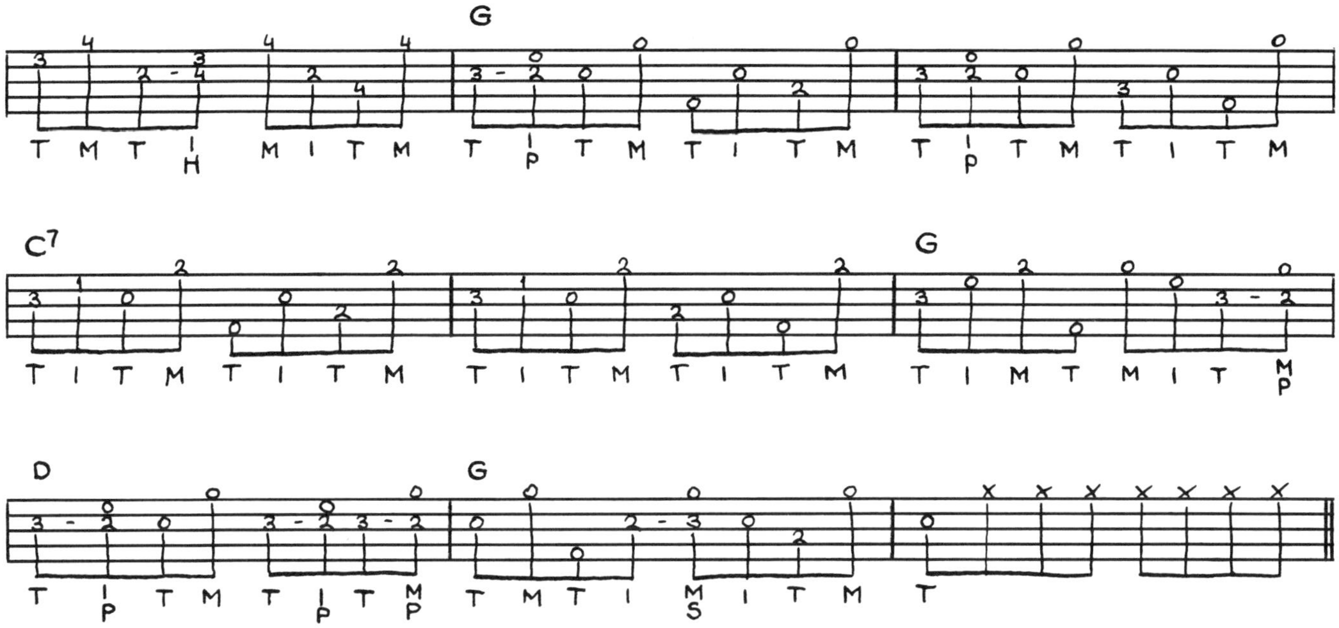

Lester Flatt and the Nashville Grass, Haskell McCormick on banjo

Armadillo Breakdown (second break)

Peter Wernick
Recorded in key of A on Country Cooking's first album.

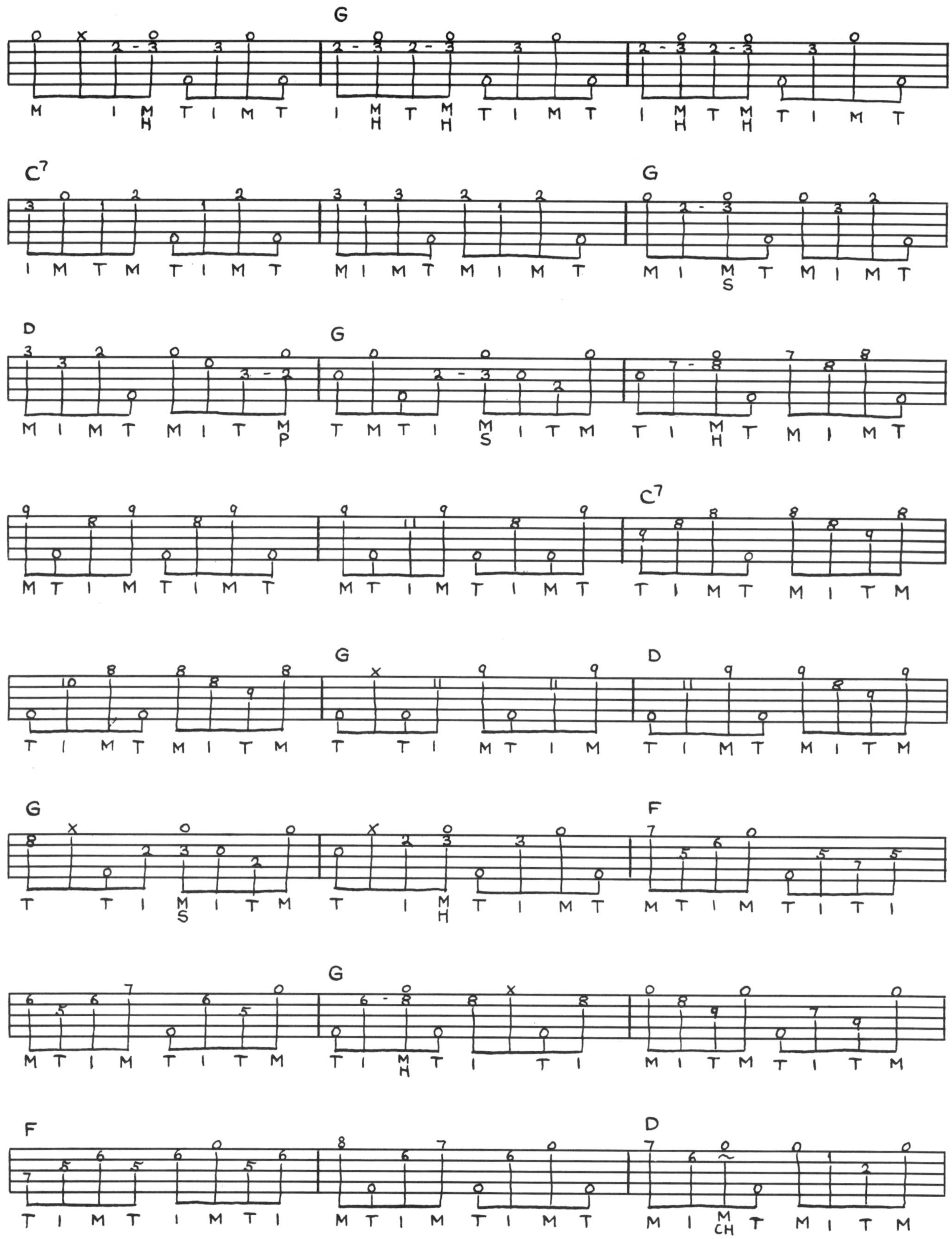

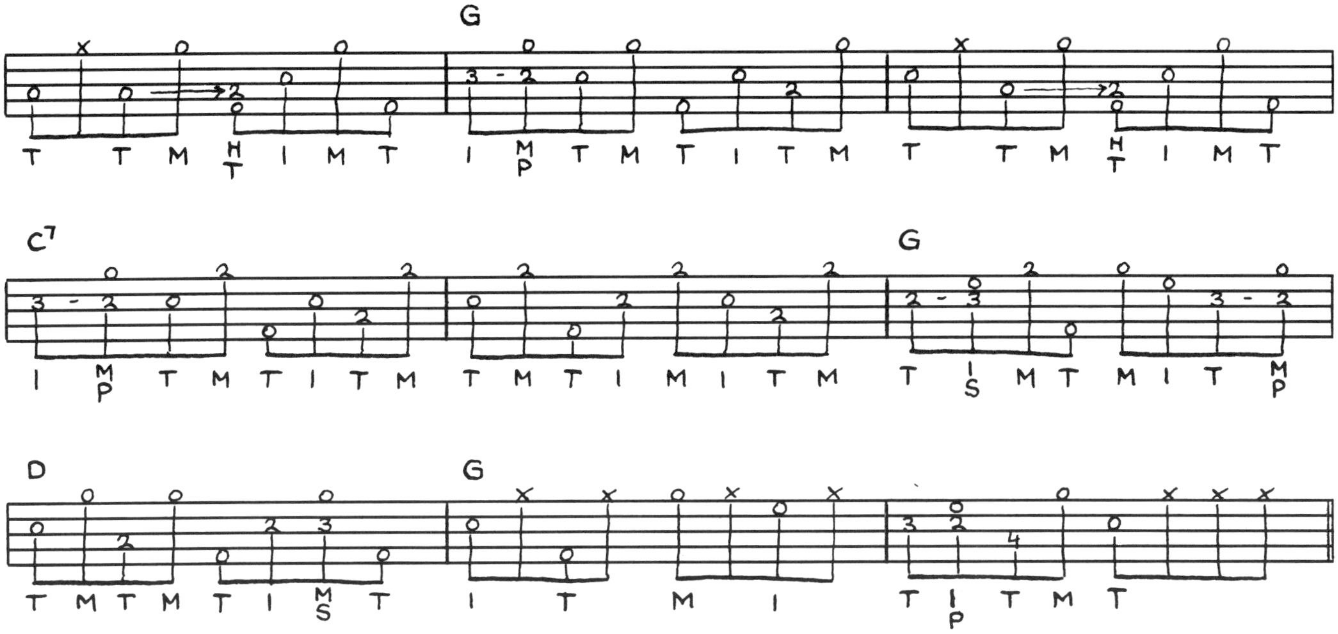

Don Stover

Tequila Mockingbird

Peter Wernick

Recorded in key of G on Country Cooking's *Barrel of Fun* album.

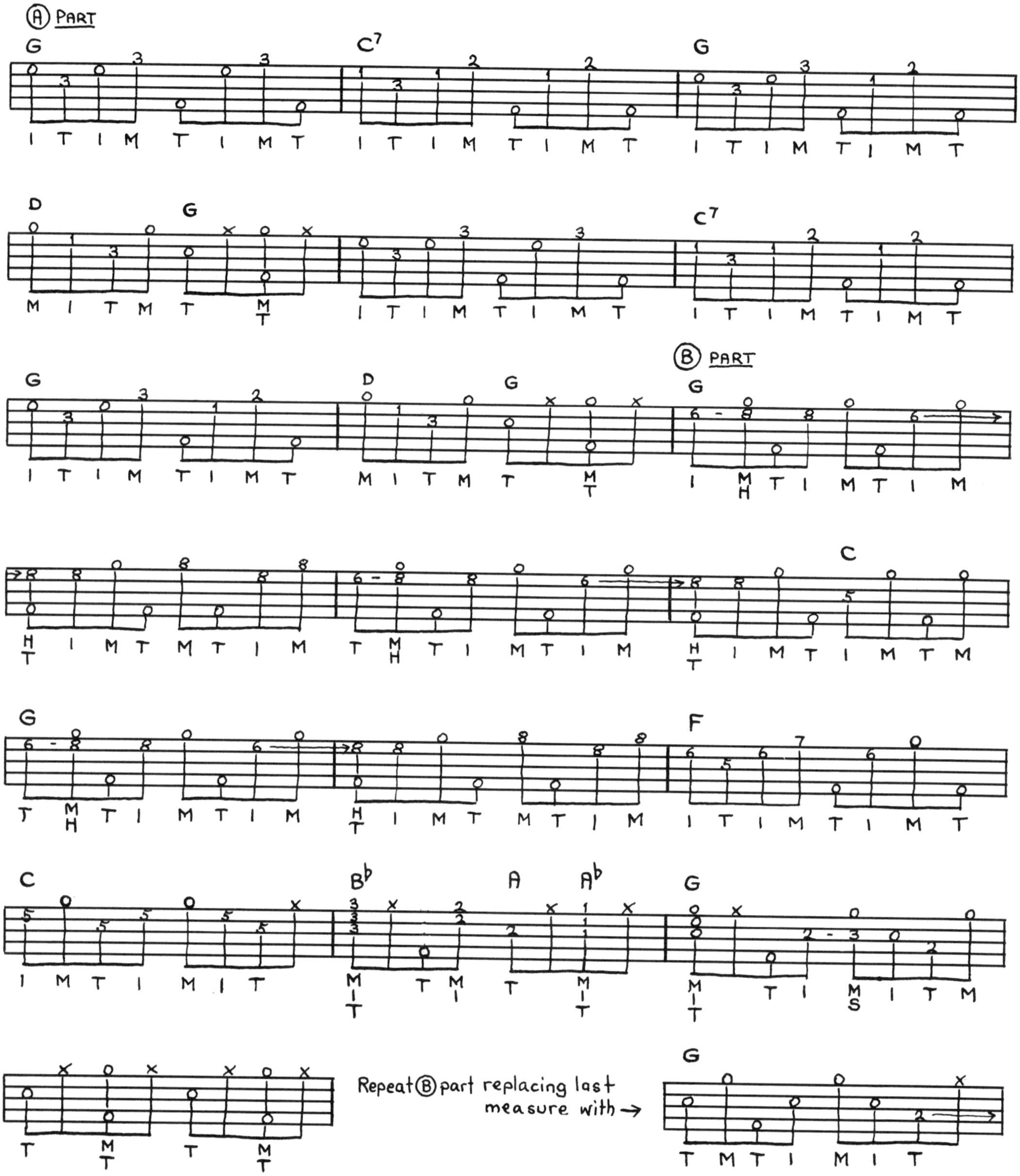

Ⓒ PART

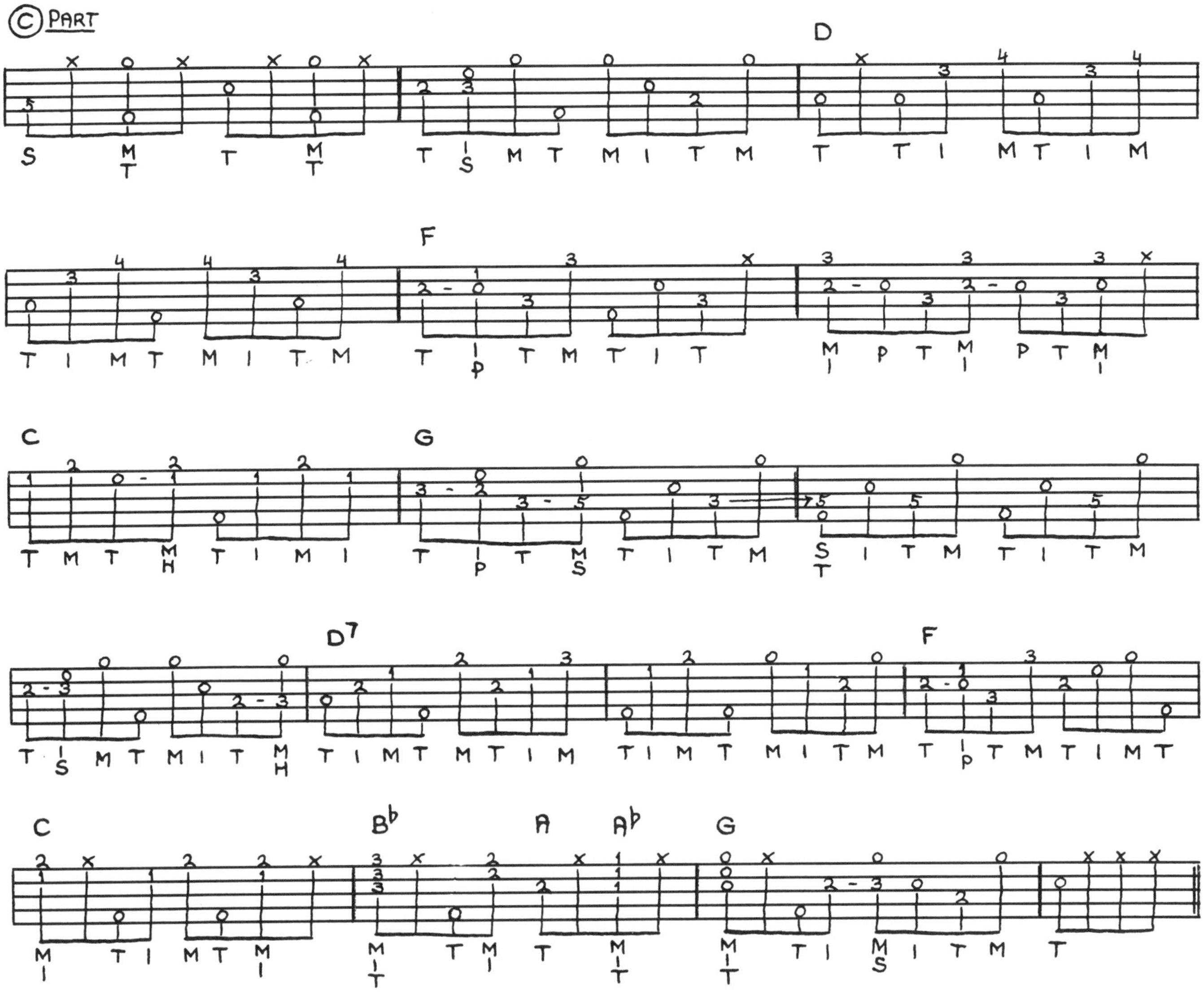

Peter Wernick

Kentucky Bullfight

Tony Trischka

As played on Country Cooking's *Barrel of Fun* album. Key of E.

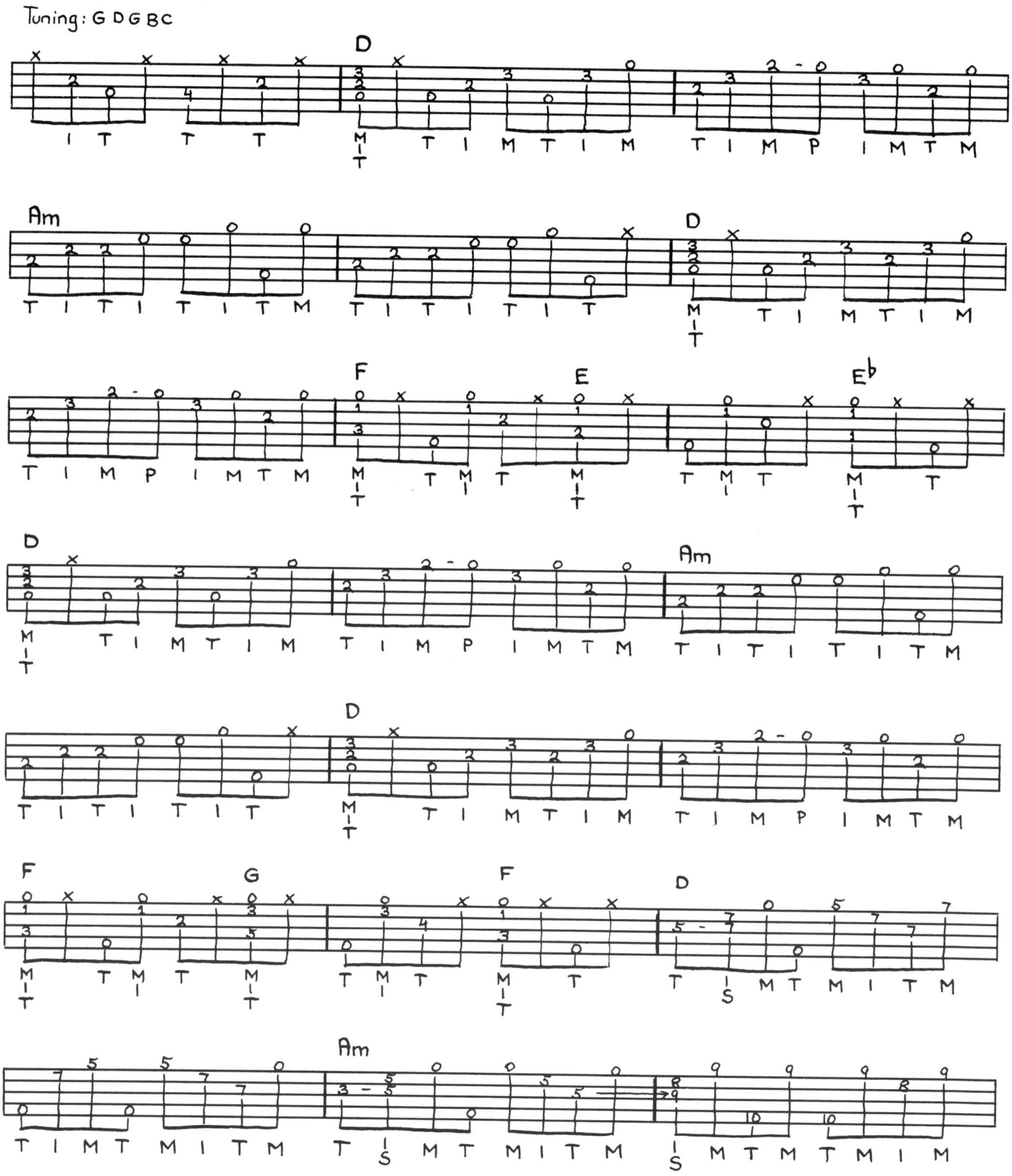

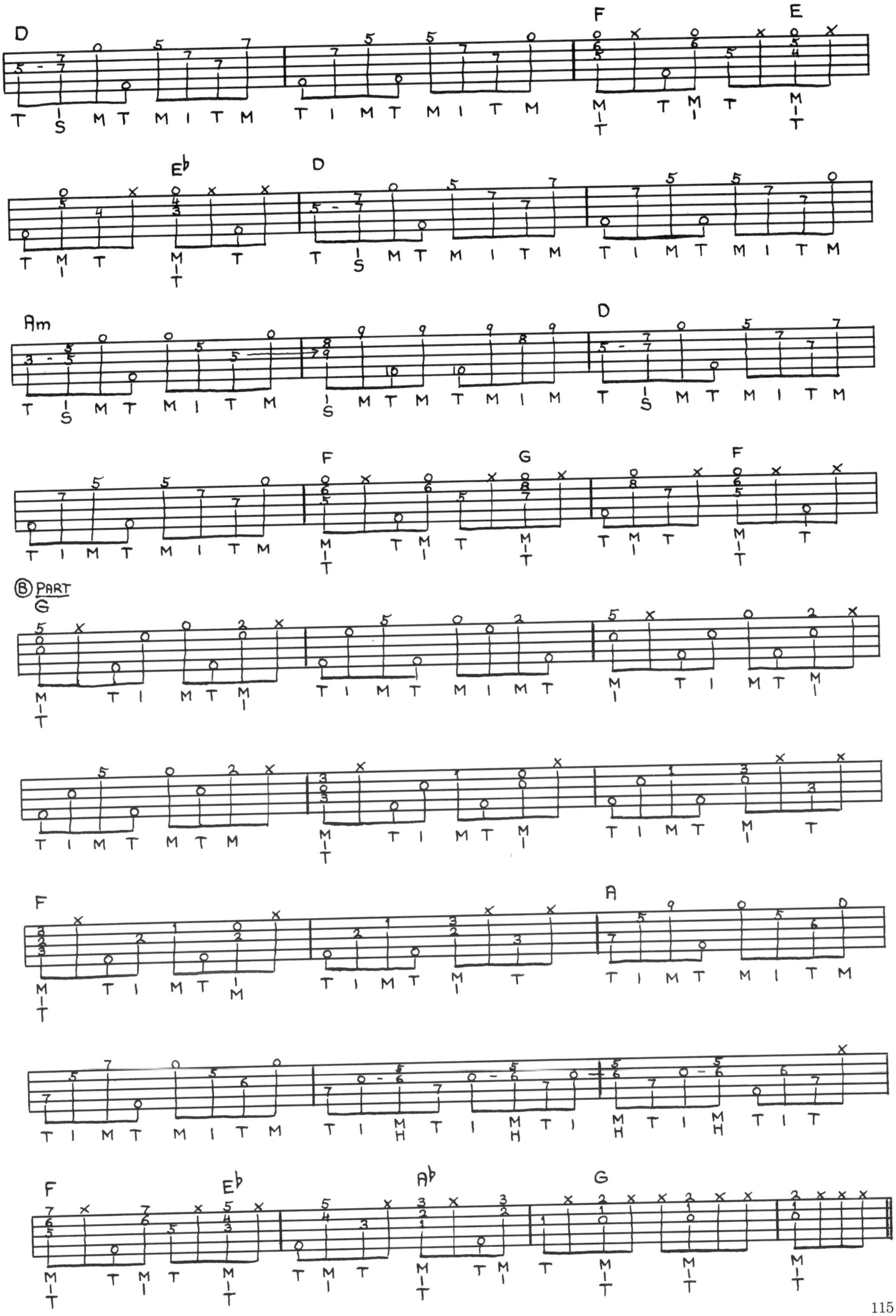
D
F
E
E♭
D
Am
D
F
G
F
B PART
G
F
A
F
E♭
A♭
G

Six Mile Creek

Russell Barenberg
As played by Tony Trischka on Country Cooking's *Barrel of Fun* album. Key of A.

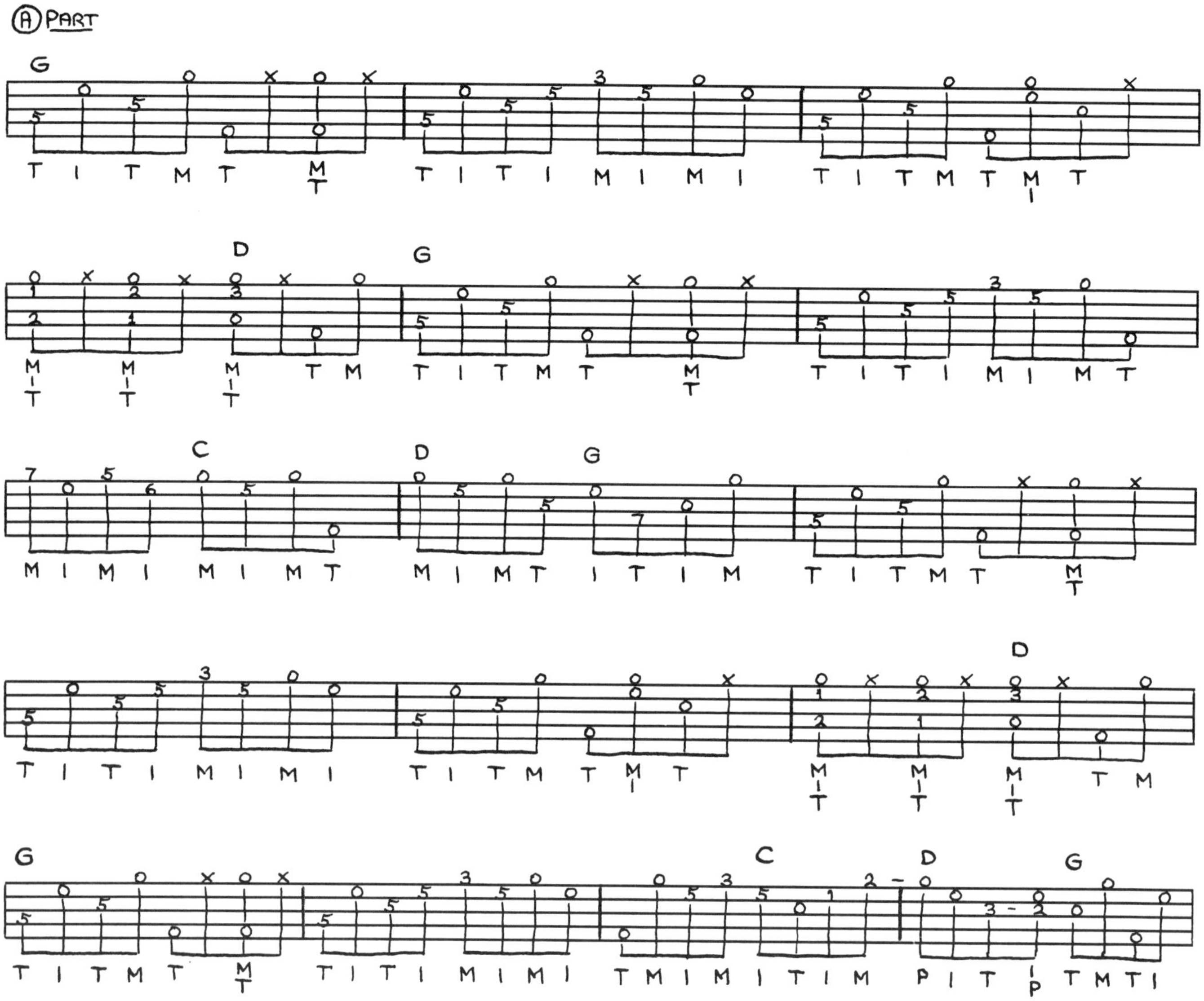

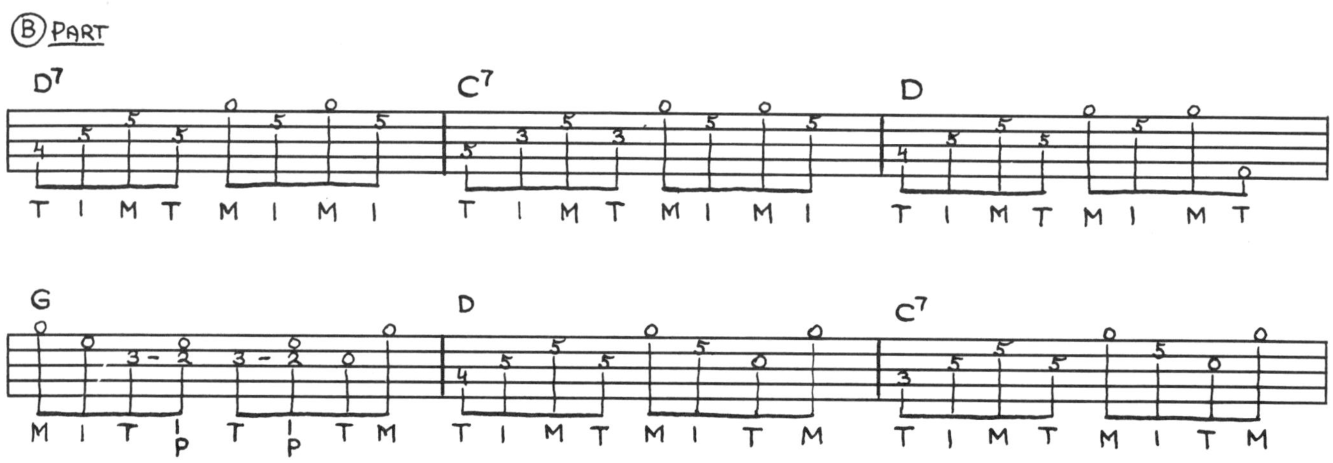

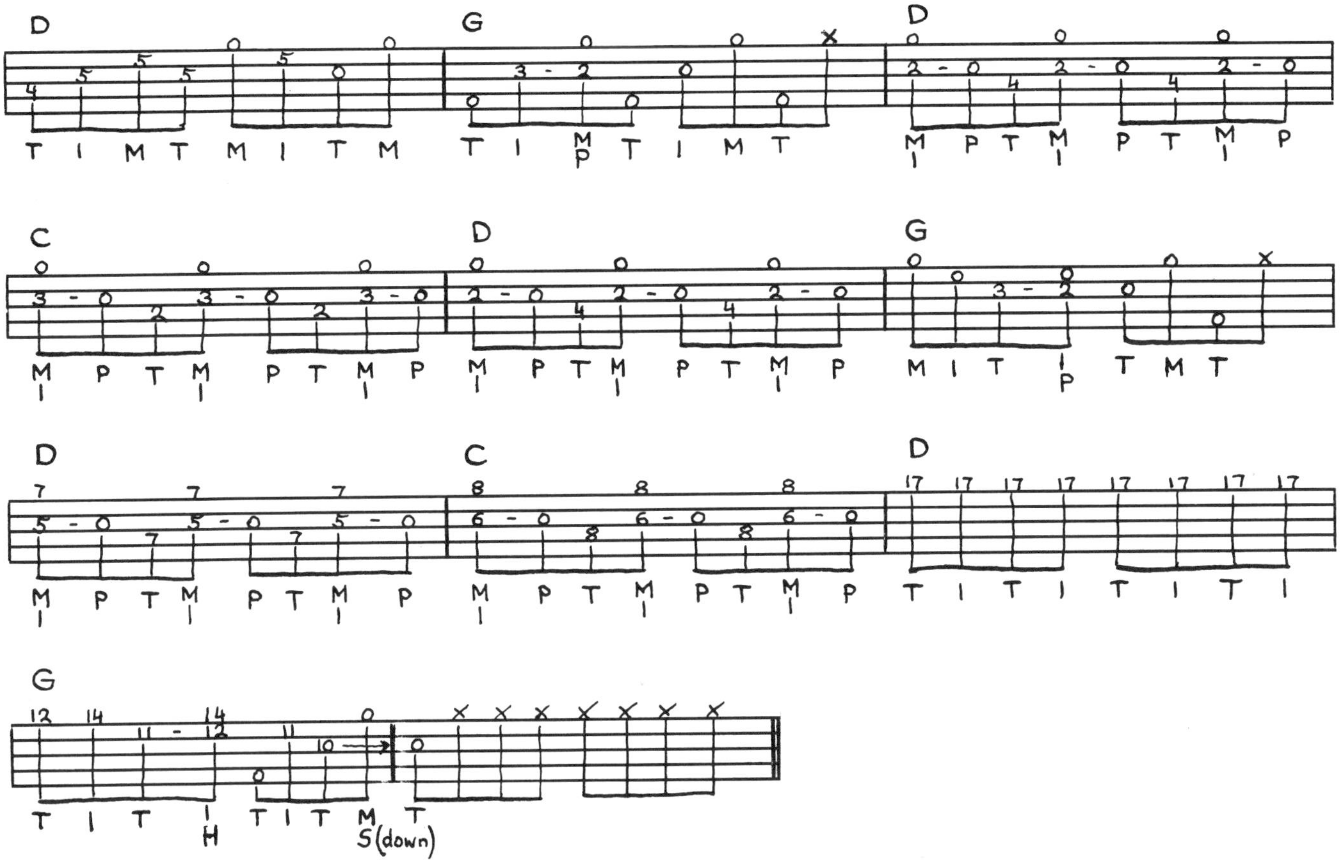

Johnny Whisnant and Raymond McLain

Barrel of Fun

John M. Miller

As played by Tony Trischka on Country Cooking's *Barrel of Fun* album. Key of B.

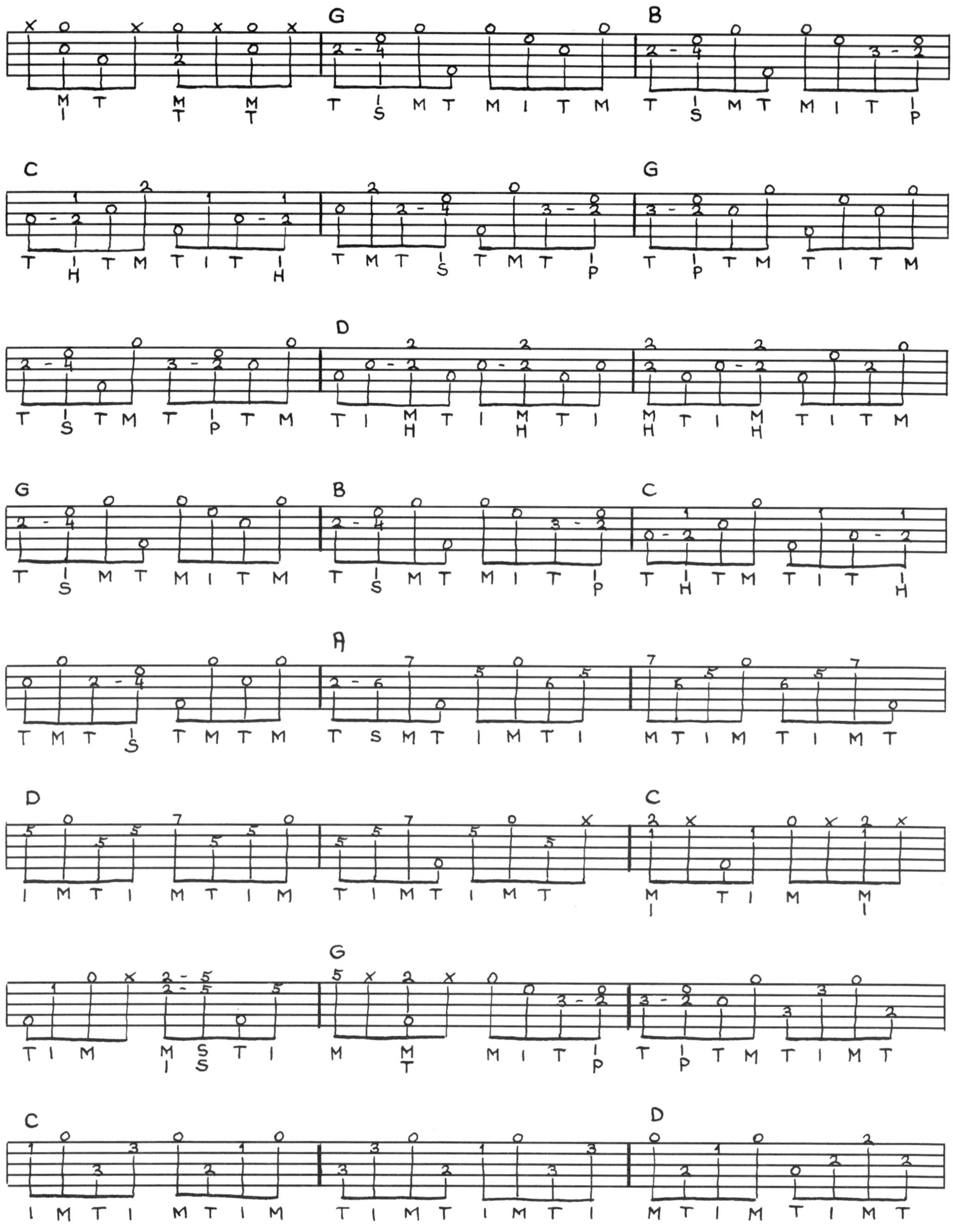

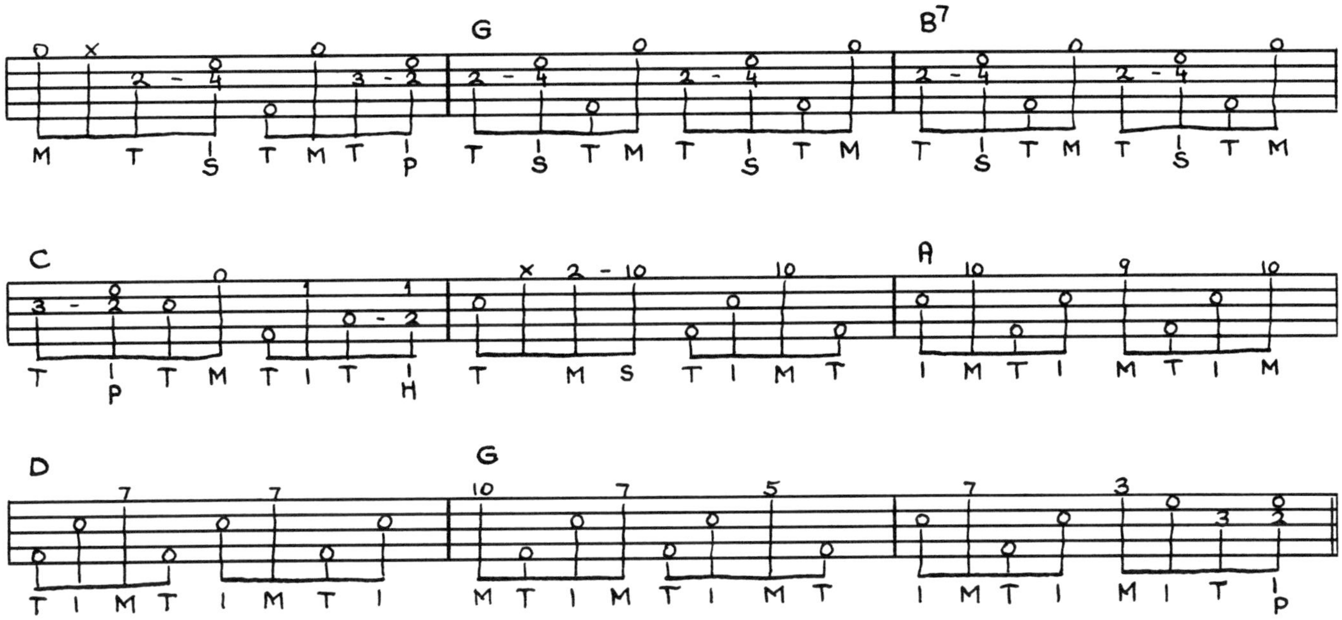

Earl Scruggs and Snuffy Jenkins

Parson's Duck

Tony Trischka

As played on Country Cooking's *Barrel of Fun* album. Key of A.

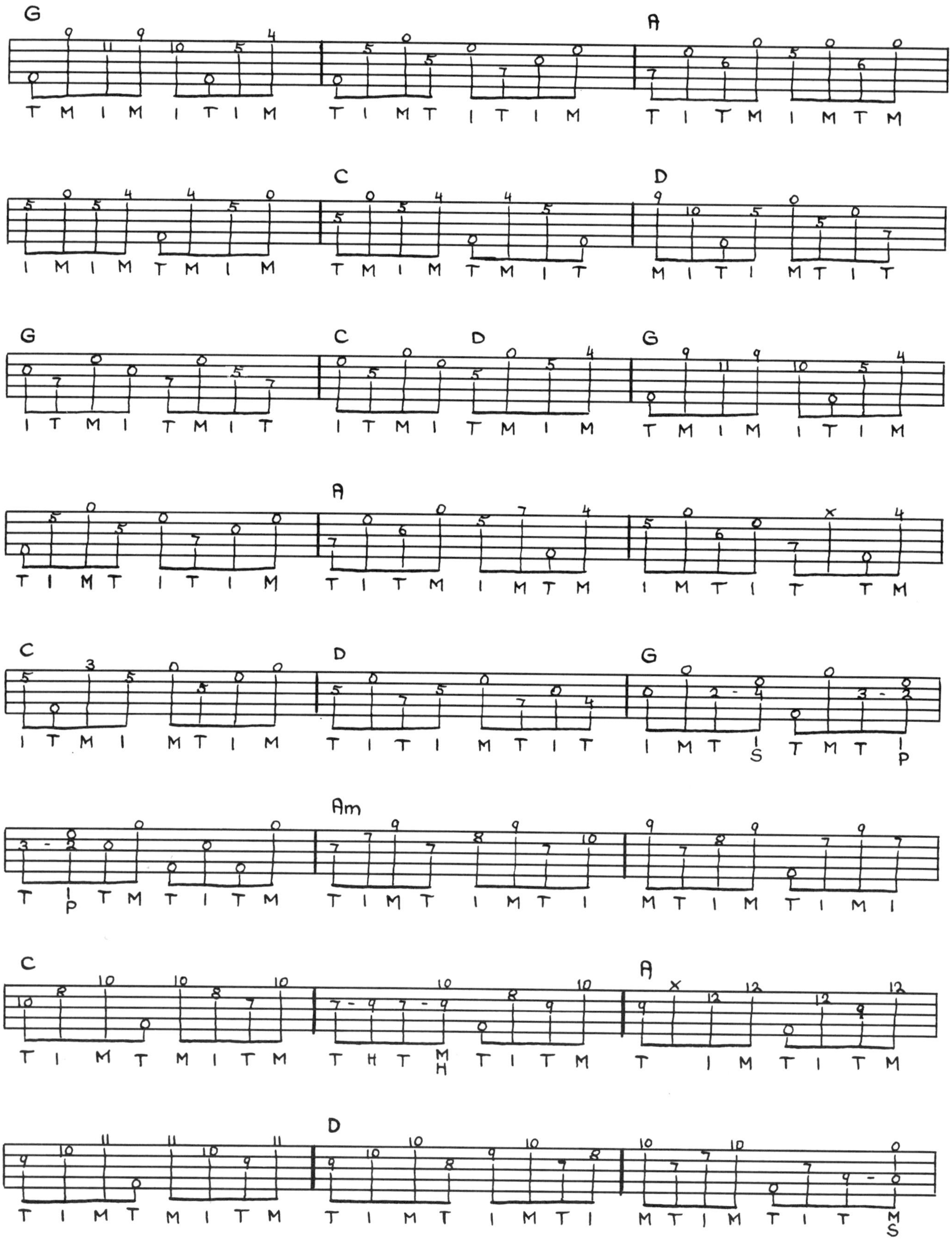

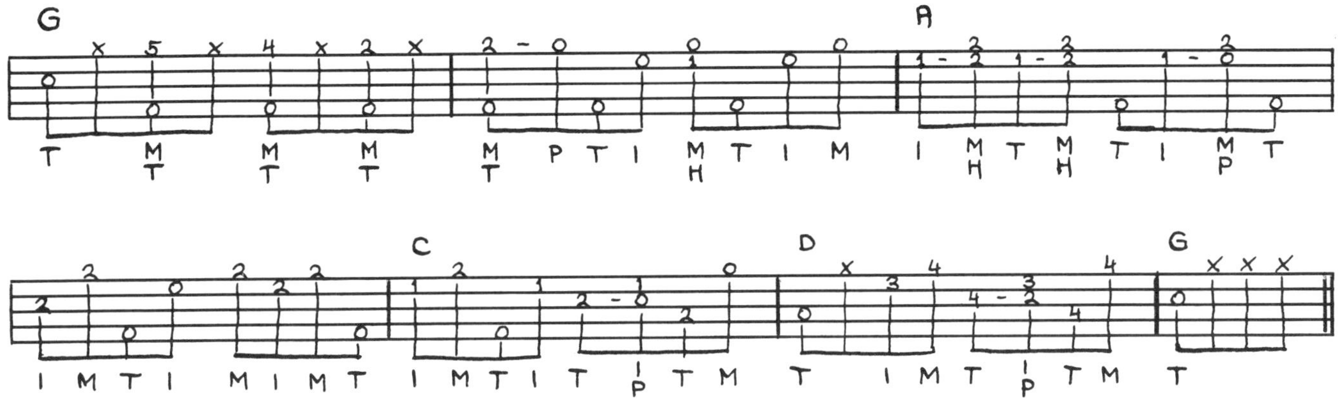

Tony Trischka

Paul's Banjo

C.P. Heaton

Paul pops up silvery snaps,
Opens the casket-dependable case.
It's (ahh) still there.

  Paul won't look at you;
  He'll look away and say,
  "Saw a rat in the barn today,"
  Then leave.

It rests cold and corpse-like comfortable
In darkest green velvet.
Pearl tuning pegs—Black Diamond strings—
Forty flecks of Hearts and Flowers pearl iridescent in ebony—
Flat tone chamber—curly maple resonator—
Mastertone seal—serial number 9473-142—
Ten pounds of pure poetic bluegrass banjo.

Paul doesn't see you.
Strap over right shoulder, he hefts his banjo.
Two National fingerpicks, Dobro thumbpick.
Deft left-hand twists, he tunes his banjo.
Doesn't see you.
Strums over the tone ring.
Smiles and touches
His prewar flathead Gibson 5-string banjo
Over the tone ring.

Then, dreading and overquick,
  They always want "Bonnie and Clyde,"
  They always want "Jed Clampett"
He leans into Reno's "Follow the Leader"
  Likes the G, F, E minor of it
With fluid tackhammer fingers
(Now he looks through you, listening
To his banjo)
Cruciform,
Working toward the single-string middle miracle,
Patters and ripples through it.

Cardboard banjo,
Stock and Maxwell House can,
Open-back Kay,
  Thumb—Index—Middle—
  Thumb—Index—Middle—
  Thumb—Index—
    On the banjo, table, pants leg, mattress
  Thumb—Index—Middle—
  Thumb—Index—Middle—
  Thumb—Index—
    All the while slowing 78s down to 33:
    Earl's Breakdown, Shuckin the Corn,
    Pike County, Dear Old Dixie,
    Paddy on the Turnpike,
    The canon.
      Scorning Grandpa Jones, Stringbean,
      Uncle, Cousin, the desecrating comedians
    ThumbIndexMiddleThumbIndexMiddleThumbIndex—
      S.S. Stewart, Kalamazoo,
      Long-neck Pete Seeger Vega (parents' error)
    TIMTIMTI—TIMTIMTI—TIMTIMTI
      Attics, hock shops, ads, rumors,
      Then, Paul found his banjo.

E minor one last time, then Reno up the neck
(D E♭ E G A B C D E D E D C)
(TI TITITITITIT)
Keith run down,
Wild double shave-and-a-haircut tag,
Harmonics on two-bits.
Over the tone ring.

The Fraternity boys say,
"Play louder and faster, Paul."
"Hey, man, that was great. Play Jed."
"Bonnie & Clyde."
"Hey, man, play Comin Round the Mountain."
"Hey, Paul, play You Are My Sunshine."
"Play something loud and fast, Paul."

Paul's banjo hangs albatross-heavy.

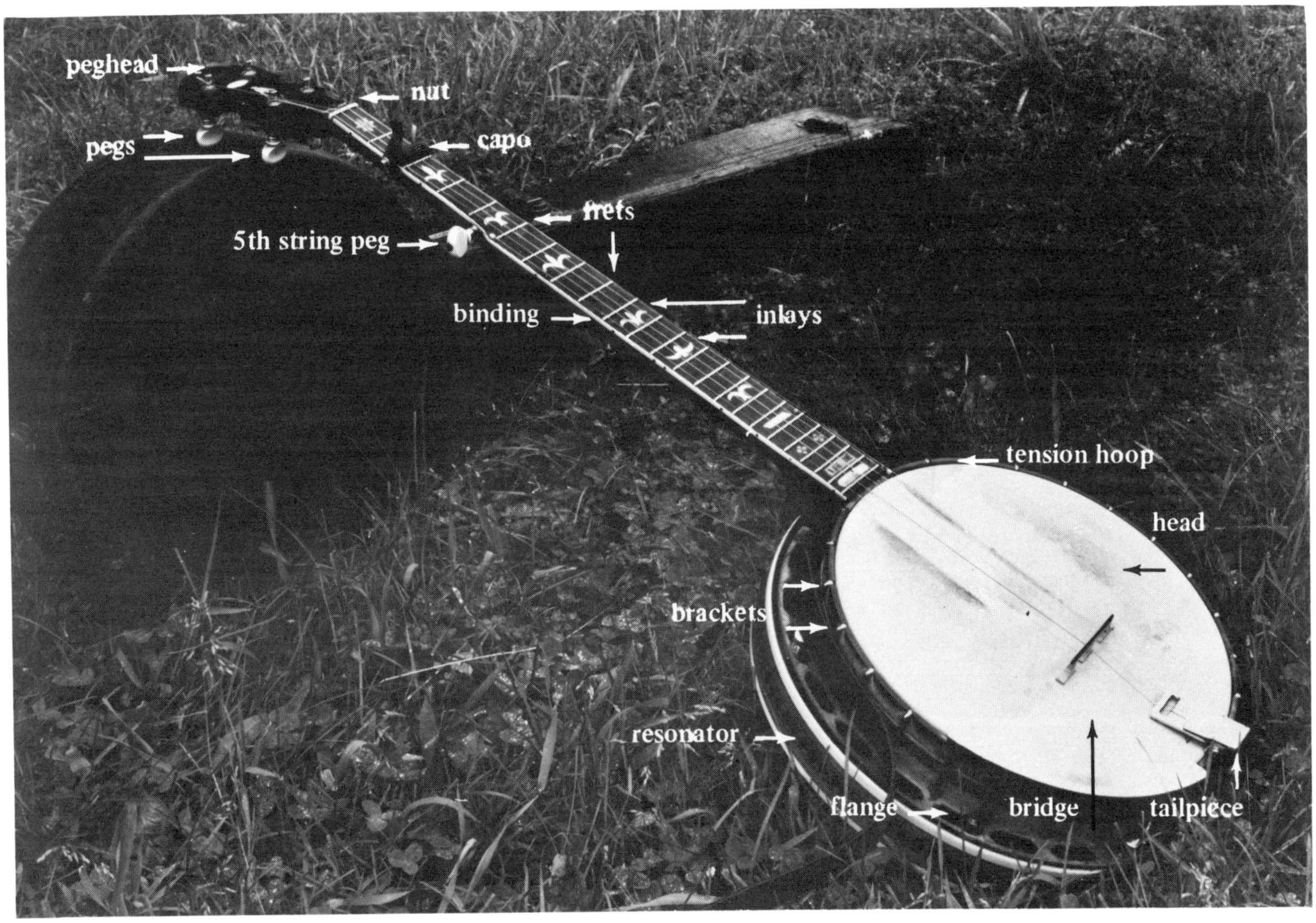
peghead
nut
pegs
capo
frets
5th string peg
binding
inlays
tension hoop
head
brackets
resonator
flange
bridge
tailpiece

Appendices

Appendix 1
Buying your first banjo

When getting a banjo it helps a great deal to have someone knowledgeable on hand. If you can't fully trust your local instrument dealer and if you don't have a friend who can help, it might make sense to pay a teacher to shop with you. Many instrument dealers don't know much about banjos and can't adjust them to sound their best. This makes it hard to make a good judgement about what you're buying. It also could mean getting less than the best from the banjo you buy, if you don't have someone around to make the necessary adjustments.

For your first banjo I would recommend something as cheap as possible, as long as it meets a few standards (or, as in most cases, can be altered by a good repairman to meet the standards):

1. *The action* (distance from the strings to the neck) *shouldn't be too high*—a quarter inch where the neck meets the body is a generous limit, though anything over an eighth of an inch could stand lowering. Lowering the action isn't too hard. Even a not-too-advanced instrument repair place should be able to do it quickly and cheaply.The trick may be to insert a *shim* (a thin wedge made of leather or wood) where the neck meets the head. Action can also be too low, causing strings to buzz, that is, to make an impure sound something like the sound of a sitar. There can be other reasons for buzzing strings, so make sure low action is the reason before you correct it. If the action is low and the banjo's bridge is less than the maximum 5/8″, you can easily raise the action by getting a taller bridge. Incidentally, the bridge should be placed so that the twelfth fret is exactly one half the way from the nut to the bridge. If it's out of place, move it. In any case, mark the proper place on the head with a pencil.

2. The banjo *shouldn't be too hard to tune.* The main factor here is the tuning pegs. If they are geared and the gears aren't stripped, you can be pretty confident that the strings won't frequently slip out of tune or be very hard to tune exactly. Often a banjo will have four geared pegs and a friction (ungeared) peg for the fifth string. Don't worry about the one friction peg. Be sure it's loose enough to move with some ease (a dab of oil can help) and tight enough to hold when you have it where you want it. For that purpose you may sometimes have to tighten the screw on the end of the peg with a small screwdriver or the edge of a dime or a finger pick. Friction pegs *can* be quite usable but on cheap banjos they're sometime troublesome. Except possibly for the fifth peg try to avoid friction pegs. Replacing them isn't difficult or overly expensive.

3. *Tone,* of course is an important factor, but to tell the truth, I have never heard a banjo which, when properly adjusted, didn't sound halfway decent. Fixing up a banjo usually means not much more than tightening the head until it's pretty taut (won't give more than an eighth inch when pressed near the bridge with the thumb). If a banjo sounds sort of noisy it can probably use tightening. For this job all you need is a bracket wrench, which is like a skate key and is available at music stores. Until a banjo's head is tightened you can't really tell how the instrument will sound. If you're looking at a banjo for possible purchase and the head is loose you might ask to tighten it before deciding. If you're dealing with a music store they might tell you that tightening the head, besides being a hassle, puts a bit of stress on the instrument (which they'd rather avoid unless you're going to buy it). Tightening the head does not really put undue stress on the instrument and you should insist upon hearing it with a tightened head before deciding. Tightening the head involves tightening the brackets which pull down on the tension hoop on the outside border of the head. This is a job to do carefully; a head which has been tightened too much can break. A good rule of thumb is to tighten all the brackets finger-tight, and then go back and tighten them all one or two quarter-turns more. Incidentally, another way of correcting a noisy sound is to stuff some cloth in the back of the head. To quote Pete Seeger, "A handkerchief is too small, a bath towel too big, a diaper just right."

4. It's especially important to look out for *a warped neck,* especially on a cheap instrument. You can detect a warp by sighting down the length of the neck. If it's not *perfectly* straight, both from front to back and from side to side, you have a problem. It might not be an important problem (a warp of 1/16″, which you can check by laying a yardstick or other straightedge along the fingerboard, is not too serious), but warped necks often go on warping, and they become unplayable when they're too warped. However . . . on your first banjo, which you won't have too long anyway if you retain interest in playing, I wouldn't worry about it unless the warp approaches ⅛″. In any case, this is another flaw which can sometimes be fixed easily. If the instrument has a *tension rod,* a metal rod which goes straight through the length of the neck, a warp can sometimes be simply corrected by adjusting the rod. It's delicate—don't do it yourself unless you know how. When buying a banjo, look to see if the instrument has a tension rod. It's a sign of quality. The quickest way to tell is to look for a small flat piece of plastic held to the peghead by screws (this is to cover the opening through which the rod can be adjusted).

5. *Improper fretting* is a problem rare among new banjos but not uncommon among older ones. A fret that is too high will produce the same note as the fret behind it. A low fret or one worn down by use can result in a buzz. If you want to be fastidious, go up each string one at a time to make sure the string gives a different, clear tone at every fret. Again, most music repair places can adjust or change bad frets without too much trouble or expense.

As you can see, most flaws in banjos are not serious. When looking at a banjo try to get a sense of the cost of any repairs which may be needed (if possible, get an estimate from the instrument repair place which will do the work) and figure those costs in when considering whether to buy.

One thing *not* to worry about is a missing bracket or two.They are inexpensive and easy enough to replace. On a cheap banjo a missing one or two will hardly make a difference. A missing string, bridge, or tailpiece is similarly easy and inexpensive to replace.

Another thing not to worry about is the presence or absence of a resonator. A banjo doesn't need a resonator to sound pretty good, and you can't look for a sound better than "pretty good" on an inexpensive banjo. I'd say that on an inexpensive banjo the biggest advantage to having a resonator is that it prevents the ends of the brackets from rubbing against your clothes (I wore out what was then my favorite sweater with my first banjo).

The reason I recommend getting no more than a cheap, half-decent banjo at the start is that it's possible to start learning on it, and you don't have to make a big financial commitment. Banjos for $120 or less are not too hard to find in music stores (not in 1979 anyway), especially cheap ones (though some stores don't carry cheap instruments). Then there's always the hock shop or auction or want ad circuit, where you might even find a good one for a low price. However, be extra careful with people who don't have a reputation to guard and who may have nothing to lose by overcharging you.

Incidentally, instruments, unlike most other things, do not usually depreciate in value. They don't tend to wear out, so don't think of newness as something worth paying extra for.

When you have clearly decided that you intend to be playing banjo for a while, and somewhat regularly and seriously, you are ready for a better banjo even if you're not very good yet. A better banjo is worth the investment because 1. it's easier to sound good on a good banjo; and 2. the better you sound, the more you're inclined to practice, which will improve your playing.

In buying your second banjo you obviously have to be more careful and selective because it is a more expensive and permanent purchase. Criteria for a second banjo are discussed in Appendix 4.

When you're ready for your second banjo it's easy enough to sell the first, particularly if you've kept it in decent shape. You can often sell it to the local music store, especially if you bought it there. You'll probably take a loss but think of the loss as a rental fee for having the banjo a year or whatever. If you put ads in the paper or on bulletin boards and sell directly to another person, you can probably recoup your original expense plus inflation.

You may be one of those people who don't take to the banjo and find it collecting a lot of dust. If you started with a cheap banjo, you can sell it as above and not have to feel guilty about being wasteful. For that matter, you can do the same with a more expensive banjo. If you're patient about finding the right price for it you don't have to worry about taking a significant loss, as long as you didn't overpay for it in the first place and have kept it in good shape.

Appendix 2
Banjo accessories: What else you should get

Besides the banjo, you should have the following.

1. An extra set of strings. You need extra strings in case the one you're using breaks. You should also have an extra set ready to replace the old one every couple of months in order to freshen up the tone. If you buy a used banjo, especially one that hasn't been used for a while, change the strings. Sometimes the strings on an old banjo are older than you are, and produce a poor sound.

There are many different brands of strings, all the same except in regard to gauge. Gauge simply means thickness, and it affects how hard the strings fight back when you fret them with your left hand or pick them with your right. Different gauge strings create differences in tone and in the feel of the strings. At the beginning, get light gauge strings to make it easier on your fingers. After you've been playing a little while and your fingers have toughened up, try experimenting to see what you like. I prefer heavier strings (Liberty mediums) but I am in the minority. Most people use Earl Scruggs Vega light gauge strings or other brands of comparable gauge. When buying strings, don't worry too much about brand names. Buy according to gauge and price. Some brands sell identically-made strings at different prices.

When buying banjo strings make sure to ask for five-string banjo strings. To put them on, simply hook each loop over the appropriate hook on the tailpiece (if there aren't enough hooks, double up some strings), and run the string over the appropriate groove in the bridge and the nut. Thread it through the hole on the appropriate peg. To keep the string from slipping it helps to kink the string in the opposite direction from the way it's wound and to leave enough slack at first so that when tightened to pitch the string is wound three or four turns around the post. Winding the string downward along the post instead of over itself is said to minimize string breakage and make tuning easier. See the diagram.

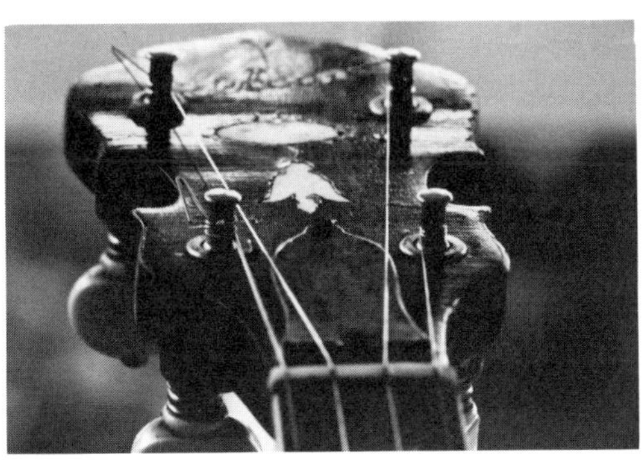

2. You will need a bracket wrench for tightening and loosening the head. It's like a skate key—a small socket wrench with "ears" for easier twisting.

If your banjo has had the same head on it for more than a couple of years, you might get a better tone by changing it. A new head usually runs about $10 to $12 (1979 prices), which is a lot to put into a cheap banjo unless you are planning to keep the instrument for a while or unless the improvement would be very significant. The improvement probably won't be dramatic unless the head you have on is cracked or ripped, or if the head is made of skin instead of plastic. At one time banjo heads were always made of animal hide, but that started changing in the fifties. Now it's rare to see a skin head on a banjo. Players who prefer old time styles like frailing use skin heads, but it's risky to tighten them as much as is necessary to produce the bluegrass sound. They also change with the weather (unlike plastic) and it's a pain to have to continually tighten or loosen the head.

3. All bluegrass banjo players use picks. The standard combination is a plastic thumb pick and two metal finger picks. It's important to take the time to find a good thumb pick—one that fits comfortably without slipping, while having the right length and shape. The right length and shape is something you will have to decide for yourself after experimenting. Most people use clear plastic Dobro brand thumb picks, but I prefer the ones with blunter points which usually come in an assortment of awful colors. I used my last thumb pick for over six years, at first wearing down the picking edge to a nice smooth surface and eventually wearing away the edge enough to require a replacement. I don't recommend metal thumb picks because the metal edge tends to grate against the strings, especially the wound fourth.

Although I've seen plastic finger picks in the stores, I've never seen an experienced bluegrass picker use anything but metal picks. There are two good types of metal picks: Dunlop and National. Dunlops are now available in several gauges. They are also about ten cents more expensive. Metal picks come in one size but it's easy to bend them to fit your finger or to change the angle at which the pick hits the strings. Some people straighten the picking edge, some increase its curve, and people sometimes adjust the angle of the index and middle finger picks differently. I like them just the way they are. You can also change the size or shape of your plastic thumb pick by filing it or by bending it after soaking it in hot water.

4. To play in different keys you will need a capo, a sort of clamp which holds all the strings down at one fret. Don Reno is the only bluegrass banjoist I know of who doesn't use a capo (although he used to). What he does is amazing, but he makes it difficult for himself to play in some keys. You don't have to play in many keys if you're just practicing, but for playing with others I'd say you *need* a capo, Don Reno notwithstanding. Also, playing along with records is an important part of your learning, and for this, too, you will need a capo.

There are a few types of capos around. Some hold the strings down more firmly than others, which is an asset, but they are also usually more clumsy, which is a liability. A standard elastic-plus-bar capo runs about a dollar.

5. To go with the capo you will also need a fifth string capo or a couple of small nails in the neck to slipip the fifth string under, in order to raise the pitch of the fifth string when you change keys.

The fifth string capo is a strip of metal that runs along the fifth strings side of the neck and has a little hook or "finger" attached which can slide along the strip. When not in use it hooks over the string on the non-playing side of the fifth string nut near its peg. When you need it, though, you can just slide it up to the proper fret and it holds the string down. There are two main disadvantages to using a fifth string capo. One is its cost: $10-$25 including installation, enough to make it not worth doing on an inexpensive banjo. The other is clumsiness: while it is a convenience when it comes to retuning, most fifth string capos get in the way when you try to hook your thumb over the top of the neck to fret the fifth string in up-the-neck positions. Some people solve this problem by fretting the fifth string not with the thumb but with one of the other four fingers. There is one type of fifth string capo which isn't clumsy. It adds only 1/16″ to the width of the neck and can even be recessed to add no width at all. The fretting part of this capo presses the string down harder than other capos do—this is another advantage. For more information, write to the inventor, Rick Shubb, 1701 Woodhaven Way, Oakland, California, 94611.

Instead of a fifth string capo, you can use two small nails in the neck. Their placement at the seventh and ninth frets make it easy to adjust the fifth string for playing in A or B, the two most common keys bluegrass is played in (through that can vary according to the range of the singers' voices). The nails aren't actually nails, which would be too big—the standard item is a little hooked spike which holds tracks in place on model train sets. Check your friendly local model train supplier.

Putting in the nails is an easy but delicate job. You may want to have it done by a good instrument repairman, just to be sure. If you do it yourself be careful! Here's how: make sure the nails are staggered, that is, on either side of the fifth string so that the string can be pushed down *between* the nails without touching them. Also, point the hook at the top of each nail away from the normal path of the string. This will prevent the string from slipping out from under the hook. See the diagram.

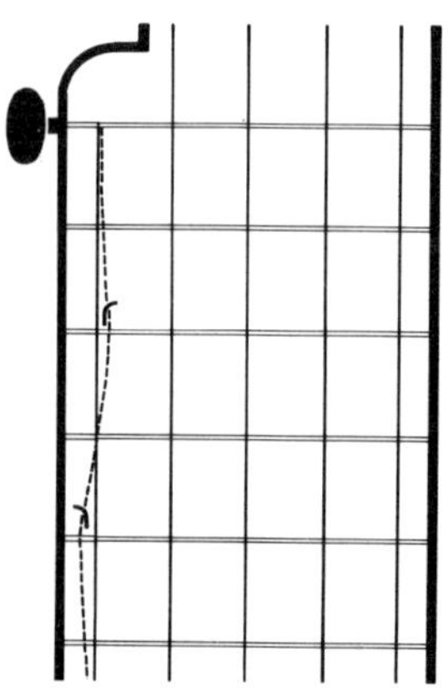

Since the nails are a little off center, slipping the string under them stretches the string a little and raises the pitch a little higher than you want. When tuning up, make a small adjustment after putting the string under the nail. Having to make these small adjustments all the time can be a bother and that's the main advantage of a fifth string capo over nails.

6. Sooner or later you'll need a strap, for, when people play bluegrass together, they usually stand up. There are some attractive adjustable cloth straps available for a few dollars, but you can also easily make one of your own out of tough scrap cloth. Attach it to brackets near the neck and tailpiece and adjust it to a height you find comfortable. I'll warn you though—the *style* is to wear it mostly above your belt and some people will think you look just terrible having it lower. So if you want to be *in*, check yourself out in a mirror before going someplace where you'll be on view. There is no one accepted fashion for wearing the strap over your shoulder. Some put their head through it, some don't.

7. If your banjo doesn't already have an armrest you should get one. You'll see why when playing in the summer months with short sleeves on. Even if you don't perspire much, it will be enough to leave its mark on an unprotected head, especially a skin head.

Optional additions are pointed cowboy boots, a ten gallon hat, a string tie, and a country drawl. None of these are required, though there are always a few who seem to think so. In my opinion, people who get wrapped up in appearances usually do it as a substitute for being wrapped up in the music. One of the reasons I like bluegrass festivals so much is that they're one of the few kinds of events in which a lot of very different-looking people get together and find out how much they have in common.

Appendix 3
How the banjo works and how to maintain it

There's not too much you really need to know about how a banjo works. There is a lot that is nice to know, though, especially if you're a do-it-yourself type who likes tinkering with things to try to make them better. Many banjo players like working on their instruments, learning about their construction, history, etc. If you're interested, take a look at Tom Morgan's article "Gibson Banjo Information" (Appendix 5). Morgan is a leading authority on banjos and is very thorough and clear. For more information on this and other articles, I suggest writing to Morgan at Morgan Springs, Rte. 3, Dayton, Tenn. 37321. Also, in Earl Scruggs' instruction book, published by Peer International, there is a section on building your own banjo–(which is a highly expensive and complex job). Looking through it will increase your understanding of the anatomy of banjos.

The basic idea is that when you play a note on the banjo the string vibrates. The number of vibrations per second creates the specific musical tone (for example, 440 vibrations per second is A). A string will vibrate faster (and give a higher pitch) when it is made either shorter or tighter. What the left hand does when it frets the strings is to alter the length of the string which is permitted to vibrate. The frets play an important part here. Stringed instruments were originally fretless, so that when you pushed down a string, the part of the string which vibrated was the part between your finger and the bridge. With frets, you push the string down *over* the fret so that the string vibrates between the *fret* and the bridge (a precisely measured distance), not between your finger and the bridge (a variable distance depending on the exact placement of your finger).

When you pick the string, it vibrates, creating the note. The note would be very quiet were it not for the sounding apparatus on the instrument. Every type of stringed instrument is based on the same idea (vibrating strings)–it's the sounding apparatus that makes instruments sound different. In the case of an acoustical (non-electric) guitar, the string vibrates through the bridge and through and over a sound chamber with a hole in it. With an electric guitar, each string's vibrations are amplified electronically by a microphone-like device under the string, called a pickup. With a banjo, vibrations are transferred through the bridge to the tight, thin head stretched over what is usually a metal hoop (tone ring) which vibrates also. There is a sound chamber in a banjo, either open backed, or enclosed by a resonator. A banjo can be muted a great deal by keeping the bridge or head from vibrating freely (Try strumming the banjo with someone holding their hands flat on the head.). The tension of the head and the thickness of the bridge, both of which affect the resistance offered to the strings' vibrations, affect the tone and the volume of a banjo–a tight head and a thin bridge tend to increase volume up to a point and produce a "thin" as opposed to a "tubby" tone.

The resonator's job is to increase volume. One way it does this is by taking the sound which would go toward your stomach and bounce it out in front of you, adding volume. The shape and positioning of the resonator have important effects on the tone. (If you want to know more about this, check "Notes on Stringed Instruments" by David Sturgill in the January 1972 issues of *Bluegrass Unlimited.*)

The positioning of the tailpiece also has an effect on the sound. The lower the tailpiece, the greater the tension of the strings being pulled down over the bridge and the greater the volume and sharpness of tone.

Unless you enjoy experimenting with your banjo there are really only three things you'll ever have to do to it to keep it in shape: change the strings, keep the head tight, and keep the bridge in place. In addition, changing the head and the bridge are good things to do from time to time (every couple of years). Besides keeping the banjo clean you may want to polish the metal and wax the wood occasionally. Using a good quality wax, such as paste wax, will protect the wood against moisture, and keep the neck smooth and easy to play on. Materials for this are available in musical instrument stores. (see Appendix I: Buying Your First Banjo)

Restringing a banjo is a pretty self-evident task. It's something that should be done every couple of months or so: *more often* if your hands perspire a lot and make the strings sound dead, or if you leave the banjo out on a humid night and a lot of rust collects on the strings (from oxidation of the metal), or if you particularly like the sound of new strings and don't mind changing them often; *less often* if you can't afford six sets of strings a year (they're about $2.00 a set).

Strings last longer if you keep the banjo in its case (especially an airtight case) when you're not playing, and if you clean them after playing with a cloth, and periodically with some light oil like Three-In-One or even Wessen (you'll be surprised at how much rust comes off sometimes); or use the Dave Bromberg method, which is to boil old strings in water (take them off the banjo first of course). This method supposedly renews the strings, but they go dead again a bit more quickly than do brand new ones, and they're also more likely to break. If you kill strings at the rate he does, you may want to try this method.

To change the head, start by removing the tension hoop, which is what holds down the head. Since the brackets are holding down the tension hoop, you have to loosen them first. Take your bracket wrench and loosen away, until every bracket is clear of the hoop. Then, off come the hoop and the old head. The new one goes on by the reverse process, except that tightening the brackets has to be done as follows.

After putting the tension hoop down over the head and the brackets in place over the hoop, slightly tighten any four brackets at opposite corners. Then slightly tighten all the brackets between. The idea is not to pull down on any part of the head or tension hoop more than any other. Otherwise, the tension on the head might be uneven and the tension hoop could warp.

Tighten all the brackets a turn at a time until they're all finger-tight, then add one or two quarter turns. Try periodically pressing the head with your thumb to see how tight it's getting.

The bridge must be placed correctly or the banjo will fret inaccurately. The twelfth fret should be exactly halfway between the nut and the bridge. There are a number of ways to check this without a ruler. Because of the idiosyncrasies of banjos I can't promise that each way will give the same results.

Method 1: The note on the 12th fret should be exactly one octave higher than the open string. You need a good ear for that one.

Method 2: For this, you need to know how to play *harmonics,* or *chimes,* so here's a quick lesson: when the bridge is correctly placed, if you pick a string while placing a finger very lightly near its halfway point, you will get an unusual ringing note which is unlike the normal banjo sound. The clearest *harmonic* is the one played at exactly half the length of the string. The idea is to adjust the bridge so that the harmonic is best right over the 12th fret, which is supposed to be the halfway point.

Method 3: The pitch of the harmonic should be the same as the string fretted at the 12th fret. On a banjo with high action this method (and method 2) may not work.

Once you have the bridge placed correctly, mark it with a pen, drawing the outline of the bridge's feet on the head. Then when you change strings next, you'll know exactly where to put the bridge without having to use all those methods.

Align the bridge so that it's perpendicular to the neck (though in some cases angling it slightly helps the strings to fret more accurately), and be sure the strings are centered over the neck.

One other important point about caring for your banjo: avoid temperature and if possible, humidity extremes, which can warp or even crack parts of your instrument. Leaving a banjo (or any other instrument) in a car for very long on a cold day is taking a risk. Also, on a hot day the inside of a car or a trunk becomes super-hot, a bad environment for any instrument, in a case or not.

If you plan to store your banjo for a while, try for a stable climate. If the instrument doesn't have a tension rod (at the right tension), loosen the strings.

Appendix 4
Getting a better banjo

Once you've decided you've had it with the banjo you started with and want to get something better, you are faced with a wide choice. There are good new banjos for as little as $300-$400 and as much as $4500. And then there are the particularly rare and/or fancy old Gibson Mastertones that go for even more.

The less expensive banjos can be quite good. As of this writing, 1979, such companies as Iida and Deering put out well-made, good sounding banjos in this range. They do not sound as good as many banjos in the $800-$1000 range, but when they're set up well they come closer than the price differences would indicate.

The classic bluegrass banjo is the Gibson Mastertone. Mastertones have been made for about sixty years, and the pre-World War II models are considered the most valuable due to the quality materials and workmanship in construction. Another factor contributing to the high market value of a Mastertone is the scarcity of the instruments: most serious banjo players don't consider their banjo-buying days over until they've landed a good pre-war Mastertone.

Since most old Mastertones were originally made as tenors, it's common to find "conversions." The most typical is an original pot with a 5-string neck added on. Since the neck could be either factory made or constructed by a single craftsman, the quality of conversion necks can vary considerably. To learn more about old Mastertones, read the articles by Tom Morgan and George Gruhn in appendices 5 and 6 respectively.

Post-war Mastertones vary greatly in quality. They were quite good until the mid-60's when Gibson started to cut corners on important aspects of construction; particularly the type of metal on the tone-ring. They got worse and worse until the early '70's when Gibson suddenly brought the quality back up to earlier standards. During the '70's, however, the quality again slipped to a low level. For this reason, don't assume a Mastertone is good just because it's a Mastertone. In fact, many homemade necks have the typical "Mastertone" inlay at the upper frets, just for show! So, don't go by the name, go by the banjo itself.

Fortunately, many other companies have made Mastertone-style banjos. Some of the current brands are Ibanez, Stelling, Gold Star, Great Lakes, Allison, Ome, Hohner, and Saga. Older manufacturers and models are mentioned in George Gruhn's article. As good banjos have become more in demand and banjo technology has improved and spread overseas, more and more companies have started producing quality banjos. The result is that there is an ever-widening selection of brands and models to choose from.

Unfortunately, shopping for a good banjo isn't easy. It's rare to find a store that carries more than one brand of high-quality banjos, even large music stores in big cities. The best way to get an idea of the selection is to hang out in the parking lot at bluegrass festivals and check the various banjos that people are playing.Most banjo players are happy to talk about their banjo and would probably let you play it. Some might even offer to sell it to you—many instruments, not just banjos, are sold and traded at bluegrass festivals. In fact many people, anticipating this, go to bluegrass festivals prepared to buy or sell a banjo. I would warn possible buyers that there are risks involved here. Individuals can't give meaningful guarantees. They aren't accountable for unforseen problems or defects that appear after the transaction, especially when the festival is over and buyer and seller are probably hundreds of miles apart. Selling stolen instruments is not unheard of either. If you buy a stolen instrument and the original owner finds out, the banjo returns to the owner and you get burned.

If you are interested in an old banjo (like a pre-war Mastertone) you might be able to find one through a dealer. The advantage of this is accountability, and the disadvantage is the higher price tag because of the dealer's cut. The alternative is to buy directly from an owner, which is probably what you'll end up doing since not too many dealers have good old banjos. You can find individuals selling banjos at festivals, as I said, or you can look in the classified ads of such publications as *Bluegrass Unlimited, Pickin',* or *Banjo Newsletter.* (Addresses given in Appendix 7.)

Or you can look in a newspaper classified section or run a "wanted to buy" ad of your own. If you're lucky, this could put you in touch with someone who "wouldn't mind getting some cash for Uncle Fred's old banjo which has been collecting dust in the attic for years, anyway." Sometimes Uncle Fred's banjo is a fine old Mastertone and you have yourself a find. But don't get your hopes too high!

What should you look for in a quality banjo?

Mainly sound, in my opinion. I don't see how a serious musician could consider anything else more important. Durability and playability are also factors. Appearance is as much of a factor as you want to make it.

Tone is largely a matter of personal taste. For a sharper, brighter, more responsive sound, an arch-top model is ideal because of the smaller vibrating surface of the head. Most banjos are flatheads and give a fuller sound. Volume, clarity and tone quality are important. These are all variables which can depend a great deal on the way the banjo is set up. Of course, different banjos have different potentials, based on their construction. Usually, hitting a few notes gives you a good idea of the basic sound of a banjo even if it is in need of adjustment. Tom Morgan's article (Appendix 5) should help you if you want to learn more about the relationship of construction to tone.

Playability is not too hard to check—by playing of course—though it takes a while to get used to the feel of an unfamiliar instrument. Factors affecting playability are: size and shape of the neck, material of the fingerboard (hard smooth woods like ebony are preferred), finish of the neck, size and shape of the frets. The quality of the tuning pegs (how responsive and free from slippage) is quite variable and quite important.

When checking out a banjo with a non-factory-made neck, it might be worth checking fret placement. Even good craftsmen have been known to slightly misplace a few frets, causing intonation problems that can be difficult to discover and correct. First make sure the bridge is place correctly by comparing the pitch of any string fretted at the 12th fret with the 12th-fret harmonic on the same string. Then, using a strobe-tuner, check the pitch produced by each fret on the first string against the standard pitch. Another, more simple way of checking the intonation is to take the strings off and compare the fret placement on the neck in question with a quality factory-built neck.

The durability of a banjo is also a matter of construction. Most good banjos should last indefinitely if well cared for. However, if you are considering spending a lot of money on a banjo it's worth the trouble to get some expert advice. It's not always easy to find an expert, especially an impartial one, but if you do you may find out that the banjo you are considering has an important though subtle defect or that the company which makes it has an uneven reputation or is about to fold, etc.

Appearance and uniqueness are important factors governing banjo prices, but of course they have nothing to do with playing. Many banjo players take pride in their instrument's age, or the fact that it's "all original" (not altered since manufacture), or one of a certain well-known series, or has a certain neck inlay pattern, or has a certain type of pattern on the resonator (a part of the banjo no one ever sees unless you make a point of showing it), or has engraving on the metal or carving on the wood, or is gold plated, etc., etc. The variations are endless. If you'd like to learn more about them, read George Gruhn's article.

Rual Yarbrough and elaborate resonator

APPENDIX 5

GIBSON BANJO INFORMATION

This article was included originally as the companion to the Gibson banjo catalog reprints

Tom Morgan, Revised March 1979

Recent popularity of the banjo and a need for wider dissemination of various bits of information have prompted this writing. Much of the information is based only on opinions formed during approximately twenty years of experience working on banjos, while the instruments themselves were made over a period of 60 or more years. It should then be remembered that many variations are likely to have occurred.

During the years banjos have been manufactured, one strong contrast is noticeable. During the time of its wide popularity around 1920–1930, the tenor banjo was the style. The people then playing 5-string banjo were apt to be country musicians, and often were unable to afford the more lavish instruments. For this reason, the majority of these older, nicer instruments will be tenor banjos. The recent popularity of the 5-string often makes it desirable to convert these.

Gibson banjos used a designation of RB for regular banjo or 5-string, TB for tenor banjo, MB for mandolin banjo, and so forth. Therefore, reference to a model –00, for example, should be understood to represent the different possible models that were, or may have been made (MB–00, RB–00, etc.).

The shell or rims were made to be an interchangeable basis for either of the different types, and a mandolin banjo can be converted to a 5-string banjo by installing a different neck. Problems in fitting may be encountered due to several shapes of the heel, and two sizes of lag screw (8-32 and 10-32 threads) being used. Also, shell diameters vary from about six inches in some banjo ukes to a 24 inch banjo bass. The most popular sizes were 10½ and 11 inches, with the 11" size the only one well-suited for upgrading with one of the better MASTERTONE tone rings.

In reference to lag screws, the more recent ones are 10-32 metal threads on the outer end, and wood threads to hold onto the heel of the neck. This larger size is preferred for strength. Should the wood strip out, an oversized hardwood dowel can be glued into the heel, and the lag screw re-installed by drilling an appropriate size pilot hole.

In several older instruments, the lower lag screw, which takes the greater stress, was made as showin in sketch B on the following page. This L shape is fitted in two holes drilled appropriately, thus anchoring firmly into place. A cover plate of maple, ebony or celluloid was then glued on to seal the installation. A piece of filler wood between the lag screw and the plate is often distinguishable. BUT when this lag screw refuses to turn with firm pressure with a pair of pliers, it is very likely that it *isn't* the wood thread type, and further pressure will only cause further damage.

The three shapes of heel commonly found are shown, followed by the three types of shells to which they correspond:

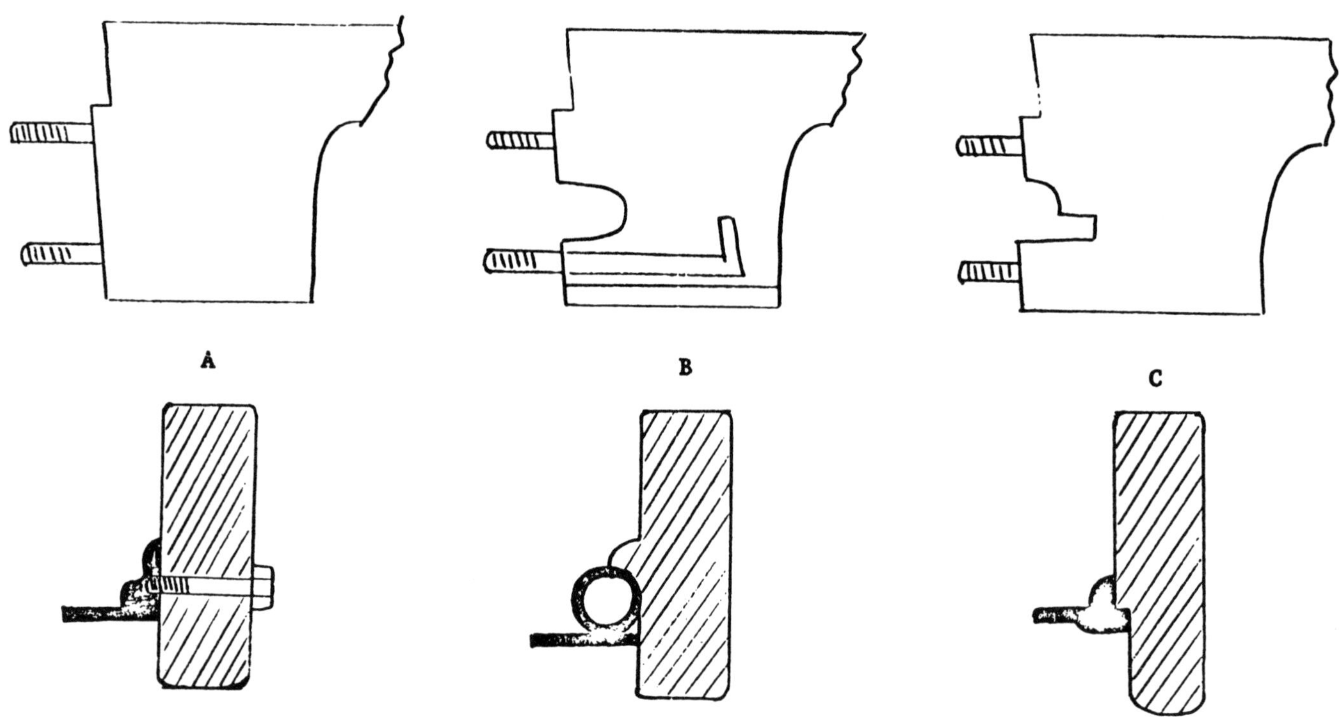

TYPES OF SHELL

A–*Plate and shoes, with bolts through the shell.* It would appear this is Gibson's oldest banjo since the shoes were in use previously in other makes, but this could also have been the less expensive method in somewhat later times. These have been seen in 10½ and 11" diameters, and usually have diamond shaped holes through the brass resonator plate making it easily distinguishable from the more conventional style. It should be noted the shell is laminated construction, ¾ inch thick, and has proved to be fully functional when an 11" one is fitted with a MASTERTONE tone ring.

B–*2-piece type, tube and plate.* This shell construction is the more desirable in many respects. It is very solid; the resonator plate of brass can be easily engraved and replated; it shows no tendency to bend up out of the resonator due to bracket tension.

C–*1-piece resonator flange.* Although many expensive Gibson banjos were made with this type of flange, there are several disadvantages. This flange is cast of white or "pot" metal, is breakable, pulls upward due to bracket tension, is not suited for engraving, and is difficult to replate. In the early seventies, the Gibson Company returned to the tube and plate flange as part of a general trend to improve their banjos. Unfortunately, the thin layers of wood rim used can shear off where they are contoured to stop the tube if the bracket tension is sufficient.

Stretcher band (tension hoop)

Several types have been made through the years. Shown are three styles, excluding the top-tension type described later in this paper.

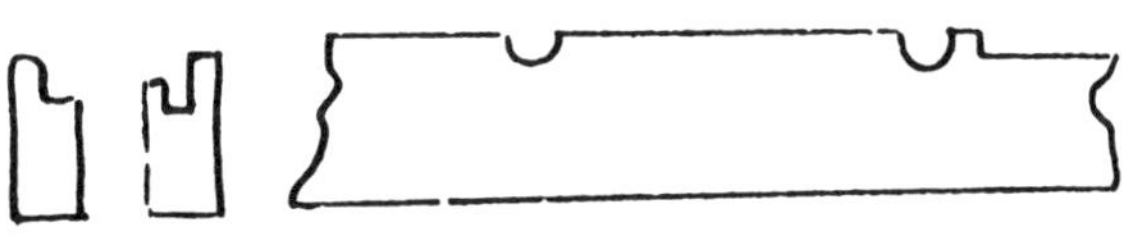

A B C

A–Was originally used on the least expensive models such as –00. It uses a flat-type bracket, and though it looks somewhat less desirable, it is made of solid brass and is therefore more functional than pot metal ones.

B–*Split-type.* This one is also of solid brass and uses flat brackets. Was used on early models such as the trap-door and ball-bearing models, and was engraved on the gold-plated models.

C–This type utilizes round brackets, and having been in production for several years, is found in solid brass as well as cast white metal. Numerous solid brass ones were stamped "E-2" on the inside, and a pre-war, gold-plated, engraved banjo would invariably have a brass stretcher band. It is rumored they will again be made of this material beginning in early 1971. Unfortunately, the resonator flange on some of the later gold, engraved models, such as the –18 and –800 were made of pot metal.

Apparently Gibson went back to brass tension hoops as part of the up-grade effort referred to above.

A nickel plated stretcher band can often be found with the plating worn thin and the brass showing through. These are suitable for engraving and re-plating. The white metal ones tend to "flare out" at the top due to bracket tension, when the head is kept up to maximum tightness.

WOOD RIM CONSTRUCTION

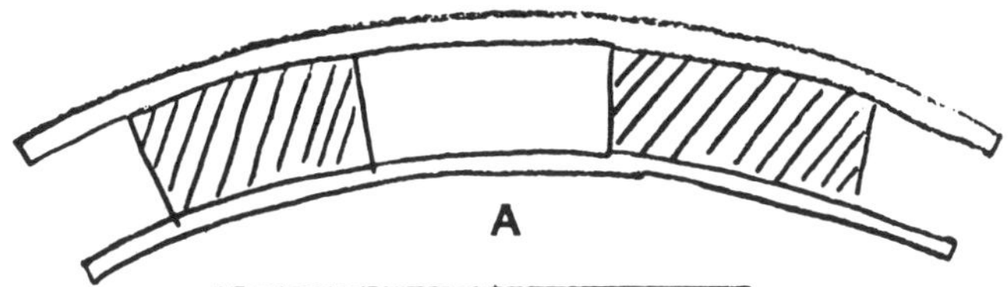

A

B

A–*Hollow type* is rarely seen, but is generally conceded to be Gibson's poorest instrument. It has been seen in several sizes including 11 inch and a 14 inch guitar banjo. Due to the thin walls, the MASTERTONE tone ring wouldn't be apt to be properly fitted to this shell, although the one-piece tubular ring as in the trap-door type might be suitable to improve tone. This shell used the tubular method for holding the brackets, but had no resonator, so the plate wasn't used.

B–*Laminated type rim.* All the other Gibson banjos seen have had rims of laminated maple varying from 3 to 6 or 7 ply, with the exception of models built after the early seventies: they have approximately 15 ply. It should be noted that some shells, though 11" in outside diameter, may have a thinner wall thickness than the normal ¾ inch at the top, and therefore aren't well-suited to up-grading with a different MASTERTONE tone ring.

Tone Rings

First, it seems worth mentioning that several models used a ring of ¼" round brass, and experience with this approach indicates the results don't justify calling it a "tone ring." Hence, reference will be made to different models describing them in some detail, but "tone ring" will only apply to a tubular improvement to the above, or more likely in reference to a standard 2 piece ball-bearing, 1 piece arch-top, or flat-type MASTERTONE rings.

Some very plain banjos were marketed just before and during depression times under the model –00. These sold complete, first for $30.00 and then $27.50, and though the shell was laminated and solid enough, it used only a turned bead in the wood at the outside top edge (see sketch) for the head to bear on. This model is one previously referred to as having only 5/8 inch wall thickness at the top, and installation of a solid-arched or flat MASTERTONE ring would allow 1/8 inch of the metal to overhang. Acceptable results have been achieved by using the 2 piece ball-bearing tone ring parts on this type shell, but further effort to install the springs, ball-bearings and washers doesn't seem practical. First, the wall thickness may not be sufficient, a more solid union of wood and metal seems desirable, and the original feature of "taking up the slack" with the springs due to humidity and temperature change is no longer necessary with the advent of plastic heads.

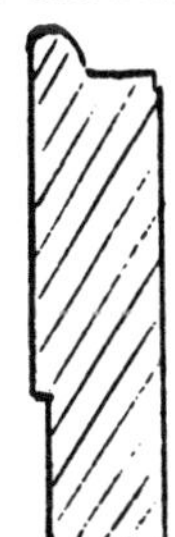

Care should be exercised so the wood is cut properly to allow the inner tubular ring (with bead) to project above the outer ring if this conversion is attempted.

This model is seen only with the one-piece cast resonator flange.

¼ inch solid brass ring. This type has been manufactured for several years under different model numbers. The most recent is the –100 and –150 in which the ring is smaller and rests on the inside edge to give a raised-head effect. Pre-war designations of –1, –2, and –11 are known, and the ring is often placed to the outside edge giving the banjo a "flat-head" appearance. It is important to realize this isn't a MASTERTONE flat-head as described later in this paper. An easy was of differentiating between the two is by checking under the head, from the outside of the banjo. The metal of a MASTERTONE ring will be visible there, where only the finished wood rim will show in the less expensive models.

Of some interest in those having only the ¼ brass ring is the model –11, which is often referred to as a "blue-banjo." This model has been made under three known trade names of Gibson, S.S. Stewart, and Kel Kroyden. It has a simulated mother of pearl fingerboard, peghead veneer and resonator veneer with red, blue and greed decorations, and the remaining wood parts painted blue or black.

The metal parts of these models are identical with cast one-piece flange and stretcher band of white metal. The laminated ¾ inch thick shell lends well to up-grading, but refinishing of the painted shell, resonator rim and neck is recommended.

½ inch tubular "tone ring." This was Gibson's first serious approach to a tone ring, but wasn't designated MASTERTONE. It is found both with and without holes, and was used on the "shoes and bolts through shell" and "trap-door" types. It is easily recognized from the outside by the large radius there the head makes contact, and the fact that there is no metal visible under the head (see sketch).

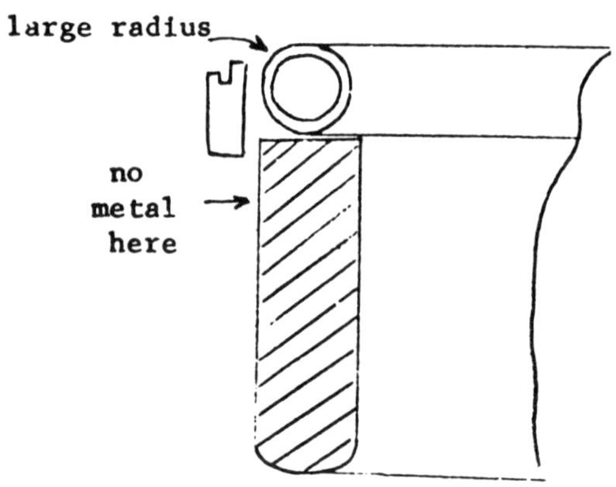

This type of shell is best suited for frailing, but with a standard resonator, plastic head, etc., has been set up to perform fairly effectively as a bluegrass banjo.

Quite a number of variations have been seen such as 12 sets of ball-bearing and spring sets suggesting a transition toward the standard ball-bearing MASTERTONE.

Trap door banjo. This name is currently used to describe the older banjo which featured a flat resonator, held closely to the shell by screws, but hinged to allow open or closed playing, thereby changing tone and volume. They always used the tubular method for holding the brackets, a split-type stretcher band with flat brackets, and models have been seen from very plain to very fancy, concerning the wood, inlay and hardware used.

These usually were 10½ inches in diameter, and the wall thickness of the shell isn't suitable for upgrading with a better MASTERTONE tone ring.

The descriptions offered here should be a guide to help in acquiring or modifying a banjo, but it should be emphasized that unusual variations may turn up. For example, an 11" thin shell, much like the trap door, was found. The unusual part was the resonator which was made of celluloid with felt-padded, slip-on braces built into it, and shaped as shown in the sketch.

Ball-bearing (or floating-head) MASTERTONE. This was the earliest shell construction to be designated MASTERTONE, and incorporated several ingenious devices to further its value in its day. The tone ring parts are basically two pieces, with an outer ring fitted to the side of the shell, and a tubular ring supported by 24 ball-bearings, washers and springs combinations. The tubular piece is actually 3 pieces brazed together, using the ½ diameter round tube seen in less elaborate models previously described, but with a small bead placed high on the inside tangent to create a raised-head configuration, and a scalloped filler ring to prevent side-to-side movement.

These usually had a large number of holes drilled through the tubular part of the tone ring as shown in the sketch, and it is the distinguishing feature looking from the inside. An easier way is the outer ring often had small holes around its bottom edge which are visible from the outside, but in some cases these holes are absent, and positive identification must be made from within.

These always used the plate and tube type resonator flange, and the ¾" thick shell wall is suited for conversion to a flat-head tone ring by removing 1/8 inch from the top of the wood rim. It is generally felt the holes for the ball-bearings and springs should be doweled in for this conversion. Hardwood dowel (preferably maple) should be used, and the holes likely will need drilling slightly to 3/8 inch to avoid any chance of forcing the shall laminations apart. Conversion to a solid arch-top MASTERTONE ring isn't recommended, since the top of the wood rim would need to be built up 1/8 inch for proper fit.

The ball-bearing MASTERTONE is probably the nearest to an ideal banjo to be used intermittently for frailing and Scruggs' style picking, *without adjustment*, but it is not considered to be in the upper bracket for bluegrass alone.

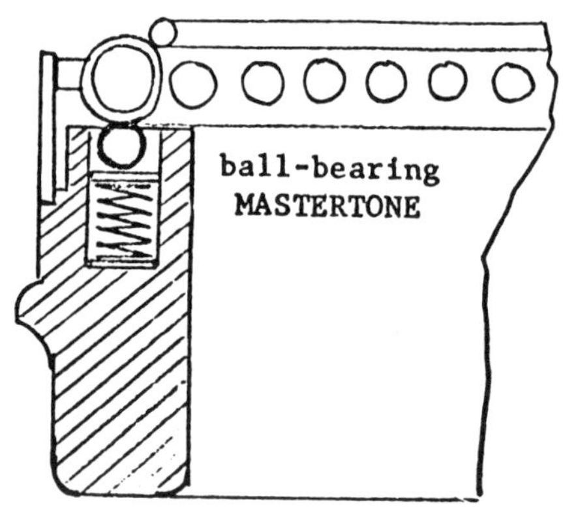

When fitting a flat tone ring to a ball-bearing shell, there is no contact of the metal to wood on the side of the rim except at the extreme bottom where a small shoulder is cut to form an automatic fit for this ring. There is much room for discussion about whether this lack of "fit" would affect the tone, but satisfactory results have been gotten without installing a strip of wood to fill this space. In the event it was felt necessary to do so, only maple should be glued neatly into place, and the proper fit reached.

Raised head (arch top) MASTERTONE. The pre-war version of this tone ring usually had 40 holes as shown below, but in some cases there were *no* holes. They generally have a sharp type of tone, but the clarity seems to diminish slightly as the higher notes are played. Compared to the flat-style ring, the vibrating area of the head is less, creating a more treble effect.

A

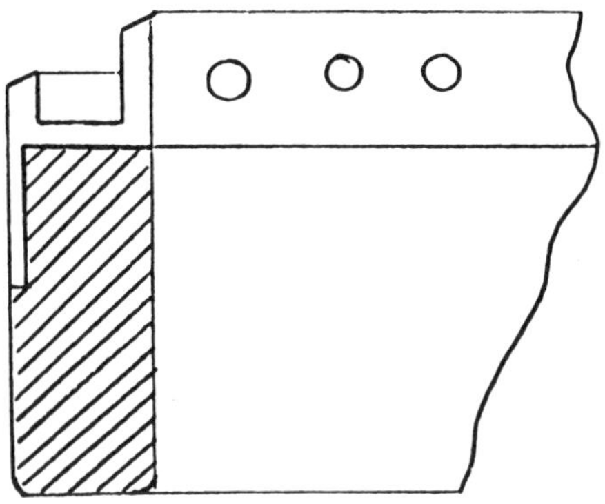

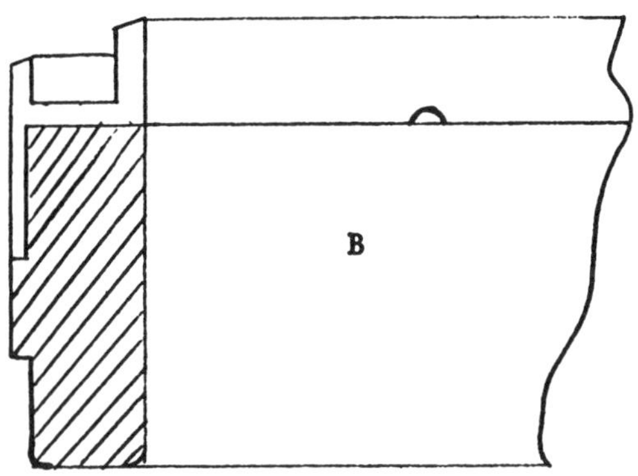

The pre-war arch-top rings are found on shells with one or two-piece resonator flanges. The post-war version of this tone ring is almost identical in construction, can be interchanged with pre-war ones, but can be identified by 4 equi-spaced holes drilled diagonally from inside to outside and appear as half-circles as shown in B, above. The arch-top wood rim can be converted to accept a flat MASTERTONE ring by removal of ¼ inch from the top surface only. A lathe is recommended for this operation.

Flat-head MASTERTONE. This model is generally considered best for bluegrass. It has a full, bassy tone in the open positions and becomes clearer in the higher positions. It is more often seen with 20 equi-spaced holes as shown in sketch A, but also has been seen with *no* holes. In case an original flat-head were found with no holes, every effort should be made to set the banjo up for best results before any consideration should be given to drilling in the missing holes.

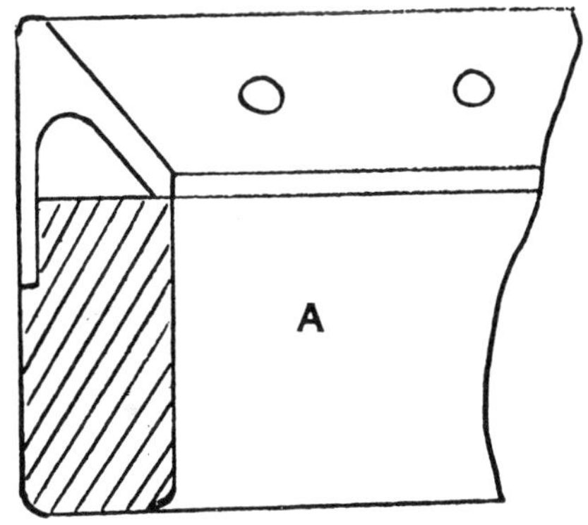

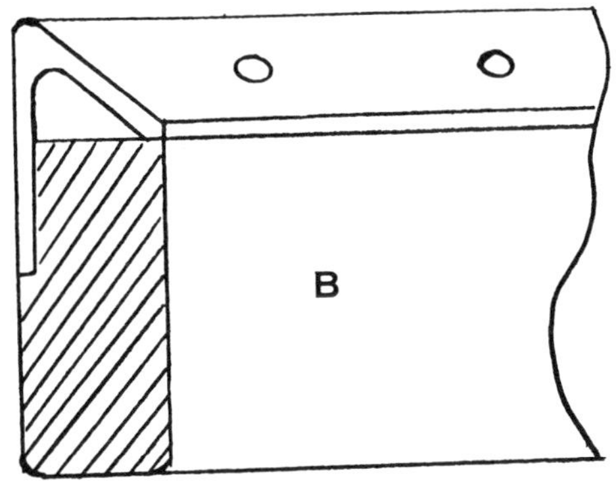

One notable variation, seen only in a gold-plated model to date, is a "light-weight" tone ring which had a low angle as shown in B, above. Since this type tone ring has only been seen on a shell with 2 piece resonator flange, this may have been an experimental transition from arch-top influences. Other observations are that the metal seems to be a different alloy, the face with the holes is thinner, decreasing the overall weight and solidity of the ring, and the tone seems to be sharper than the heavier, high-angle ones.

Recent flat-head MASTERTONE tone rings. As the demand for bluegrass banjos continued to grow in the late sixties, Gibson returned to the flat-top banjo as a standard model. These rings are shaped much like the pre-war ones, can be interchanged on a shell, but generally don't have as good a tone quality as the older rings.

These intermediate-age flat rings have been seen with 19, 20 and 21 holes, and in some cases the holes are not equi-spaced. Unless it is obvious by the odd number of holes, it is very difficult to distinguish between a pre-war and a post-war flat ring except when close examination and comparison with a proven original is possible.

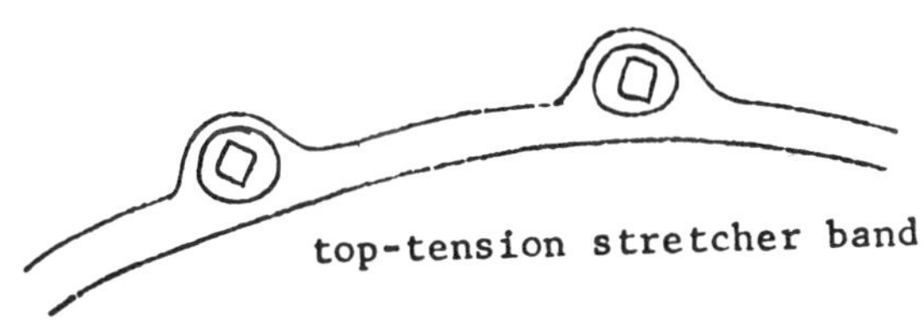

Top-tension MASTERTONE. These are recognized by a stretcher band as shown in the sketch, and were so called due to the brackets' being movable from the outside with a square head much like drum-head tighteners.

They were manufactured under model numbers –7, –12 and –18 just before World War II, always in conjunction with a flat tone ring, and the stretcher band was apparently cast from the same bronze-like material as the tone ring. The extra bulk of the metal in close proximity to the tone ring seems to give a type of tonal result somewhat like the bassy body and depth of a conventional pre-war flat-head, but being noticeably sharper in the direction of an arch-top.

They were made with only the one-piece resonator flange, and the cast metal frequently shows stripping of the threads. A very suitable answer to this problem is now available in the form of a spring-like insert to replace the threads, and called a "helicoil." They require special tools for insertion, but do not create any noticeable change in the appearance of the banjo.

The top-tension MASTERTONE weighs considerably more than the average Gibson banjo due to heavier brackets, the bulk of the stretcher band, and the fact the resonator, being of solid walnut or maple, is left flat on the inside, and turned with a hump in the center approximating ¾ inch thick. Also, the necks of this period were rather bulky, and the keys were large box-type in the style of the "bowtie" –150 and –250 models.

Getting the Best Sound from a Banjo

There are many areas which can affect the sound of a banjo, and the more important ones can be covered first. The *head* must be very tight to achieve the ultimate in bluegrass sound. For frailing, etc., a progressively looser head is practical to suit the taste of the individual. The porous nature of a good skin head, under optimum conditions of low humidity and tautness, produces a tonal quality that is hard to equal; however, plastic heads are more practical.

It is very important to have a *tail-piece* functional enough to place the strings at any desired level from "touching the head" to about 1/8 inch of clearance. Within these limits, the most desirable point to suit the individual can be found by comparison. Kerschner "Unique," Waverley, and Grover "Presto" are some of the good, old ones, but the final test is whether it will hold the strings closely enough to the head. The length of the tailpiece has an effect, also, and one that is too long or too heavy should be avoided.

A maple *bridge* (with ebony top such as the standard Gibson 3 foot model is very important in attaining a bluegrass sound, and the 5/8 inch height is strongly recommended. The added height causes the strings to project downward at a sharper angle to the tailpiece, thereby increasing the pressure on the bridge. This decreases the resistance the string vibration must overcome in traveling through the bridge and head, and results in a better sound. Also, *thinning the bridge* can improve the sharpness, based on the same principle.

The gauge and quality of *strings* can affect the sound of a banjo. The string gauge an individual is accustomed to has much to do with the "feel" or playability, and some strings tend to be too heavy or too light. A suggestion would be to use a set of Bell Brand or Black Diamond, but substitute a Gibson plectrum banjo wound 3rd string for the 4th, when a moderately heavy action is desired. The S–M strings or Vega Nu-Sound have a lighter feel.

The *resonator* can change the tone and decrease the volume where there isn't enough clearance between the back of the shell and the inside of the resonator. Four wood blocks, approximately 1/8 inch thick, placed under the flange where it rests in the resonator to temporarily raise the shell, will give an easy determination if this might be a problem in a specific case. The blocks could then be glued into place if an improvement were noted.

The *level of the stretcher band* in relation to the tone ring may or may not have any marked effect on sound, but it creates a nicer appearance if the top of the band is approximately level with the top of the tone ring. And, since solidness is apt to be a positive step toward good tonal results, the stretcher band being level may serve to aid by forming a more integral unit with the tone ring.

The *plastic head* has become the only practical way to keep your banjo sounding good. A wide variety of sizes are manufactured by Remo, Inc., under the name Weatherking, etc., but for 11 inch rims, the Stewart-MacDonald 5-Star head is recommended. A new method of "tucking" the plastic around the retainer band prevents the problem which was so prevalent in earlier plastic heads.

Adjustment of String Height, Gibson Banjo

Minor adjustment of the action (almost 1/16 inch in either direction) can be easily accomplished by inserting a nail or punch in the hole of the lower shell rod to prevent turning; then, by loosening the inside nut and tightening the outside one, the strings will be drawn toward the fingerboard. By loosening the outside nut and tightening the inside, the strings will be raised.

This operation actually expands and compresses the wooden rim, but no problem should arise as long as the wood is protected by washers under the nuts. Quite a lot of pressure can be exerted, but the limit of 1/16 in either direction would be a fair rule of "how far" to go. Also, using a different height bridge or trimming the existing one is possible, but the 5/8 inch bridge is recommended, when practical.

Major adjustment of string height requires reshaping the heel, or shimming at top or bottom may be used as a temporary solution.

Correcting Neck Warp

The truss rod feature in most Gibson instruments is helpful in controlling warpage due to string tension and change of climate. Tightening the nut is only effective when the warp is upward in the direction of the string tension, and a warp in the opposite direction causing the strings to "buzz" on the 2nd or 3rd frets should prompt first a check to be sure the truss rod is not *too tight*.

Tuning Gear

Planetary type tuning pegs are generally conceded to be best, and are available in both pre- and post-war styles.

The Kroll geared 5th peg has eliminated the problem of lesser types that were always too tight, or slipped.

Keith-Scruggs pegs are highly recommended as special effects tuners in that they function as two regular tuners (rather than drill extra holes in the peghead) and are made to very exacting specifications.

Appendix 6

BLUEGRASS INSTRUMENTS
ORIGINAL VS REPRODUCTION

GIBSON BANJOS

By George Gruhn (with Douglas Green)
GTR Inc., 111 4th Avenue North, Nashville, Tennessee 37219

Discussing original and reproduction guitars and mandolins was a relatively easy matter, in that there was only one mandolin (the F-5) and two guitars (prewar D-28 and D-45) which have commonly been reproduced. All this changes in tackling the Gibson banjos, because these banjos came originally in many styles and models, with many different tone rings, headstock shapes, inlay patterns etc., etc. that this task is vastly complicated.

In order to clarify things, we are going to undertake a rather detailed discussion of 1) tone ring styles, 2) headstock shapes, and 3) style numbers before trying to sift out the originals from the fakes.

But first, a word or two on Gibson banjos and their popularity in bluegrass music is in order. Just as Bill Monroe has had a tremendous effect on the choice of the F-5 as "the" bluegrass mandolin by his admirers, so Earl Scruggs has had much to do with the fact that most bluegrass banjoists prefer Gibson banjos, and among Gibson banjos prefer those with a flat tone ring. Although Vega, Paramount, Epiphone, Bacon and Day, and others have made excellent bluegrass banjos, it is the Gibson which has become the most popular by far among bluegrass banjoists, and the standard against which all others are compared. Likewise, although many banjoists prefer the quick, crisp response of a raised head banjo (Larry McNeely and Ralph Stanley, to name two), most bluegrassers seem to be seeking for that heavy, popping, tone so characteristic of Earl Scruggs.

So it is these banjos, the Gibson Mastertones, made between 1924 and the beginning of World War Two on which we will concentrate.

STYLES OF TONE RING:

1) Ball bearing—this was a two piece tone ring supported by springs and ball bearings. Introduced in 1924, they were made until 1927. The earliest ones had holes on the outside, and are easily recognizable, while later ball bearing banjos are identical in outside appearance to the later raised heads. The stretcher band (also commonly called the tension hoop) is typically thin and grooved—as opposed to notched—and has brackets with the flat tops which fit into this groove. They have a 3/4" shell and a two piece flange.

2) Raised head—a one piece ring made from 1927 until World War two. The earliest do not have any holes at all in the tone ring, while later ones have forty holes. They have a modern bracket and notched stretcher band arrangement. The earlier ones had a two piece flange with a 3/4" shell, while the later one, went to a one piece flange and a 5/8" shell. Postwar raised heads are distinctive in that they have 4 crescent shaped holes in the ring.

3) Flat Head—a one piece ring, made with either no holes or twenty holes. As far as Gibson catalogues are concerned, they are listed as coming only on top-tension banjos, but in fact were available as a custom feature on any model during the middle and late 30's. Most have a one piece flange and a 5/8" shell, and they used the modern bracket and stretcher band arrangement. Early postwar flatheads have 19 holes on the tone ring, while the more recent made have 20.

4) Top Tension—a highly distinctive arrangement in which a specially designed stretcher band is fitted with drum bolts which tighten into the tension hoop from the top, making it possible to tighten and loosen the head without removing the resonator. The resonator itself is highly distinctive, in that it is flat on the inside but carved on the outside. These banjos came with one piece flanges and 5/8" shells. Because of the carved resonator and the amount of metal used in this arrangement, this was Gibson's heaviest banjo ever — almost 15 pounds!

STYLES OF HEADSTOCK SHAPE:

1) "Fiddle" headstock—to no ones' surprise, this is so called because it is shaped like a violin. All ball bearings, and of course many others, had this headstock shape. Ralph Stanley's banjo has this "fiddle" headstock.

2) "Double cut" headstock—found only on one piece flange banjos: Don Reno's banjo has this style.

3) Top tension headstock—a modernistic design, shaped much like a guitar headstock, which only came on top-tension banjos.

STYLE NUMBERS:

Style numbers come in two parts, the first part a letter or letters, and the second a number. The letters stood for the type of neck on the banjo, while the numbers signified the ornamentation of the instrument. The letters were TB (tenor banjo), PB (plectrum banjo), RB ("regular" banjo—these are the five strings), GB (guitar banjo), and MB (mandolin banjo). Tenors were the most popular, probably accounting for more than 90% of all Gibson banjos originally sold, followed by plectrums which were uncommon, and five-strings, which were rare. Guitar-banjos and mandolin-banjos were actually in their heyday before the introduction of the Mastertone, and consequently few Mastertones were made in these neck arrangements. With the exception that the notch cut in the tension hoop was wider on the GB and RB models than on the PB or TB, the bodies on all these Mastertones are the same: in other words, a PB, an RB and an MB have the same body, and with a 5 string neck, both sound the same.

1) Style 3—These were first issued with ball bearing tone rings, fiddle headstock, 2 piece flanges 3/4" shells, nickel plated parts, a plain maple resonator and neck, stained red mahogany in color, with single binding on neck and back of the resonator only and diamond shaped inlays on the fingerboard. The second series was the same as the first, except that they had a rasied tone ring, modern-type bracket and tension hoop arrangement, and purfling on the top *and* back of the resonator. The third series had a one piece flange, double-cut headstock, mahogany neck and resonator, bound top and bottom, and with two purfling rings on the back of the resonator. A very few made in the thirties had wreath pattern inlays (and flat rings), but by far the greatest number had big inlays (much like Gibson's new reissue).

2) Style 4—First series: ball bearing, nickel plated parts, mahogany neck and resonator, multiple binding on top and back of resonators, and narrow concentric rings on the back. The shell was like the number 3, but they came with the fiddle headstock, the "hearts and flowers" inlays, triple binding on the fingerboard. Second Series: raised heads, with the modern tension hoop and bracket arrangement. Third series: came with raised 40 hole tone ring (with a very few flat), a one piece flange and 5/8" shell, double cut headstock, the "flying eagle" inlay pattern (similar, but more refined, to the postwar RB-800), and were chrome plated. The resonator and neck were walnut, and had concentric inlaid rings of wood purfling in the resonator.

3) Granada—First series: ball bearing tone ring, curly maple neck and resonator, hearts and flowers inlay pattern, fiddle headstock, and the binding on the fingerboard and the concentric rings on the back of the resonator are of checkered wood purfling. Second series: same as first series except the tone ring is the raised head. Third series: a different Granada entirely, which came with a triple bound resonator, (top and bottom), one piece flange, 5/8" shell, triplebound fingerboard, a flying eagle pattern (with a rare hearts and flowers), curly maple neck and resonator, double cut headstock, and no wooden purfling. All Granadas had gold plated metal parts, and were engraved on the stretcher band and the name "Granada" on the tailpiece.

4) Style 5, or Deluxe—first series: ball bearing tone ring, curly walnut neck and resonator, wreath inlay, pearloid bindings, greenish and yellow wood marquetry, fiddle headstock, engraved and gold plated parts, with the word "Deluxe" usually engraved on the tailpiece. Second series: same as the above, but with a raised head tone ring. In our experience, we've only ever seen one flat ring style 5, which was probably a custom order. We'll probably never see another.

5) Style 6—we have seen no ball bearing in a style 6. This style came with either the raised or flat ring. They were gold similarand engraved, and came with an inlay pattern quite similar to hearts and flowers, but fancier. The neck and resonator were curly maple, with the resonator bound top and back in white, and the neck bound either with checkered black and white binding or with gold sparkle. The fingerboard and headstock face also had matching checkered or gold sparkle binding. The checkered pattern is earlier, and the later ones tended to have the gold sparkle. Typically, they have two piece flanges with 3/4" shell.

6) Bella Voce, Florentine, and All American—These are exceptionally collectable banjos, which have carved painted necks and resonators, gold plating and engraving, and were Gibson's top of the line, mainly custom order instruments. They were available in so many custom ordered features such as choice of wood (white holly, dark walnut, natural maple and others), purfling (wood, gold sparkle, plastic, pearloid), and painting scheme, that Gibson once bragged that 27 different choices of Bella Voce and Florentine were available.

I. Bella Voce—Carved on the resonator, with a pattern showing a lyre, a horn, and a banjo entwined in vines. It had its own distinctive pearl inlay pattern on the fingerboard and headstock. It came typically with a raised head, although as always, exceptions are possible.

II. Florentine—The carving and painting of the seal of the city of Florence on the back of the resonator gave this banjo its name, although, oddly enough, the hand painted scenes on the fingerboard are of the canals and the sites of Venice. The fingerboard and headstock are pearloid (called, in common parlance, "mother-of-toilet-seat"), and the headstock is trimmed in white rhinestones, with "Gibson" written in red rhinestones, and a bouquet of flowers (which looks more like a multiple-scoop ice cream cone) in various-color rhinestones. They came with both raised and flat rings.

III. All-American—A patriot's dream, this banjo has the American eagle carved in the resonator (the same one that is on the reverse of a dollar bill), and a headstock hand carved in the shape of an eagle holding a shield. The fingerboard has scenes from American history, beginning with Columbus' discovery, going on up (as you go up the neck) to battles of WWI. These were also available in raised head or flat.

7) Top Tension—These don't fit into any of the above schemes, for about 1937 Gibson scrapped all previous banjo designs and came out with an entirely new Mastertone: the top tension, which was the only Mastertone offered. These banjos were offered in three styles:

I. Style 7—had a maple neck and resonator, and had single white binding on the top and back of the resonator, and the fingerboard. The finish was dark, the model parts were nickel plated, and the headstock was bound in white. The name Gibson is inlaid in the headstock in the later, heavier script. The inlays in the neck are like the RB-250, except that there were three slashes in the each side of the "bowtie", giving the design something of an American Indian look.

II. Style 12—same as the above, except that it was chrome plated, had a walnut back and resonator, triple bindings, and the neck inlays were stepform blocks, typical of top tensions only.

III. Style 12—same as the above, except that the neck and resonator are curly maple, with a golden brown sunburst, and the metal parts are gold plated and engraved.

Since Gibson banjo parts are so interchangeable, many originals have been altered, many postwar banjos have been doctored up to look like prewar, many ball bearings and raised heads have been converted to flat heads . . . etc., etc., etc., the list is nearly without end. This, coupled with the enormous number of models made, make telling original from reproduction *very* difficult. In addition, there are a number of mail order establishments who offer high quality interchangeable parts.

As stated before, original flat head banjos are very rare, and original five strings with flat heads are infinitely more rare. Out of a thousand seen at a festival which look like original prewar flatheads, chances are that not one will be a real original, and in fact, 99.9% of all flat head, five string banjos are copies or are in some way modified.

Many of these, of course, are not intended to fool or defraud anyone, but banjos in particular are the instruments the unscrupulous will try to sell as original, because they are—of all bluegrass instruments – the most often faked.

While it is hoped that this article will be of help in discriminating originals from fakes, the best course, as always, is to buy from some person or dealer whom you can trust, and who will be willing to give legal certification that the instrument you are buying is original. It is better to get an original from a reputable dealer at the going rate than to get a bargain from Joe Blow, only to find out later that it is worth half what you paid for it because it is a fake.

This lengthy preamble has served, hopefully, to make the distinction between Mastertone model styles, tone ring arrangements and etc. clear. Now we proceed to the specifics of telling originals from reproductions:

1) Label and Serial Number—The originals have a yellow, oval guarantee sticker, edged in black. Reproduction labels are now available, but usually these are stuck on, and can be peeled

off, which the originals cannot, but we understand a good original type is coming out soon——the art of the copyist is always improving. When a conversion flat tone ring is put in an original raised head or ball bearing shell, usually this label has to be cut, and while a cut label is often the sign of tampering with original, it is not necessarily so, for we have seen several original flatheads which had cut labels; probably these were custom ordered, and a shell already made up by Gibson for a raised head was simply altered at the factory, cutting the label in the process.

A serial number is placed in three places on an original instrument, providing a good way of telling whether parts have been switched. One number is stamped on the inside of the shell (although some had this stamp on the back of the headstock in the late 30's), another is written in chalk or red paint on the inside of the resonator, and a third number is stamped or penciled at the heel of the neck.

2) Catalogue Description——While most guitars and banjos adhere faithfully to catalogue description, banjos often do not——in fact, they deviated notably. We have seen several late Style 4 with a Bella Voce board, and we've seen two banjos which had Florentine resonators, nickel plated parts, Style 6 headstocks, and style 1 (not a Mastertone) fingerboards. These and many other deviations are factory original, although in general 99% still follow the catalogue description. With banjos, however, these deviations occur more often, and the key to discovering originality is by the way the parts match——their contexture. Certain distinctive characteristics just fall into place: 5/8" shells have a one piece flange and double-cut headstocks. Just as 3/4" shells, two piece flanges and fiddle headstocks go together. Thus a fiddle headstock on a banjo with a one piece flange would be very suspicious. Also, parts should be from the same period: i.e. Planet tuners are original on a Ball-bearing, but not on a late 30's. Again, what to look for is contexture——a banjo may be weird as far as catalogue description, but its parts should match up in time. A mish-mash of 1925 and 1940 parts is highly suspicious indeed, but strange mixtures, if parts are all of the same age, are highly possible.

3) Workmanship——Excellent with the occasional execption of inlay, which varied considerably, from sublime to clunky, although it was usually quite good. The woodwork and binding on originals is uniformly excellent.

4) Body Dimensions——Mastertone size is so standardized that this is not a problem on banjos. If the body dimensions are off, it is almost certainly a fake.

5) Purfling and Binding——All but a few very early ball bearings used white celluloid. A lot of fakes use ivoroid where Gibson didn't. Also, most of the binding and purfling have proved extremely hard to duplicate although better copies are constantly being introduced. The art of copying is getting better and better, so often the newer the copy, the harder it is to tell from original.

6) Inlay——This was discussed under the different styles. One point: most copyists rout out the fingerboard and place inlays into it, while Gibson originally cut through the boards in most cases——once again, the advantages of machinery. Because of this, most copies have much thicker fingerboards than the originals, which are usually about 1/8".

7) Finish——Gibson did excellent quality finish work, and a dribbly, grainy, or splotchy finish is a sure sign that something is amiss.

8) Wood——Normally the resonator and neck matched up, no matter what type of wood was used. Fingerboards, interestingly enough, were made of rosewood, except on the Style 6. Most copyists use ebony, but with the growing scarcity of good quality ebony, rosewood boards, like the originals, may well soon be reappearing on copies. And, interestingly, although most copyists use ebony (or sometimes rosewood) facing on the headstock, Gibson used a light wood (usually maple) *stained* black! This is also true of guitars and mandolins.

9) Parts and Fittings——Much has been covered in our description of styles, but there are a few points which should be noted. One is tailpieces, for an original prewar five string tailpiece is extremely hard to get . . . most copies use converted four string tailpieces. Frets are another thing to watch for . . . the original frets were very small and quite distinctive, and most copyists do not use them. Also, the machining marks on the old tone rings are extremely distinctive, and quite unlike the copies of the tone rings being made currently by various people . . . Prewar tuners, as might be expected, are extremely hard to find, and, as we said earlier, they should match the banjo generally in period of construction. Gibson used about 15 different types and brands of tuners, and an article could be written about these alone, but suffice it to say at this point that the tuners should be correct for the year and the style of the banjo. One final thing: on the old necks made for banjos with two piece flanges, the co-ordinator rods fitting into the studs in the body of the banjo fitted into a non-turnable stud (the one closest to the heel of the neck), a small fitting which most copyists do not have.

10) Cases——Prewar five string cases are, as might well be expected, a great rarity. If the banjo has one, it is a point in favor of its originality, but of course this does not necessarily hold true. Also, a plectrum or guitar-banjo case will fit, and cases can be switched.

11) Distinctive Marks of the Maker——As we said, with guitars and mandolins, the workmanship on these instruments is like handwriting, and infintesimal differences can be spotted. For the large part, because much of the original work was machined, while most copyists work strictly by hand. The copies are also like handwriting . . . they are the handwriting of *their* maker, and Gibson's handwriting is very distinctive.

With this article, our series on reproduction vs. originals comes to an end. Although we could not describe everything in detail, we hope that it will be at least a step forward for our readers, who hopefully will have an improved understanding of the subtle things to look for when picking out that certain instrument you've been saving for. We wish you good luck, we hope you find what you want, and if there are any question, technical or otherwise, or otherwise, or suggestions for further articles, we welcome them all, at the address listed at the front of this article.

Appendix 7
Records

As a native of a big city, I don't think I could possibly have learned how to play bluegrass without having spent a lot of time listening to records. Unless you're fortunate enough to get to hear live bluegrass often, you'll have to rely on records quite a bit.

It's important to realize that when you take up bluegrass banjo you're learning more than just how to play an instrument, you're learning a whole style of music. Records will help you to develop a close familiarity with the sound and feeling of bluegrass. Since you will be learning banjo, you should be listening to how the banjo contributes to the sound, and how the bluegrass band helps the banjo.

Another benefit that comes from listening to records is the chance to learn some bluegrass material. When people first get together to play bluegrass they usually pick out songs to play that everyone knows from records. The more records you're familiar with, the more likely you will be to fit in quickly with other musicians.

As a banjo player you should get some records which emphasize the banjo. But don't overemphasize it–all the instruments are important. In fact, if you're one of those who is tempted to overemphasize instrumentals over vocals (as I did when I was starting), try to resist the temptation. Bluegrass is basically vocal music, built around songs and singing. Keep your ears open to what's happening vocally as well as instrumentally. If, when you eventually become a member of a bluegrass band, your playing reflects the attitude that playing is more important than singing, you won't be helping the band much.

Getting records is a tricky business because many good bluegrass records are hard to find, especially those that are out of print or about to be. (This unfortunately has been the fate of some of the very best bluegrass records. Sometimes, though, they are reissued.) Getting bluegrass records is easier than it used to be thanks to a few recent phenomena: good mail order services and bluegrass magazines, and bluegrass festivals. There are at least two mail order services that offer a huge selection of records (almost any bluegrass or old-time recording in print, and some out of print) at good prices. They are County Sales (Dept. PW, P.O. Box 191, Floyd, VA 24091) and Roundup Records (Box 474-PW, Somerville, MA 02144). You might also try Uncle Jim O'Neal (Dept. PW, Box A, Arcadia, CA 91006) or Record Revival (Dept. PW, 7121 W. Vickery, #118, Ft. Worth, TX 76116).

The two leading bluegrass magazines are *Bluegrass Unlimited* ($8/year; Dept. P, Box 111, Broad Run, VA 22014) and *Pickin'* ($12/year, Dept. P, 401 N. Broad St., Philadelphia, PA 19108). Both publications review new records and tell you how to get them. They also provide other valuable services, such as articles and information about the music, musicians, instruments and instrument repair, who's playing with whom, where, when, etc. In addition they carry ads promoting festivals and shows–the main places where bluegrass buffs meet. If you are serious enough about bluegrass banjo to be picking on a regular basis, I recommend subscribing to at least one of these magazines. It should be mentioned that although bluegrass is its specialty, *Pickin'* does cover some kinds of acoustic music outside of it, and devotes more space to instruments than does *Bluegrass Unlimited*. Another publication, *Frets*, ($15/year, Box 615, Saratoga, CA 95070) is devoted to acoustic "roots" music, and often spotlights bluegrass performers and instruments.

Of special interest to banjo players is the *Banjo Newsletter* ($9/year, Dept. P, Box 1830, Annapolis, MD 21404) which includes a wealth of tablature, columns, and articles exploring every conceivable aspect of banjos and banjo playing. It is mostly, but not exclusively, bluegrass oriented, and includes record reviews and record-buying information and advertisements.

You can also buy records directly from artists, and the easiest way to see artists is by attending bluegrass festivals. These festivals have been the focal point of bluegrass music since the first few were produced in the mid-60's. One or more of the top groups in bluegrass plus some lesser known ones are brought together, usually in an outdoor setting over the weekend. People come from all over, paying $10–$25 to drench themselves in bluegrass for a couple of days. They set up their campers and tents right on the grounds and when they aren't listening to the noon-to-midnight shows, they're off somewhere playing. Not only do the artists bring their records, but there is often a record dealer or two who set up a large assortment of their stock for sale. At one bluegrass festival you will find a better selection of records than you would at almost any local record store. Also, the middleman in this case is either the artist or the bluegrass dealer, who probably needs your business more than the record shop does.

That's how to get records. Now the question is which records to get. For this purpose I have put down some basic information–enough to give you an idea of which records might suit you best.

The major groups

Bill Monroe I list first because he is rightfully considered the father of bluegrass. The name bluegrass comes from the name of his band– the Blue Grass Boys. Many of the best known figures in bluegrass played in his band early in their careers, learned a lot, and finally went out on their own. They include: Earl Scruggs, Lester Flatt, Jimmy Martin, MacWiseman, Don Reno, Sonny Osborne, Carter Stanley, and Del McCoury. This process is still going on, even with Monroe approaching his seventies. Monroe originated the bluegrass band style and helped Earl Scruggs shape his banjo style which is the basis for all bluegrass banjo playing. Monroe's band features his powerful tenor singing and mandolin playing, and usually more fiddle than banjo. You can't be a bluegrass musician without being well acquainted with Bill Monroe's music.

Monroe has recorded for two companies since the early '40's: Columbia and MCA (formerly Decca). The Columbia material is the earlier and ends around 1950 when the basis for the present standards of bluegrass style were still taking shape. The sound is less driving and more primitively recorded than most of today's bluegrass, but it is very inspired and cohesive. Much of it features Lester Flatt and Earl Scruggs, who together with fiddler Chubby Wise comprised what many people consider the original, "classic" bluegrass band during the years 1945-48. Some of the Columbia material is pre-Scruggs, when the banjo–if it was used at all–was used for rhythm and not lead. The best of this material is available on a Rounder re-issue, *Bill Monroe with Lester Flatt and Earl Scruggs*, and *16 All-Time Greatest Hits* on Columbia.

Monroe has been with MCA/Decca since the early '50's. He makes one album a year and they are usually quite good. I particularly recommend either of his two "Best of" releases: one is a two-record set; the other, a single LP called *Bill Monroe's Greatest Hits*. Otherwise, my favorites are *The High Lonesome Sound* (beautiful songs and singing with Jimmy Martin–but with little banjo), *Bluegrass Instrumentals* (mostly fiddle–little banjo again), and *Bluegrass Ramble* (not quite as distinguished, but lots of banjo playing).

The other artist whose work I think is absolutely indispensable to any bluegrass collection, however small, is–you guessed it–*Earl Scruggs*. Although some people dispute that he originated the three-finger roll style of banjo playing, no one would disagree that he has done far more than anyone else to refine it and popularize it. It's fitting that traditional bluegrass-style banjo is often called "Scruggs style."

Lester Flatt and Earl Scruggs left Bill Monroe's band in 1948 and soon formed their own group, The Foggy Mountain Boys. They recorded for Mercury for a couple of years. This band was driving and incredibly smooth, both vocally and instrumentally. Luckily, their recordings are still floating around on various labels. Anything of theirs that you find on Mercury, Gusto, Pickwick–or any other label except Columbia and Columbia reissues–is from this period.

The recordings are not high fidelity, especially after rechanneling for stereo, but they are great.

Flatt and Scruggs moved to Columbia in 1950, where they stayed until their split in 1969. Throughout the '50's and into the '60's they played outstanding, classic bluegrass and popularized the form all over the country. With the folk boom in the early '60's, though, the producers at Columbia thought they would have more commercial potential if they had a smoother, gentler sound. The result was a series of uninspired albums featuring inappropriate material and very little banjo playing. There are two live albums of the group on Columbia which have many good moments, but all the other Columbia albums seem quite dreary compared to the sound that made Flatt and Scruggs famous. Their earliest Columbia LPs are out-of-print gems: *Foggy Mountain Jamboree, Songs of Glory,* and *Foggy Mountain Banjo* which consists entirely of banjo instrumentals. There is a *Greatest Hits* set on Columbia and a few Harmony reissues which feature some of the earlier material, but the best '50's Flatt and Scruggs presently available can be found on two Rounder reissues, *Blue Ridge Cabin Home* and *The Golden Era*, and a County reissue, *The Golden Years.* There are also some bootleg LP's of live shows. The audio quality varies greatly, but the music is always first rate. I strongly recommend any records of 1948-62 Flatt and Scruggs to anyone interested in learning bluegrass banjo.

Since Flatt and Scruggs' split, Scruggs has become more experimental, supplementing his usual style with new types of instrumentation and new people. He is still on Columbia and has a rock n' roll group with his sons Randy, Gary, and Steve, called the Earl Scruggs Revue. On some records Earl's banjo is hardly heard at all, but when it is, particularly on their live albums, it's clear that he still has the master's touch.

Lester Flatt resumed a more traditional style with his group, the Nashville Grass, until his death in 1979. They recorded quite a few albums, mostly for RCA, and included a succession of top-notch banjo players: Vic Jordan, Haskell McCormack, Kenny Ingram, and Blake Williams. As good as their music was, I would first recommend vintage Flatt and Scruggs.

Ralph Stanley and his late brother Carter are among the most influential bluegrass artists of all. Their music is pure "mountain soul" based on haunting singing, beautiful two-, three- and four-part harmonies, and an uncluttered band sound that hits home every time. With the exception of more index leads, Ralph's banjo style is similar to Scruggs'. Still, his sound is unique, and has an instantly recognizable stinging, singing tone. He's also been known to perform and record using the old-time clawhammer style.

The Stanley Brothers and the Clinch Mountain Boys began their career in the late '40's and became popular bluegrass artists in the '50's through various radio shows and many great recordings. Most of these were on King, some were for Mercury, Columbia/Harmony, Starday, and a few others. Many of the King records are now available on Gusto, and they are generally excellent, particularly King #615.

Since Carter's death in 1966 Ralph has recorded for the Rebel, Michigan Bluegrass, King, and Jalyn labels. The band has been a consistent standout through occasional personnel changes, and put out many fine albums–some recorded in a single day. Some of the best on Rebel are *Plays Requests, The Old Home Place,* and *Live at McClure Festival*, a double album which includes many cuts from other excellent traditional bluegrass bands. For a good taste of what mountain music is all about, you can't beat a live, stick-to-your-ribs show by Ralph Stanley and the Clinch Mountain Boys.

Don Reno succeeded Earl Scruggs on banjo in the Blue Grass Boys in 1948. He has gone on to become one of the best known bluegrass performers through his partnerships with guitarists Red Smiley and Bill Harrell. He is presently the sole leader of the Tennessee Cutups, who now include two of his sons.

Reno's great knowledge of the banjo neck and his fancy single-string style have earned him a high position among influential banjo players, although some fault him for his lack of right hand finesse. His techniques are often based on guitar styles, and he happens to be a fine guitar player. Many Reno and/or Smiley and/or Harrell records feature a good proportion of slow heartsongs or gospel numbers. Reno's playing on these slower tunes is good to listen to, especially for the player who isn't sure of what to do when the tempo calls for something slower than a roll.

The majority of the recording made by this band were for King (now Gusto). They've also been on Dot, Monument, King Bluegrass, Wango, Rome, and now CMH. Some of my favorites are *Best of Reno and Smiley* on Gusto, and *Country Singing and Instrumentals* and *Wanted*, which was originally recorded for King and hopefully is still available through Gusto. Some of Reno's best playing is on these records.

Jimmy Martin has been in the bluegrass field for over thirty years, and recorded on MCA (Decca) until the late '70's when he signed with Gusto. He played five years with Bill Monroe, worked a short while with the Osborne Brothers, and finally, in the late '50's, formed the Sunny Mountain Boys. The band changes personnel frequently but Jimmy's recordings have been quite consistent through the years. They feature his great lead singing, tight trio singing, and ultrasolid instrumentation. Sometimes his material is a bit hard to take–for instance, novelty numbers like "Dog Bite Your Hide" and "I'm Going Ape Over You" –but considering the overall quality of the band, it doesn't matter. The banjo playing is always first-rate and always sounds the same because Martin has one style that he likes and makes everyone play to suit his taste. His first banjo player was J.D. Crowe and since then there have been Bill Emerson, Vic Jordan, Alan Munde (playing Martin style, not his usual style), Kenny Ingram, and many others. They all do very well, playing similarly to Scruggs, but with a little more bounce.

I would rate all Jimmy Martin albums about equally high. His two sacred songs albums are extra good on singing, and his instrumental album is extra good on banjo playing. In fact, I would say that it is one of the very best records for bluegrass banjo players to listen to and study, because it has so much good-sounding easy-to-follow banjo playing on it.

The Osborne Brothers have long been the most commercially oriented of the major bluegrass bands. Their beautifully blended harmonies, Bobby's high clear vocals and Sonny's banjo wizardry have been their trademarks as regulars on the Grand Ole Opry and as major label (MGM and MCA/Decca) recording artsts in a career that goes back to the early '50's. The Osborne Brothers have a high reverence for bluegrass traditions, and have recorded several fine albums of straight-ahead bluegrass, but over the years they have kept up with the commercial Nashville Sound and have made quite a few hybrid style records.

Sonny is a one-of-a-kind musician and person, always willing to take chances and try bold approaches. One of his most notable experiments was adding a sixth string, a low G, onto his banjo in 1970, but he gave it up a few years later. His playing on slow songs is about as personal and soulful as bluegrass banjo playing can get, sometimes using "jazz" notes and chords. For Sonny's banjo tips and philosophy, see his monthly column in *Banjo Newslatter.*

One of the best Osborne Brothers albums was recorded for MGM in the late '50's when Red Allen was with them. This material and some early '60's cuts have been released on two Rounder Special Series records. *The Osborne Brothers*, and *The Osborne Brothers with Red Allen* are both highly recommended as "classic" Osborne material. One of their best efforts for MCA, *Yesterday and Today*, contains one side each of straight bluegrass and bluegrass-pop (including their biggest hit, "Rocky Top"). Possibly still available from MCA is a two-record set of their greatest hits culled from over ten years on that label.

In the late '70's, Bob and Sonny signed with CMH records, and have turned out several fine efforts, particularly *The Bluegrass Collection*, an excellent two-record set of the greatest hits of the Osborne Brothers, Bill Monroe, Flatt and Scruggs, et al.

Like the Osborne Brothers, *Jim and Jesse* (the McReynolds Brothers) and the *Virginia Boys* have flirted with the Nashville Sound, though with somewhat less success. As a bluegrass band they have had some of the best sidemen in the business (on banjo, Allen Shelton, Bobby Thompson, Carl Jackson, Garland Shuping, and Vic Jordan), and can lay down some of the smoothest, surest singing and picking around.

In addition to their fine duets, they feature Jesse's cross-picking mandolin style which imitates the three-finger banjo roll using only a flatpick.

Jim and Jesse's early '50's recordings for Capitol were reissued in a two-record set, but it is now out of print. The only early Jim and Jesse records now available are their first two Epic albums from the early '60's—*Bluegrass Special* and *Bluegrass Classics*, now combined as a set on CSP—featuring some strong material and the solid, creative picking of Allen Shelton. Shelton's bouncy, punchy style is one of the best ever in bluegrass, and is a model for anyone learning banjo. He has a good record of instrumentals on Rounder called *Shelton Special*. Another Jim and Jesse record from the Shelton era, well worth getting, is a two-record set of radio transcriptions. Also recommended is the *Jim and Jesse Show* on Prize, which features good bluegrass material and the fine picking of Vic Jordan. Unfortunately, Bobby Thompson is heard on only a few cuts of a few Jim and Jesse LP's. However, as a Nashville session player for over ten years, he has turned up on many records, commercials and sound tracks such as the *Hee Haw* theme.

The Country Gentlemen, formed in 1957, can be seen as the newest of the old groups, or as the oldest of the new. They were the first to modernize bluegrass with contemporary material, unusual chord progressions, and the like. Through years of personnel changes they have maintained their characteristic sound, humor, and airtight delivery under the direction of Charlie Waller, who is the only remaining original member. Many greats of bluegrass have worked with the group for several years at a time, including mandolinists John Duffey, Doyle Lawson, and Jimmy Gaudreau; and banjoists Eddie Adcock, Bill Emerson, and James Bailey.

Of the banjo players, Eddie Adcock is probably one of the most unique, with a recognizable, "plunky" sound and a big bagful of flawless guitar-style and single-string licks. He is now, with his wife Martha, the force behind The II Generation, a quasi-bluegrass group with whom he also plays electric guitar. Bill Emerson, known for his absolutely sure and smooth sound, has been in Country Current, a U.S. Navy band, since leaving the Gentlemen in the early '70's.

Almost all of the Country Gentlemen's records are in print, even the first few on Folkways. Almost all the rest are on Rebel or Zap, with the exception of a few on Starday, Vanguard, and Mercury (all recommended and all out of print). The Country Gentlemen are consistent enough so that it's hard to go wrong with any of their records, but I recommend the three Folkways records of the early band, and their series *Yesterday and Today*, Volumes 1-5, on Rebel for a sampling of some of the group's best material over the years.

The Seldom Scene formed in the Washington, D.C. area in the early '70's and soon became known for their unique brand of polished modern bluegrass. Their sound is more gregarious than lonesome, and like the Country Gentlemen (with whom mandolinist John Duffey and bassist Tom Gray started) their material is relatively progressive both musically and lyrically. The creative and tasteful banjo playing of Ben Eldridge has been a strong point of the group from the beginning. Eldridge's solid Scruggs basis and chromatic highlights make him one of my favorites. All of their albums are recorded on Rebel, and if you're new to bluegrass and traditional-style singing doesn't appeal to you, some good Seldom Scene records would be especially recommended. Listen particularly to *Live at the Cellar Door*, a two-record set of excellently-performed modern and traditional Scene hits.

J.D. Crowe started playing banjo with Jimmy Martin as a teenager, and during his five-year stint became "the" Jimmy Martin-style banjo player. His powerful, economical sound, flawless timing, and choice licks put him among the most highly respected banjo players. Some call him the best.

About 1970 he started *The New South*, which has included many of the best young bluegrass pickers and singers: Tony and Larry Rice, Doyle Lawson, Ricky Skaggs, Keith Whitley, and Jimmy Gaudreau. The group is always smooth and professional at appearances and on records, but the sound is not always bluegrass. Some records have a definite pop-country flavor, with drums, pedal steel, and J.D. on banjo-dobro. For excellent bluegrass I recommend Rounder #0044, (with Ricky Skaggs and Tony Rice), and of earlier vintage on Lemco, *Rambling Boy* (with Doyle Lawson and Larry Rice) and *Bluegrass Holiday* (with Red Allen and Doyle Lawson).

The Newgrass Revival was formed in 1971 by some members of what was then the Bluegrass Alliance. Led by creative dynamo Sam Bush, the group does rock-style material and arrangements with bluegrass instruments. This is no small project, but the power and drive of the four musicians carries it off, even without a drummer. On banjo is Courtney Johnson, a rare example of a strong and punchy melodic-style player. In keeping with the group's approach, his solo flights are experimental and laced with minor and chromatic-scale notes.

Even if rock music isn't your "bag," I strongly recommend taking in a live Newgrass Revival show. Their energy and talent comes through loud and clear in a way that a record can't duplicate. Their two best records consist of a "live" recording—*When the Storm is Over*— and *Barren County*, both available on Flying Fish, like all except their first album, which is on Starday.

The Country Gazette is the only group west of the Mississippi to gain major national recognition in the bluegrass field. Originally based in California, their smooth high vocals and polished incorporation of non-bluegrass influences made them the leading exponents of what could be called the "California bluegrass sound." Now they are based in Texas and Oklahoma, stomping grounds of Alan Munde, the group's only remaining charter member. Munde is unquestionably one of the top banjo players today, a master of both the straight-style (he picked with Jimmy Martin for two years) and the melodic-style, which he plays with impeccable taste and technique.

The Gazette has recorded for United Artists and Flying Fish. Most highly recommended, though out of print, is *Don't Give Up Your Day Job*, which was recorded for United Artists when the great fiddler Byron Berline was in the group. Also recommended is *Out to Lunch* on Flying Fish, which should be in print and easier to find. The group now records for Ridgerunner. For more concentrated doses of Alan Munde's playing try his solo album *Banjo Sandwich* or *Sam [Bush] and Alan Together Again for the First Time*, a superb instrumental LP, both on Ridgerunner.

Somewhat less active in bluegrass today are some top-rate veterans who have made a lasting conrribution to the field.

Red Allen is a standout bluegrass singer whose records on County, Melodeon, and Folkways are as driving and soulful as you can get. On any Red Allen record you are likely to find excellent straight-ahead Scruggs-style banjo, played by such notables as Porter Church, J.D. Crowe, Bill Emerson, and Pete Roberts (who edits *Bluegrass Unlimited* magazine under his real name, Pete Kuykendall). The Folkways *Red Allen and Frank Wakefield* record from the mid-60's includes some great melodic picking by Bill Keith.

Mac Wiseman never works with a band of his own, nor is he best known for his bluegrass records. However, his association with bluegrass goes back a long way and he is still regularly featured at bluegrass festivals. His warm full voice is not particularly bluegrassy, but he has fit in very well on records will Bill Monroe, Flatt and Scruggs, the Osborne Brothers, and Lester Flatt. The few records of his own which use bluegrass accompaniment are generally quite good, especially those recorded with the Shenandoah Cutups, with the fine banjo playing of Billy Edwards, or his early recordings for Dot. These are now reissued on Dot and ABC, but are not especially strong on banjo.

The Shenandoah Cutups, without Mac Wiseman, are one of the finest traditional bluegrass groups going today, and have made several solid records for Revonah, County, and Rural Rhythm.

The Lilly Brothers, Bea and Everett, haven't performed together regularly for some time, but their sweet duet singing, often backed by the forceful banjo of *Don Stover*, can still be heard on some fine records available on County, Rounder, and Folkways. Don Stover is still active and has released some enjoyable old-time flavored LPs of his own on Rounder and Old Homestead. Lately he has started a group with veteran guitarist Bill Clifton and mandolin player Red Rector.

Del McCoury, Larry Sparks, Earl Taylor, James Monroe, Hylo Brown, Carl Story, Charlie Moore, and the Goins Brothers are some of the other most noted bandleaders whose groups always feature good solid bluegrass banjo playing. All are known for their quality music, though band personnel may not be consistent from year to year.

There are other well-known and well respected banjo players who have been associated with particular groups. Roy Lewis of the Lewis Family, the leading bluegrass gospel group (on Canaan Records), is an exceptionally solid banjo man. So is Walter Hensley, who is often heard with Earl Taylor and on some records of his own with the Dukes of Bluegrass. Doug Dillard, who first gained fame with the Dillards, and is heard on their first three Elektra records, has recently teamed with Byron Berline and recorded for Flying Fish. Raymond McLain of the McLain Family Band is an innovative virtuoso and can be heard on the family's records on their own label, Country Life. Jack Hicks has used his fancy melodic style very effectively on records with Buck White and The Down Home Folks (on Ridgerunner and County).

There are large numbers of fine Scruggs-style banjo players whose names I haven't mentioned. They are carrying on the bluegrass banjo style in its pure form even after its originator has left his own ranks to play rock n' roll. You can probably hear a few exceptional pickers at any good bluegrass festival—often in the parking lot!

New Banjo Records

Recent years have seen a development of interest in using the banjo as more than a bluegrass instrument. Quite a few players based in bluegrass have expanded their repertoires into other realms, written new tunes, and recorded instrumental records all of which have helped forge the present "banjo revolution."

And so we now have records of bluegrass banjo players playing ragtime, swing, modern jazz, and calypso banjo. The classic bluegrass instrumentation has been supplemented by synthesizer, flute, bells, choruses—even symphony orchestras. Banjo technique has also expanded to deal with chord forms and rhythms outside the usual boundaries of bluegrass. There's no doubt that the field will keep expanding. Still at the bottom of all of it is the three-finger roll developed by Earl Scruggs, and very often you find the three-finger melodic approach developed within bluegrass by Bobby Thompson and Bill Keith. Where it will lead no one knows, but as of 1980 we have quite an array of bluegrass-based banjo instrumentation records.

The first and biggest-selling of these records was *New Dimensions in Banjo and Bluegrass*, which was recorded in the early '60's by New Yorkers Eric Weissberg and Marshall Brickman. Their melodic flights inspired many banjo pickers back then and the record *really* took off when it was repackaged to include the *Deliverance* movie version of "Dueling Banjos." In fact, it was the nation's best selling album for several months in 1972-73, and will probably always be available, though the label may change.

Although *Dueling Banjos* may lead by several lengths, here's an alphabetical list of some of the second-best selling modern banjo albums:

artist/group	**album(s)**	**label(s)**
Jimmy Arnold	*Strictly Arnold*	Rebel
Brown and Sullivan and Company	*Magnum Banjos*	Sequatchie
Country Cooking with Tony Trischka and Peter Wernick	*14 Bluegrass Instrumentals* *Barrel of Fun*	Rounder
Fred Geiger	*Newgrass* *Swing Banjo*	Ridgerunner
Dave Griffiths	*Working Man's Banjo*	BMA
John Hickman	*Don't Mean Maybe*	Rounder
Vic Jordan	*Pickaway* *Banjo Nashville*	API Sugar Hill
Bill Keith	*Strictly Clean and Decent*	Rounder
Bill Knopf	*Banjo Album*	American Heritage
Larry McNeely	*Banjo Album*	Flying Fish
Susie Monick	*Melting Pots*	Adelphi
Alan Munde	*Banjo Sandwich*	Ridgerunner
Butch Robins	*Forty Years Late* *Fragments of My Imagination*	Rounder
Fred Sokolow	*Bluegrass Banjo Inventions*	Kicking Mule
Roger Sprung	*Grassy Licks* (several others)	Folkways
Tony Trischka	*Bluegrass Light* *Heartlands* *Banjoland*	Rounder
Peter Wernick	*Dr. Banjo Steps Out*	Flying Fish

A list of progressive banjo players would not be complete without mentioning *John Hartford* although he has never released an instrumental album. His standard fare consists of original songs—often with banjo accompaniment and nothing else. His banjo picking, though based on Scruggs style, remains lilting and original. Of his close to a dozen albums, my favorites are *Morning Bugle* (Warner Brothers) and *All in the Name of Love* (Flying Fish).

Of particular interest to banjo players using records as a practice aid is a play-along banjo record by Country Cooking. It is a typical bluegrass record with fourteen selections, except that the banjo (played by yours truly) is separated in one stereo channel so that it can be isolated from the sound of the rest of the band by using the balance control. For more information, write: Dr. Banjo, 7930 Oxford Road, Longmont, CO 80501.

Sonny Osborne and Rual Yarbrough. The banjo is the six-string Rual made for Sonny.

Index
of songs and tunes in tablature

All the Good Times Are Past and Gone, 80

Armadillo Breakdown
two breaks, 108

Ballad of Jed Clampett
beginner version, 27
intermediate version, 42

Banks of the Ohio, 76

Barrel of Fun, 118

Buffalo Gals, 100

Cedar Hill
two breaks, 66

Chromania, 89

Cripple Creek
intermediate version, 38
advanced version, 102

Dark Hollow
normal version, 74
for muted banjo, 95

Devil's Dream, 84

Huckling the Berries, 106

In My Mind to Ramble, 52

Jesse James
melody, 44
harmony, 92

John Hardy, 98

John Henry, 99

Kentucky Bullfight, 114

Little Birdie, 70

Little Maggie, 45

Lonesome Road Blues, 96

Mountain Dew, 43

November Cotillion, 107

Old Joe Clark, 54

Orange Mountain Special
two breaks, 86

Parson's Duck, 120

Pow Wow the Indian Boy, 103

Rabbit in the Log, 71

Sailor's Hornpipe, 85

Salt Creek, 104

She'll Be Coming Round the Mountain
beginner version, 25
intermediate version, 40

Six Mile Creek, 116

Tequila Mockingbird, 112

Will the Circle Be Unbroken
beginner version, 28
intermediate version, 41
advanced version, 97

Worried Man Blues
beginner version, 26
intermediate version, 39